YouTube in Music Education

Thomas Rudolph
James Frankel

Hal Leonard Books
An Imprint of Hal Leonard Corporation
New York

Published in 2009 by Hal Leonard Books
An Imprint of Hal Leonard Corporation
7777 West Bluemound Road
Milwaukee, WI 53213

Trade Book Division Editorial Offices
19 West 21st Street, New York, NY 10010
Printed in the United States of America

Book design by Kristina Rolander

Library of Congress Cataloging-in-Publication Data

Rudolph, Thomas E.
YouTube in music education / Thomas Rudolph and James Frankel.
    p. cm.
Includes bibliographical references and index.
ISBN-13: 978-1-4234-7938-3
ISBN-10: 1-4234-7938-6
1. Music--Instruction and study. 2. YouTube (Electronic resource) 3.
Video recordings--Production and direction. I. Frankel, James. II. Title.
MT1.R88 2009
780.71--dc22
                                        2009044591

www.halleonard.com

To My Family:

Alison, Abigail, and Isabelle
—James Frankel

To My Children:

Liia, Gusten, and Kalev
—Tom Rudolph

Contents

CHAPTER TWO

YouTube Tour

CHAPTER THREE

Creating a YouTube Account 41

CHAPTER EIGHT

What to Do If Your School Blocks YouTube

CHAPTER NINE
Equipment for Producing Quality Videos 185

CHAPTER TEN
Creating Music Videos and Student Applications 201

Introduction

There is no doubt that you have been exposed to the "buzz" about YouTube, the video-sharing website that receives millions of visits every month. There is a plethora of videos on YouTube, many of which can be useful in the music classroom. Your students are certainly familiar with the site, and we are excited to share some unique ways that YouTube can provide you with a relevant teaching tool.

The Focus of the Book

This book was written with both the beginning and experienced YouTube user in mind. Its intention is to provide music educators with a clear understanding of how to use YouTube and implement some of its many pedagogical applications in the music classroom. It includes comprehensive information on how to effectively navigate the YouTube website; how to search for relevant videos; how to create a YouTube account for use with your students; how to create a YouTube community for your students; and how to create and upload your own videos. The book will also examine concerns regarding the use of YouTube in the classroom, including copyright issues, accessibility, and protecting student privacy. Several chapters share ideas and concepts for the pedagogical use of YouTube in the music curriculum. The book also includes what to do if your institution blocks YouTube; other video resources for teachers such as SchoolTube and TeacherTube; and technical information on how to show YouTube videos in the classroom as well as recommended equipment for producing quality videos.

Companion Website

A companion website for this book can be found at www.youtubemusiced.com. It includes links to many of the videos mentioned in the text; downloadable lesson plans written by teachers who use YouTube as part of their curriculum; a Q&A section that addresses how to use YouTube and some of the issues raised in the text; an FAQ section on copyright issues in relation to YouTube videos; a condensed how-to guide for viewing and posting videos on YouTube called *The YouTube QuickStart Guide*; a blog containing relevant videos, news, and developments concerning YouTube; and links to related websites. This site is updated frequently and will serve as an additional resource for the text.

Companion YouTube Channel and Group

Along with the companion website, we have also created a YouTube Channel, located at www.youtube.com/MusicClassroom. Here you will find an introductory video explaining our rationale for educators and administrators to use YouTube in the classroom. This video can serve as an advocacy tool for teachers who are trying to convince their school and/or district-level administrators to unblock YouTube for teacher use in the classroom. Many of the videos mentioned within this text are also located on this channel. These videos are "safe"—they do not infringe on copyright—and can be used in the classroom for any purpose.

We have also created a YouTube Group called MusicClassroom, which we encourage you to join. The purpose of this group is to allow educators to connect with other teachers from around the globe to share their music lesson ideas, related videos, and stories about how they use (or are prohibited from using) YouTube in the music classroom. To join our group, simply visit our YouTube channel and click on "Join This Group."

Conventions Used in This Book

Throughout the book you will find various tips for using YouTube, as well as several YouTube Teaching Strategies. If you are new to YouTube, we suggest you read the chapters in order starting with chapter 1. If you are an experienced YouTube user, you can simply read the chapters that are relevant to you.

Contacting the Authors

We welcome your feedback. You can post a comment to one of the videos on our YouTube channel or contact us via e-mail:

Tom Rudolph (tom@tomrudolph.com)

James Frankel (jtfrankel@hotmail.com).

Chapter One

An Introduction to YouTube

In this chapter, you will be introduced to some unique ways that YouTube can be integrated into music education. These concepts will be further developed in the chapters that follow.

The main topics in this chapter include:

- ▸ The attraction to YouTube
- ▸ Musically YouTube: auditions, creations, and distribution
- ▸ YouTube Symphony Orchestra
- ▸ YouTube and mash-ups
- ▸ Showcasing your talents on YouTube
- ▸ Why YouTube works in music education
- ▸ A brief history of YouTube
- ▸ Educational applications

How many times have you sat down at your computer to watch random strangers make fools out of themselves on YouTube, only to look up at the clock and be surprised at how much time you've spent on the site? What is our fascination with watching reporters slipping up on live television, or a skateboarder falling down a flight of stairs? Why do we become glued to the screen watching clips of old television shows, or a car accident caught on tape? For decades our culture has had a voyeuristic tendency—everything from watching our own home movies on 35mm film to the wildly popular *America's Funniest Home Videos,* which is still running after an incredible 19 years on television.[1] For whatever the reason, our fascination with these video forms of entertainment can explain the extraordinary success of YouTube.

The Attraction to YouTube

With its user-friendly interface (see chapter 2), YouTube has made it possible for anyone to post their videos online in minutes—to an audience that far eclipses that of any one night of *America's Funniest Home Videos*. It is quite common for videos to be viewed millions of times—even those containing seemingly innocuous scenes of everyday life. Video sharing has become an integral part of Internet culture, with millions of new videos uploaded daily. An astonishing 44.1 percent of all videos posted online are hosted on YouTube.[2]

Students Are Using YouTube

While YouTube viewers represent nearly every demographic imaginable, the students we teach are perhaps the most active uploaders of content to the site. Armed with cell phones equipped with video recording capabilities, students are posting video clips showing everything from personal video blogs intended for their friends to view either on YouTube or on social networking sites such as MySpace and Facebook, to fistfights in the schoolyard. Many students have secretly videotaped their teachers during class and posted the videos to YouTube for their classmates to view and comment upon. Other videos show students lip-syncing to their favorite songs. While there are numerous examples of harmless clips showing people doing silly things, there are also examples of bullying, foul language, violence, and distasteful content. The site does not have any type of rating system for the content of its videos (like the MPAA system), and many parents and educators feel uneasy about allowing children to visit the site unsupervised.

The YouTube Culture

These issues aside, YouTube has quickly become a main component of our culture, often serving as a central point of conversation at the office cooler. Television news and gossip shows often show YouTube videos as part of their broadcasts. "Have you seen the video where…" seems to be a common start to a conversation. The education world, however, seems to be somewhat reticent to allow YouTube into the classroom. For a wide variety of reasons, many of which will be discussed later in this book, educators are often prohibited from accessing YouTube in their classrooms. This book hopes to illustrate why educators in general, music educators in particular, parents, and administrators should consider opening up access—specifically in the music classroom.

Musically YouTube: Auditions, Creations, and Distribution

On Wednesday, April 15, 2009, a group of 90 talented young musicians assembled on the stage of Carnegie Hall in New York City and made history. Under the baton of noted conductor Michael Tilson Thomas, the world premiere of a new orchestral work, written by Tan Dun, was performed by a very unique symphony orchestra. What made the orchestra unique was not how well the members played (after all, the only way to get to Carnegie Hall is to practice), or the instrumentation of the ensemble, but how the group was selected. As any professional classical musician will tell you, the audition process for most orchestras in the world consists of an invitation to audition (often garnered by a recommendation or by the submission of a recording of required excerpts) followed by a series of "blind" auditions where the musician performs on stage behind a screen to shield his or her identity from the panel of judges. This helps to ensure a fair process, where the best player of the day wins the seat, and avoids any appearance of bias favoring one musician over another. What made the audition process for this particular orchestra unique was where it took place and who judged the musicians. Instead of taking place in a concert hall behind a screen, the auditions took place on arguably the biggest virtual stage in the history of humankind, and instead of being anonymous, the entire world could see who was performing. The auditions took place on YouTube, and the whole world helped to judge them.

YouTube Symphony Orchestra

The YouTube Symphony Orchestra project began as a partnership between YouTube and the London Symphony Orchestra to "create the world's first collaborative orchestra."[3] The idea was simple: commission a composer (Tan Dun) to write a new work (*Internet Symphony no. 1—Eroica*), and post the individual parts online for musicians across the globe to download and practice. Musicians could then post videos of themselves performing the parts, as well as selected repertoire, for the YouTube community and a selected panel of judges to evaluate. To facilitate this idea, YouTube created a dedicated channel (see Fig. 1.1) for the project, located at www.youtube.com/symphony. Visitors to the channel could watch a welcome video featuring Tan Dun explaining the project. After viewing the video, visitors were encouraged to select their respective instrument, after which they could download not only a PDF file containing their part, but also two videos: one of Mr. Dun conducting the orchestra from the perspective of the selected part, and one that included a master class featuring a member of the London Symphony Orchestra that provided helpful tips and suggestions on how to best perform the part. All of this content was free to download and view and was licensed through a Creative Commons agreement.

Fig. 1.1
YouTube Symphony Channel

The deadline to submit videos for consideration was January 28, 2009. The YouTube Symphony project was first announced on December 1, 2008, at a press conference in New York City featuring Michael Tilson Thomas, Tan Dun, and famed Chinese pianist Lang Lang. The idea, launched by two YouTube employees at an offsite retreat about a year ago, is being greeted enthusiastically by the classical music world, which Tim Lee, one of the project's initiators, tactfully described as 'hungry for innovation.'[4] At the press conference, the two goals of the project were announced: 1) to create a mash-up performance (described below) video containing excerpts from the many videos submitted; and 2) to feature a live performance at Carnegie Hall.[5] Some would describe the press conference as "a moment in the sun" for the classical music world, because the genre was finally being noticed by kids, who used the site. Between the time that the YouTube Symphony project was first announced and the time of this writing, over 23,000 people had subscribed to the channel, and over 3,000 videos were submitted by users.[6] These videos were collectively viewed over 13 million times during the audition process.[7] The only rules governing the submissions were that the musician had to be at least 14 years of age, and they had to submit the two required videos. All musicians were encouraged to submit videos, even if their instrument was not represented in the score.[8]

In February 2009, the YouTube community was given the opportunity to vote for the 200 finalists selected from the over 3,000 videos that were submitted. Concurrently, the YouTube Symphony Project panel of judges evaluated each performance. On March 2, 2009, the YouTube Symphony Channel posted the results of the auditions, selecting 90 musicians to participate in the concert. The musicians comprised professionals and amateurs alike from more than 30 countries worldwide. Each participant that was selected received an invitation to travel to New York City—all expenses paid. The results were posted via an interactive seating chart of the orchestra (see Fig. 1.2), where visitors could click on each instrument to view the video(s) of the winning musician(s). The audio quality of the videos was surprisingly good, and provided judges with a very clear representation of each performer's musical abilities. On April 15, 2009, *Internet Symphony no. 1—Eroica,* along with several other works, was given its world premiere by this extraordinarily unique group of musicians, who had met only a few days earlier. The concert event—which was subsequently posted in its entirety on the YouTube Symphony Channel—was truly exciting. A sold-out Carnegie Hall audience greeted each selection performed by the ensemble with enthusiasm. Videos from the audition process were played for the audience, as well as short videos that spotlighted some of the musicians. Many of those who were unsuccessful in their bid for a seat on the stage were in attendance. The music and the musicians were connected to each other by a website—perhaps the single most popular website on the Internet to date—YouTube. For full-length videos of the concert, visit: www.youtube.com/symphony.

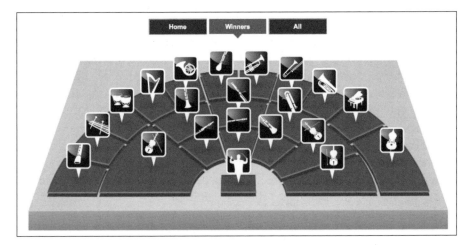

Fig. 1.2
YouTube Symphony interactive seating chart

While some might argue that this entire project and event was purely a self-aggrandizing publicity stunt for the organizations involved, others might argue that this was an ingenious way to use existing technology, and that the project could be easily replicated for other similar events—particularly in music education. Colleges and universities could begin to accept video auditions from prospective students—perhaps serving as a preliminary stage in the audition process. Regional and statewide music festival auditions could be conducted online as well. Students could collaborate with other students around the world—sharing their performances of selected repertoire with each other. College professors and public school teachers could post videos of their classes online so that students could study them later. While there are certainly intellectual property issues to consider with each of these strategies, the pedagogical implications for this type of online collaboration are significant, and should be explored further. This book explores these and other issues in order to provide music educators with strategies for making an idea as unique and exciting as the YouTube Symphony Orchestra possible in the music classroom.

From Works of the Masters to Works Made by Mashers

There are many other ingenious uses of YouTube in a musical context, and many of those are about as far from the classical music domain as you can get. With thousands of videos available of professional and amateur musicians either performing or teaching, the site is rife with content for a new breed of musicians—remixers and mashers. A *remixer* is someone who takes an existing musical work and creates a new version of it—either by adding their own beats and lyrics, or by sampling the works of others and incorporating those short audio clips into their work. While copyright issues are certainly involved with this practice—most of this type of remixing qualifies as infringement—the art form is a powerful example of how the Internet culture is using YouTube content. With so much material readily accessible on YouTube, a visitor can often find the musical phrase they are looking for within seconds. A *masher* is someone who takes existing material and layers it over other materials. A masher differs from a remixer in that he or she is simply combining new material with existing material. The manipulation and layering of these materials on top of one another is what defines the mash-up. The creativity comes in when the new work has stand-alone artistic value. Anyone can make a remix or a mash-up. Only a creative individual can make it good.

Master Masher: Ophir Kutiel

The single best example of the art of the mash-up was created by an Israeli-born musician named Ophir Kutiel—a.k.a. Kutiman—who created seven mash-ups using only videos that he found on YouTube. A professional musician with an established music career, Kutiman set out to create entirely new music using segments of the many videos that he found. By searching the expansive collection of videos on YouTube for terms such as "piano," "acoustic bass," and "trombone," Kutiman selected hundreds of videos and then edited out fragments of each to begin the laborious process of layering them on top of one another to create a new work. To help you understand this process, imagine taking a video of each member of your concert band performing a chromatic scale with various articulations—say staccato and legato. Once you have the video of each performance on your computer, you would then extract the audio from each video and cut up each audio file into smaller files containing each individual note. Now that you have all of this, you would then reassemble these individual notes to create an existing band score—say the *First Suite in E-flat for Military Band* by Gustav Holst. Sounds like an incredible amount of work, right? Now imagine creating a completely original work with that same information. That is exactly what Kutiman did—seven times. Kutiman spent three months in his bedroom splicing and dicing over 100 videos for samples of singers and instruments—from guitars, pianos, drums, and harps to synthesizers, a bouzouki, and even a cash register.[9]

Thru You Website

After creating seven new compositions, Kutiman then created a website for the project called Thru You (www.thru-you.com), where he posted not only the audio files, but the accompanying videos that included the original clips as well (see Fig. 1.3). In addition to the videos, Kutiman also posted a video of himself describing his creative process, as well as a video that credited each of the videos that he used. The site quickly gained the attention of a number of music bloggers and mentions on the social networking site Twitter. In fact, some consider Kutiman to be the first music sensation found on Twitter.[10] The site quickly became overwhelmed with traffic and crashed temporarily. While the site was down the videos were posted to YouTube

Fig. 1.3
Thru You homepage

by an account holder so that everyone could view them. And the YouTube community did just that. Within days, the videos had been viewed millions of times.[11] In addition to Kutiman's work, users also began viewing the individual clips that he used—perhaps out of disbelief that he could have created such an incredible mash-up.

The first video of the series is titled "The Mother of All Funk Chords" (see Fig. 1.4), and contains clips from 22 separate videos—everything from an instructional video featuring famed drummer Bernard "Pretty" Purdy, who plays a 16th-note shuffle throughout the piece, to an 11-year-old trumpet player named Leon (www.youtube.com/watch?v=tprMEs-zfQA). The video takes its namesake from a clip posted by guitar teacher David Taub (www.nextlevelguitar.com), who demonstrates what he calls "the mother of all funk chords"—the 9th chord.

Kutiman's work starts off with Pretty Purdy asking, "Well, what can I do?" followed by responses from Taub and others. After a preview of some of the other clips used in the video, a huge 9th chord is performed by layering notes from the many musicians featured in the videos, and then the funk groove begins. What follows is an incredible display of both creativity and technical skill.

Fig. 1.4
"The Mother of All Funk Chords"

Getting Permission

One of the criticisms of Kutiman's work is that he did not ask permission to use any of the clips in his work, although he clearly credits each video on his site. While quite a few of the videos that he used indicated that users were free to use and share their videos, others did not. Contacting each individual in the videos would have been relatively easy to do, but Kutiman didn't. This certainly raised some concerns among users—some more than others. While many of the comments from YouTube users were very positive, some expressed concern over Kutiman's use of their material (all of which is protected by copyright) without their permission. Indeed, Kutiman has brought a tremendous amount of attention to the people shown in the video. David Taub's free funk guitar lesson went from a few hundred views to well over 100,000 views in days. One user, known as yisheik2, commented: "You have just witnessed a pinpoint moment in the history of music and production techniques. Incredible. Completely blown away and inspired."[12]

However, another musician who was featured in a video titled "I'm New" was not so happy that Kutiman had used his video without permission. In response to another user, funkytradition (whose real name is Isaac) wrote: "No real beef...just a common courtesy of asking permission. You're incorrect about your assumptions regarding public reuse of images. There is a checkbox list when you post to YouTube if you are allowing the video to be reused, embedded, or distributed. I checked 'No,' so YouTube doesn't honor their own parameters. But, I do like what Kutiman does, and sent him my best wishes. I'm open to collaborating with people as long as I know about it from the person."[13] This comment raises some important issues of permission, copyright, and privacy, which will be discussed later in this book. What is important about Kutiman's work on YouTube is that he single-handedly created a new genre of music, and the attention he has garnered for his work will most certainly inspire others to create similar music in the future.

I Want My YouTube Music TV

Over the past few years, many musicians have used YouTube as an opportunity to market themselves to a larger audience. Used in tandem with social networking sites such as MySpace, aspiring musicians have the unprecedented opportunity to showcase their talent for the world to see. Gone are the days when demo tapes and talent scouts were the only way to get noticed by a record company. Musicians like Colbie Caillat, Ingrid Michaelson, and bands such as the Arctic Monkeys and My Chemical Romance owe a great deal of their success to the connectivity of MySpace and the power of viral marketing—a phenomenon where particular content (in this case music) can garner a high degree of attention in a very short period of time. Like MySpace, YouTube offers unsigned bands and musical acts a free place to post their efforts where a large percentage of the world's youth congregate. Many companies have noticed this phenomenon; after all, who wouldn't want access to such a large demographic? Some companies have embraced this form of advertising; others have resisted it. Those who have resisted it often cite the rampant copyright infringement that often occurs on these types of sites. Others are looking for creative ways around these issues and focus more on the potential financial gain from the publicity generated on the site rather than pulling down infringing content.[14]

The Wall Street Journal/Google Project

A March 5, 2009, article in the *Wall Street Journal*'s online edition announced a possible partnership between Google (which owns YouTube) and Universal Music Group (UMG), in which Google would create a music channel on the YouTube site that would serve as a hub for the music videos of artists signed to the various UMG labels. The project, with a working title of Vevo, would be a way for both companies to gain more advertising revenue, as the allure of free (and legal) music videos online would potentially attract millions of viewers to the site looking for videos from bands such as Beck, U2, Jay-Z, Fallout Boy, Lil Wayne, and Taylor Swift. Similar agreements between Google and music companies have been discussed in the past, such as with Warner Music Group, but in December 2008, Warner pulled all of its content from the site after the two companies failed to renew their licensing agreement.[15]

The problem of posting music videos online actually dates back to discussions between record label and television executives in the early 1980s regarding the airing of videos on the MTV network. The record companies wanted MTV to pay for each video it aired, and MTV argued that it shouldn't pay for the videos at all, as it was actually generating revenue for the record companies by driving sales. In essence, the same argument stands today. Record companies feel that free access to their video content (as well as audio content) will detract from album sales—while websites such as YouTube feel that airing free videos will ultimately drive sales. Both sides agree that a consensus will be reached somewhere down the line, but ironing out the details of who gets paid and how much is difficult. It is the intent of the potential partnership between YouTube and Universal Music to generate sufficient advertising revenue to make both parties happy. One model that seems to be working is the one that MySpace Music uses, where users can stream selected music on their personal websites. Both MySpace and the record labels involved in the agreement share the advertising revenue from the ads that appear while the music is being streamed.[16] It will be very interesting to see how similar music licensing agreements between record labels and sites such as YouTube will develop in the future.

Imitation Videos

One phenomenon that has grown out of the music videos on YouTube is the huge number of imitation music videos, often featuring teenagers dressed in similar clothing, in similar settings, lip-syncing their hearts out. If you search for a song title on YouTube, odds are you will find dozens of these videos—many of which are hilarious. Some of the best-known home-grown music videos feature users lip-syncing to the song "All the Single Ladies" by Beyoncé. Everything from a two-year-old girl to a rather large man dressed in a black leotard to the parody version that aired on *Saturday Night Live* can be found, with YouTube account holders dancing to the beat. There are also numerous examples of users singing and performing original music on their instruments. One of the single most viewed videos ever to appear on YouTube is of a young guitarist named Jeong-hyun Lim performing his rock version of Pachelbel's famed "Canon in D Major" (see Fig. 1.5). As of this writing, the video—which was posted in December 2005—has been viewed over 56 million times.

Fig. 1.5

Jeong-hyun Lim in the video "Guitar"

A recent search for the term "a cappella" on YouTube yielded more than 70,000 results. One user named Cory Vidal posted his version of an a cappella parody originally created by the group Moosebutter. The video, titled "Star Wars (John Williams Is the Man)—an a Cappella Tribute" (see Fig. 1.6), has been viewed well over 4 million times as of this writing. The ingenious aspect of the video is that Mr. Vidal layered four separate videos of himself singing the various parts of the piece on top of one another to create a single performance—a quartet featuring just him. While he clearly credits Moosebutter with the original arrangement, his version has garnered far more notoriety than the original. In fact, he has created other similar videos and has even opened a store that sells the T-shirts that he wore in the video.[17]

Fig. 1.6

"Star Wars (John Williams Is the Man)— An a Cappella Tribute"

Along with music videos, many television shows can be found on YouTube. Yet unless there are specific licensing agreements between YouTube and the networks that originally produced the shows, these episodes are considered infringements, and are often quickly pulled down from the site.

TIP   Be sure to adhere to YouTube guidelines and copyright law when posting video on YouTube (see chapter 5).

In recent years however, some networks have been entering into licensing agreements with YouTube in order to share in potential advertising revenues. CBS is one network that has licensed its programming to YouTube in exchange for YouTube creating "pre-roll" ads that air before the CBS content.[18] One reason why CBS chose YouTube over other sites, such as Hulu.com, could be because YouTube is willing to share more of its advertising revenue. Hulu hosts content from NBC and FOX in exchange for the networks giving 30 percent of the advertising revenue back to Hulu. CBS most likely pays less than 30 percent to YouTube.[19] The deals themselves aren't as significant as the concept behind them: content owners (specifically television shows and music videos) are licensing their work to be legally aired on YouTube in exchange for a share of advertising revenue. This model will most certainly lead to more and more content being legally posted to the site.

Why YouTube Works in Education

So why is all of this important to educators? Because as the focus of the content on YouTube moves away from what author Andrew Keen calls "the cult of the amateur"—the glut of amateur videos on the site—and more toward mainstream traditional media, educators will have access to an enormous pedagogical resource: an immense library of music and video that can be incorporated into any music curriculum. While there will most certainly continue to be millions of homemade videos available, there will also be a steady increase in educationally appropriate videos. Perhaps in the near future, networks such as PBS will enter into an agreement to allow the renowned Ken Burns *Jazz* series to be legally posted on YouTube in exchange for advertising revenue to offset the loss in DVD sales. Perhaps HBO will make its Composers Series available for music teachers to show their students, or even *Beethoven Lives Upstairs* and other stalwarts of the general music curriculum. As more and more companies license their content to YouTube and similar sites, educators will only benefit.

While we'll be providing specific examples in the chapters that follow of how music educators might use YouTube in their classrooms, first let's take a quick look back to find out how this simple site came into existence, and the incredible story behind its meteoric rise to success.

A Brief History of YouTube

The story that is widely reported by the media is that the idea for YouTube came about in early 2005, when friends and former PayPal employees Chad Hurley, Steve Chen, and Jawed Karim experienced difficulties sharing the videos that were taken during a dinner party at Chen's apartment in San Francisco. Jawed Karim, who was not at the party, denied that it had actually happened, so Hurley and Chen decided to create a site where users could easily upload their videos for others to see using Adobe Flash technology as the engine.[20] However the idea originated, the friends registered the YouTube URL on February 15, 2005, and by April the first video was posted to the site. The very first video posted was titled "Me at the Zoo," and featured founder Jawed Karim in front of the elephant enclosure at the San Diego Zoo.[21] The site began public beta testing in May 2005. It was not successful by any means at first, with very few videos being posted and very few visits. Then, after the founders added some social networking features such as those found on MySpace (including the ability to rank the videos, comment on them, and share them with others), the site began to attract some attention. Backed by an investment of $11.5 million from Sequoia Capital, the site was officially launched in November 2005. At that time, about 3 million videos were being viewed a day. By June 2006, approximately 65,000 videos were being uploaded to the site on a daily basis, with over 100 million views per day. On November 13, 2006, Google finalized a deal to acquire YouTube for $1.65 billion in Google stock. In addition to the incredible daily traffic to the site—YouTube is ranked as the third most visited site behind Google and Yahoo[22]—Google also inherited the legal problems that YouTube had run into in its short existence, including the well-publicized lawsuit that was filed on behalf of Viacom for copyright infringement. These issues will be discussed in detail in chapter 5.

In 2007 the site's popularity grew tremendously. In its short existence, YouTube had captured nearly 60 percent of the video-viewing market—more than all of its other competitors combined. By January 2009, more than 13 hours of new videos were being posted to the site every minute, costing YouTube nearly $1 million per day in Internet bandwidth costs.[23] YouTube's slogan—"Broadcast Yourself"—has obviously resonated deeply with Internet users both young and old. Although there is growing competition out there, it is clear that YouTube will be around for quite some time — regardless of the legal issues it is currently fighting.

Educational Applications

Now that you have a little perspective on YouTube, it is important to focus on some of the many curricular integration strategies that are possible using the site. Before doing so, however, it is equally important to first offer a rationale for why Web 2.0 technologies such as YouTube should be embraced rather than feared by educators. The students that we teach today are connected to the world in ways that most teachers could only have imagined a decade ago.

Digital Natives vs. Digital Immigrants

Marc Prensky calls this generation "digital natives" and the rest of us "digital immigrants."[24] Natives are characterized as those born after 1980 who use their cell phones as their main form of communication — whether talking to or texting their friends, sharing music or video files with others, or even playing online MMORPGs (massively multiplayer online role-playing games) such as *World of Warcraft* or *Everquest*. They also share massive amounts of personal information on social networking sites such as Facebook and MySpace, and create music and videos and share them on sites such as YouTube. They regularly comment on the videos that others have posted, embed their favorite videos into their personal blogs, and even create their own YouTube communities as a method of sharing videos with their friends.

Most educators, on the other hand, fall into the "digital immigrant" category, although some fall into the category that authors John Palfrey and Urs Gasser call "digital settlers."[25] Immigrants are those born before 1980 who still read paper newspapers, listen to CDs rather than digital music, and remember rotary-dial telephones. While many use today's technology, it has not yet transformed their lives to the degree that it has for natives. They might have a Facebook page, but they don't "live" online. Settlers are those who have fully embraced technology, but can clearly remember the days of old.

In today's educational environment, connecting instruction with the forms of communication that our students (natives) are accustomed to can serve as an important pedagogical lens through which curricular material can be presented. By incorporating Web 2.0 technology — defined as that having highly interactive, social networking features — into the classroom, teachers can connect learning with a familiar environment. Many have adopted this rationale, and regularly create podcasts, interactive websites, and blogs for their students, and use educational social networking sites such as Ning.com to bring their curricula to life. YouTube is one such technology, and the integration strategies below help to illustrate its potential. Whichever category you personally fit into — digital immigrant, digital settler, or digital native — it is not difficult to implement them.

Online Instrumental Music Lessons

Perhaps the most obvious of all the strategies is the creation of online lessons for students (see chapters 6 and 7). If you search for any instrument on YouTube and add the word "lesson," you will have hundreds, if not thousands, of videos to choose from. For example, a search for "tuba lesson" yielded around 160 results. While some of these are student-generated videos and not necessarily useful, many are quite good. One such video, created by Kevin Smith, is called "Tuba Lessons: Parts of a Tuba: How to Operate Spit Valves in a Tuba" (see Fig. 1.7). This video, part of a YouTube channel called Expert Village (a website that currently has over 120,000 videos online, with over 230,000 subscribers), gives an overview of how to release moisture from the spit valve of a tuba. It is thorough and well planned out.[26] Because many instrumental music teachers have to teach instruments that they might not be completely familiar with, having students view these videos can serve as a valuable enhancement to instruction — especially in situations where geographical or socioeconomic restrictions would make it difficult to find a suitable instructor otherwise.

Fig. 1.7
Online tuba lesson

Other Online Lessons

Along with instrumental lessons, many other types of lessons are available, including vocal lessons, music theory lessons, composition lessons, lessons on audio recording techniques, and even lessons on how to make your own music videos. A wide variety of software tutorials are available for almost any music title you can think of. A search for "Finale Notation Software Tutorial" yielded over

1,250 results.[27] As with the instrumental lessons mentioned above, some of these lessons are wonderful, and others leave quite a bit to be desired. It is really a case of caveat emptor. Many of the lessons posted on YouTube are there to generate publicity, and often ask viewers to subscribe to or visit the creator's personal or business website. One vocal lesson was posted by a woman named Rae Henry (see Fig. 1.8). Titled "Singing Lessons—Vocal Coach (Lesson 1— Breath)," it is very well put together. Ms. Henry asks viewers to subscribe to her channel, which contains links to her professional singing website where viewers may also purchase her latest CD, *Smooth Sundays*. The lesson promises more instructional videos to come, though as of this writing they have yet to appear. Educators should spend some time searching for and screening YouTube videos in order to ensure their overall quality. To avoid student exposure to the comments feature of the site, an embed code is listed on every video that can be used to embed the video in any other website—specifically, more student-friendly sites. This process will be described in detail in chapter 2.

Fig. 1.8
Online vocal lesson

Great Performances Online

Perhaps the most obvious use of YouTube in the music classroom is to show relevant videos of musical performances. Educators need only search for the name of the composition or the name of the artist to find multiple videos of various performances of a work. For example, a search for "The Beatles" yielded over 160,000 videos. A search for "John Coltrane" found 2,600. A search for "Marilyn Horne" garnered almost 400. And yes, a search for the "Jonas Brothers" yielded over 400,000 videos to choose from for the adoring fans in your classroom. The obvious question that surrounds all of these videos is: are they legal? While some have been posted to YouTube with the permission of the copyright owner, the vast majority infringe on the copyright that gives the owner the right to control the public display of their work. As the Beatles video *Help!* has been viewed well over 10 million times, there is a legitimate concern that having videos such as these available for free on YouTube will result in a potentially enormous loss of revenue (although that particular video is properly licensed and supported by advertising).

Chapters 5 and 8 will discuss copyright issues as well as the terms of service set forth by YouTube that govern this type of activity.

Yet if videos are properly licensed, they can most certainly be used in the classroom and serve as an incredible free resource for educators. Imagine being able to show students classic performances of Leopold Stokowski conducting the London Symphony Orchestra, or Louis Armstrong singing "What a Wonderful World," or Zakir Hussein playing the tabla—all for free. If a video is not properly licensed it usually gets pulled down rather quickly. If not, it is technically not "fair use" to use it in your classroom for any purpose and it should be avoided altogether. Chapter 5 explains how to find out whether a video is legal or not. Because YouTube has the potential to be an invaluable resource in the classroom, these issues should be examined closely.

Other Applications

Part two of this book, specifically chapters 6 and 7, will illustrate in much further detail many of the pedagogical applications of YouTube in music education, including specific examples of appropriate videos for use with students, and will also provide ideas for lessons using YouTube content. These ideas include:

- ▶ Having students post their own multimedia projects on the site

- ▶ Posting teacher- or student-produced video podcasts (or vodcasts) online

- ▶ Using content from the site for film scoring

- ▶ Using performance videos for student critique or discussion

- ▶ Creating a YouTube channel and/or community specifically for your students to share relevant videos

- ▶ Facilitating collaborative music-making projects by connecting students around the world

- ▶ Posting teaching videos for use when a substitute teacher is required

- ▶ Providing students with further resources to learn more about a given musical concept at home

There are obviously many other ways to incorporate YouTube into the music classroom. Chapters 6 and 7 will include lesson plan ideas submitted by music teachers around the world, as well as some of our own ideas.

Summary

This chapter has provided an overview of YouTube and its many applications in music education. The history of the site as well as the impact that it has had on our culture were included to properly frame the relevance of YouTube as an educational resource as well as its place within the culture of the students that we teach. The following chapters provide a more detailed guide to the technical aspects of using the site as well as strategies for implementing it in the music classroom. Careful attention is given to protecting student identity at all times, as well as suggestions for making the content from the site available in a more controlled environment—free from inappropriate content. It is our sincere hope that these resources will serve as a roadmap for using the site in your classroom to make music education come alive for your students.

Chapter Two **YouTube Tour**

This chapter provides a virtual tour of YouTube to help you become more comfortable with the look and feel of the website.

The topics discussed in this chapter include:

- ► The YouTube homepage
- ► Creating an account
- ► Account sign-in
- ► Modifying the module display
- ► Videos, shows, and channels
- ► YouTube Screening Room
- ► Events and contests
- ► Searching for and playing videos
- ► Subscriptions
- ► QuickList, favorites, and playlists
- ► Flagging videos
- ► Account options
- ► YouTube Help
- ► Creating a vlog
- ► TestTube

> **TIP**   Watching videos online is pretty computer-processor (and bandwidth-) intensive, so if you use a dial-up modem, videos will not play continuously and there will be some lag as the content loads. A high-speed DSL or cable connection is recommended for viewing videos on YouTube.

Chapter 1 provided an overview of YouTube, including a brief history. In this chapter, you will roll up your sleeves and become familiar with the YouTube website and the various ways you can search for and watch free YouTube videos.

> **TIP**   As you read the suggestions throughout this chapter and the book, try them out while accessing YouTube on your computer. You will learn and retain more if you apply the information as it is introduced.

The YouTube Homepage

Enter the address "www.youtube.com" into any Web browser (Internet Explorer, Safari, or Firefox), and you will access the YouTube homepage (see Fig. 2.1). Here you will find a list of promoted videos, including Videos Being Watched Now and Featured Videos. You can click on any of the video links and watch these videos without signing in. You can also close the advertisement on the page by clicking the Close Ad X box.

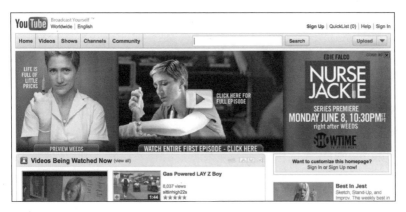

Fig. 2.1
Viewing YouTube without signing in

TIP   Any time you want to go back to the YouTube homepage, just click the YouTube icon in the upper left-hand corner of the site.

Creating an Account

If you plan on visiting YouTube frequently—especially if you plan to use it in your classroom—you should create your own YouTube account. Chapter 3 will go deeper into the various YouTube account options, but for now, you just need to create an account, which is free and relatively easy.

To create a user account (if you don't already have one) you have two options. On the YouTube homepage, you can click on the Sign Up link in the upper right-hand corner of the page. Then choose a username and password and complete the sign-up process.

You can also access YouTube via a Google account. If you have a Gmail account, you already have a Google account. Just sign in to your Google account, and in the upper left-hand menu bar under "More" you will see a "YouTube" link. Click on this link to navigate to the YouTube homepage, and follow the instructions to add a YouTube account.

TIP   Make your username something that reflects you and your areas of interest. It can be any name, but consider it carefully, especially if you are planning to use YouTube with your students. Also, there is nothing stopping you from creating two or more user accounts. You might have one for use with your students and one for personal use.

Account Sign-in

After you sign in to your account, you will see a slightly different YouTube homepage (see Fig. 2.2). YouTube automatically adjusts the look of the website to your preferences, and the more you use and customize YouTube, the more personal the links and settings will be (see chapter 3 for a detailed guide on setting up your account preferences). The YouTube homepage provides a list of categories to choose from as you scroll down the page.

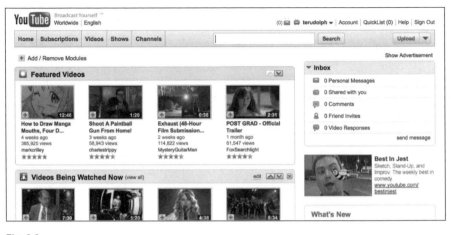

Fig. 2.2
YouTube homepage after signing in

For example, certain categories, or Modules, will be displayed, including Subscriptions, Recommended for You, Featured Videos, Friend Activity, Promoted Videos, and Rising Videos. As of this writing, this is the default modules setting. Note that YouTube is constantly updating and changing the website, so things can change without notice. The more you log in and use the site, the more content will be shown within these categories.

Modifying the Module Display

You can adjust what is displayed on your page, such as the modules that appear. Just click on the Add/Remove Modules link in the upper left-hand corner of the page (see Fig. 2.3). This will allow you to add or delete whatever modules you wish.

For school accounts, you can usually uncheck most of the options given in the Module Display. You can make changes to the module display at any time. When you are done making changes, be sure to click the Save Changes button.

Fig. 2.3
Add/Remove Modules

Main Menu

There are currently five tabs at the top of the YouTube homepage for Home, Subscriptions (see page 29), Videos, Shows, and Channels (see Fig. 2.4). YouTube changes the appearance of its homepage often, so it could look slightly different than what is described in this chapter. If you are logged in and click Home, you will be taken to your personal list of categories. The other tabs take you to Subscriptions, Videos, Shows, and Channels. This chapter will provide you with a quick overview of these.

| Home | Subscriptions | Videos | Shows | Channels |

Fig. 2.4
YouTube tabs Home, Subscriptions, Videos, Shows, and Channels

Videos

In the Videos view, you have the option to choose from the categories listed on the left-hand side of the page, or you can click on the links across the top of the page to view videos by Popular, Most Viewed, or HD (high-definition videos for better quality). The More button provides a list of options including Spotlight Videos, Rising Videos, Most Discussed, Recent Videos, Most Responded, Top Favorited, and Top Rated. Each of these will give you a different selection of videos to view.

Under Categories on the left-hand side of the window is a general list of video categories, including Music and Education. When you click on any category, the most popular videos are displayed. This is a good place to see what YouTube has to offer or to find a specific category of videos. You can also search for individual titles, which will be covered later in this chapter.

Shows

When you click on the Shows tab at the top of the window, the list on the left of the screen changes. Under Categories now appears Shows, which lists the wide variety of television shows that can be viewed on YouTube, organized by genre such as "Action & Adventure" and "Documentary & Biography."

Also listed under Categories is Movies (see Fig. 2.5). As of this writing both the Shows and Movies lists are new features, hence the "New" icon. Some of these shows may contain material you can use in your classroom.

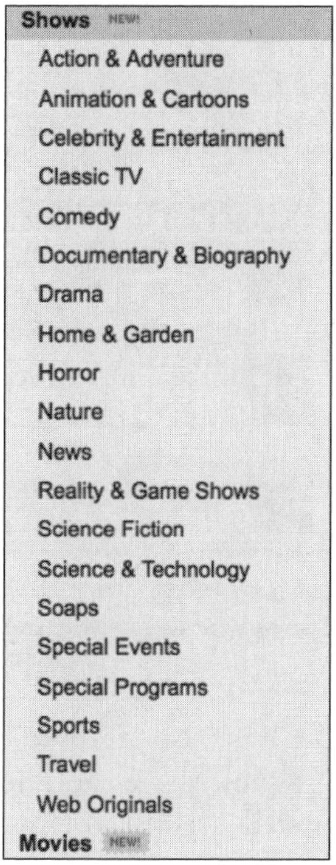

Shows NEW!
Action & Adventure
Animation & Cartoons
Celebrity & Entertainment
Classic TV
Comedy
Documentary & Biography
Drama
Home & Garden
Horror
Nature
News
Reality & Game Shows
Science Fiction
Science & Technology
Soaps
Special Events
Special Programs
Sports
Travel
Web Originals
Movies NEW!

Fig. 2.5
Shows and movies

Channels

All YouTube account holders can view their personal information on their Channel or Profile page. This is a centralized location where other users can see your public videos, favorites, comments, subscribers, video log, bulletin status, and recent activity. Users can also see stats about you, such as how long you've been a YouTube member, how old you are, and how many videos you've watched. Your channel is an easy place for people to connect with you, send you a message, share a channel, add you as a friend, or add comments to your channel.

When you access Channels for the first time, you will see a list of individual channels organized by Most Subscribed and Most Viewed. These can subsequently be organized in any manner you prefer.

The Search box allows you to look for specific videos. A search for the words "Music Education" returned tens of thousands of videos. Clicking on the Channels link on the left-hand side of the window returned 160 channels for the "Music Education" area (see Fig. 2.6).

Fig. 2.6
Channel search results for "Music Education"

See if you can find some channels that you are interested in. When you do, you can subscribe to these channels so you get automatic updates when new videos are posted. We will cover more on this later in the chapter.

YT Screening Room

When you click on the Channels tab at the top of the window, at the bottom of the list on the left-hand side you will see several additional categories, including Contests, Events, and YT [YouTube] Screening Room. YouTube provides the following information about the YT Screening Room:

> The YouTube Screening Room is a platform for top films from around the world to find the audiences they deserve. Every other Friday, you'll find four new films featured in the YouTube Screening Room. These films always appear with the permission and involvement of the filmmakers, so be sure to rate, share, and leave comments. This is your chance to not only watch great films from all corners of the globe, but also to converse with the filmmakers behind them. While the majority of these films have played at international film festivals, occasionally you'll find films that have never before screened for wide audiences. All films playing in the YouTube Screening Room are displayed within our high-quality player to give you the best viewing experience possible. Be a part of a new generation of filmmaking and distribution and help us connect films and audiences in the world's largest theater!

Events and Contests

This is an advertisement area for live events, many of which are music-related. After clicking the Events link, you can search for events by location in the Find Events search box. This is a handy way to look for local performances.

When you click on a link, you get a page that typically includes some information about the performing group or event, and a demo video. The list of events changes, so check back often to see if there are any upcoming events of interest to you. Fig. 2.7 shows a listing of a new music event that was scheduled for June 10, 2009, featuring the Network for New Music Ensemble.

 NetworkForNewMusic
Royal Theater
June 10, 2009
1524 South St. Philadelphia Map
NNM MIX: Re-Sounding/Hidden City
Composer/performer Todd Reynolds explores the musical heritage of Philadelphia's legendary Royal Theater on South Street as the Network for New Music Ensemble performs live, with a film and video installation by visual artist Laurie Olinder and filmmaker Bill Morriso (more)

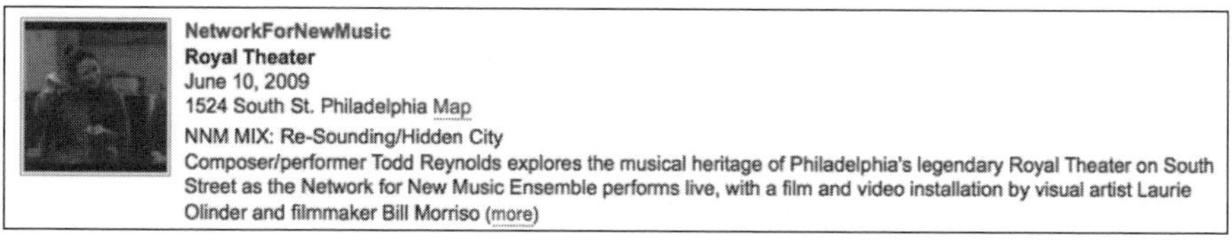

Fig. 2.7
YouTube event listing

In order to list an event, your Channel Type must be set to "Musician," "Comedian," or "Guru" status. Then you will have the option to display information related to performances. To change your channel type, go to your Account page, click on Edit Channel (under "More"), and click the Change Channel Type link at the bottom of the page.

Contests are another interesting area to explore. The YouTube Symphony, a popular contest, was featured in chapter 1. There are also frequent contests for users who remix and mash up the music and videos that have been posted by other users. Music is one of the most active contest categories on YouTube. You should consider informing your students about relevant contests, especially those that focus on creating music.

Searching for Videos

No matter what area of YouTube you are currently perusing, you can always do a search for specific items in the Search window at the top of the YouTube site (see Fig. 2.8).

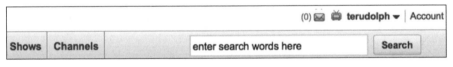

Fig. 2.8
YouTube Search window

YouTube's search capabilities lack the Google-like Boolean search options such as OR, NOT, and other terms. But you can use quotes around a group of words to search for a specific phrase, such as "trumpet lessons." Also, when you use quotations around two or more words, they will be searched as a unit or phrase, not as individual words, so this will help narrow your search.

When you start typing in a word or phrase in the search box, YouTube will begin offering suggested search terms in a drop-down menu below the search window. You will often find the exact term you are searching for after typing only a few letters. For example, if you are looking for a video about the hurdy-gurdy, you need only type

Fig. 2.9
Search drop-down list

"hurd," and YouTube will suggest *hurdy-gurdy man, hurdles, hurdy gurdy* and more (see Fig. 2.9). Then you can just click on the term that you want. This is a very helpful feature, as you will often find other related subjects in your suggested search terms.

> **TIP**   Use the search window to locate specific music education videos. Use quotations to search for specific phrases.

A search including the words "music education" returned many results that educators may find of interest, such as "National Standards for Music Education" and "The Case for Music Education." Also 43,000 other videos![1] There are more videos on YouTube than you could watch in a lifetime, so getting familiar with how to search for what you want is key.

Playing Videos

By now, if you are accessing YouTube while you are reading, you have probably already played one or more videos. When you play a video, the look of the page changes—the video screen gets larger and fills more of the page. A search for "trumpet lessons" yielded a popular lesson by the famous Clark Terry. We'll use this to review the various YouTube playback options.

The video playback options (see Fig. 2.10) include:

- ▶ **Play/Pause:** Click this button to play the video. While a video is playing, press it again to pause playback.

- ▶ **Playhead:** This shows your current location in the video. Sometimes videos will take time to load. The red bar indicates how much of the video is loaded. Once a video is loaded, you can then drag the playhead to specific locations in the video.

- ▶ **Time Elapsed:** The time that has elapsed since the start of the video. This reflects the location of the playhead.

- ▶ **Total Time:** The total time of the video. YouTube limits videos to 10 minutes total time.

- ▶ **Volume:** Click and drag on this to increase or decrease the playback volume. See chapter 4 for more details on controlling volume.

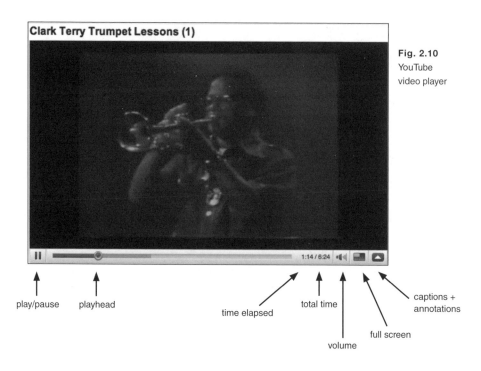

Fig. 2.10
YouTube
video player

- **Full Screen:** Click this button and the video will fill the entire screen of your computer monitor. This is the best option to use when showing videos to an entire class (see chapter 4). Press the Escape key in the upper left-hand corner of your computer keyboard to return the video to the normal size.

- **Captions and Annotations:** When you create your own videos (covered in chapter 10), you can enter captions and annotations. This button allows you to turn on each option. Captions and annotations are optional, and are not included in every video.

Subscriptions

If you are signed in, the Subscriptions tab is located at the top of the YouTube homepage. When you view a video, if you click the Subscribe button (see Fig. 2.11), you will receive e-mail notifications whenever that user posts new content on their channel. This allows you to keep up to date on a channel without having to manually check it. To manage your subscriptions, visit your Account page (via the Account link located in the top right of every page) and click the Subscriptions link under "My Videos."

Fig. 2.11
Subscribe button

Organizing Your Videos

There are millions of videos on YouTube. You will find yourself browsing through a wide range of videos. There are a few ways to organize your videos, which are described in detail in the following sections.

Creating a QuickList

There are a couple of ways to search for and watch videos on YouTube. If you are looking for a specific video, just use the Search box and click to play each video. However, if you want to save your search results so that you can easily find your videos, YouTube provides some convenient functions to make your search easier. The first option is to create a QuickList. A QuickList is a temporary list of videos that is stored in your Web browser (Internet Explorer, Safari, Firefox, and so forth). When you close the Web browser or shut down your computer, the list is erased. Think of a QuickList as a way to store your video choices temporarily for viewing. Here is how it works:

1. Log in to YouTube. Click the Sign In link and then enter your username and password.

2. Search for videos you would like to watch. You can do this using any of the search tools previously mentioned in this chapter. Search for videos any way you choose.

3. Then, when you find a video you want to watch, click the plus sign in the bottom left-hand corner of the video (see Fig. 2.12).

Fig. 2.12
Adding videos to a QuickList

For example, search for "Trumpet Voluntary Clarke" to listen to a performance of this piece. One search returned a list of 91 videos. Notice that there is a plus sign at the bottom of each video thumbnail (see Fig. 2.12). A thumbnail is a small version of a YouTube video. When you click on a thumbnail, the full screen version becomes visible. Click the plus sign to add a video to your current QuickList. The main advantage of this is that you don't have to watch the video to add it to your QuickList. You can perform several searches and add as many videos as you like to your QuickList. Then you can go to the list and view the videos. Remember, you can use the QuickList to set aside videos for later viewing.

4. When you are done searching for videos and you have clicked the plus sign on one or more videos to add it to your QuickList, you can then go to the QuickList link in the upper left-hand corner of the page (see Fig. 2.13) to view them.

> terudolph ▾ | Account | QuickList (3) | Help | Sign Out
>
> [   ] **Search**   **Upload** ▼

Fig. 2.13
QuickList link

5. When you are in the QuickList window, you can select any of the videos and play them individually by clicking on the video icon (see Fig. 2.14). You can also click the "Play QuickList" button to view the videos in order, click the check box next to any video to remove it from your QuickList, or delete the entire QuickList by clicking the Clear QuickList button at the top of the QuickList page.

TIP   QuickList is an excellent tool for a music listening lesson. You can select several videos prior to class and use QuickList to manage your selections.

If you click the + Add To link (see Fig. 2.14), you can add your temporary QuickList selections to a more permanent Playlist or Favorites. These options are detailed in the following section.

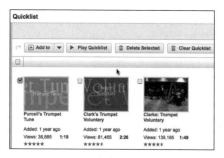

Fig. 2.14
Working with a QuickList

Saving Favorites

The next step in organizing your YouTube videos is to save videos you may want to view in the future to your Favorites. The Favorites area lists all the videos you have selected as Favorites, which will remain there until you delete them. So when you log out of YouTube, your Favorites will remain, as the Favorites area saves the videos' locations. It is a handy way to save the videos you want, and of course you can add and delete any videos you choose.

1. While watching a video, beneath the video click the Favorite button. The video will be saved to your Favorites.

2. To see your list of Favorites, click on your username in the upper right-hand area of the page and select Favorites from the drop-down menu.

3. You can sort your Favorites according to the various options shown at the top of the window, such as by Title, Time, Date Added, Views, and Rating.

4. Select the check box to the upper left of a video and click Remove to remove it from your list.

5. You can also add selected videos to your QuickList or convert them to a specific Playlist (described below).

Creating a Playlist

A Playlist is a more permanent way to save your favorite videos to your account. This list will remain even after you log out of YouTube. The Google Help menu describes a Playlist as "a collection of videos that can be watched on YouTube, shared with other people, or embedded into websites or blogs. 'Favorites' is your default Playlist, but you can create as many as you want. You can create a Playlist from the video watch page, your QuickList, or from your Account."[2]

TIP   Click on the YouTube Help link (in the upper right corner of any page) whenever you need to get a tutorial on a specific feature. There is an excellent YouTube video that demonstrates how to make a playlist. Go to the Help menu and search for Playlist: www.google.com/support/youtube/bin/answer.py?hl=en&answer=57792.

You can make your playlist public so anyone can see your list, or you can make it a private list so only your family and friends and/or students can view it (see chapter 3 for more details).

Making a Playlist from the Main YouTube Page

You can have multiple playlists, and as mentioned above, they can be public or private. You determine the type of playlist when it is created. Let's start by making a playlist.

1. To get to the Playlists area, click on your login name in the upper right-hand corner of the YouTube page and choose Playlists from the drop-down list (see Fig. 2.15).

2. On the left side of the window, under My Account, click the New tab and select Playlist.

3. Enter a New Playlist Title. Give it a descriptive name such as "Tom's Jazz Playlist." Since you can have many playlists, be as specific as possible. See Fig. 2.16.

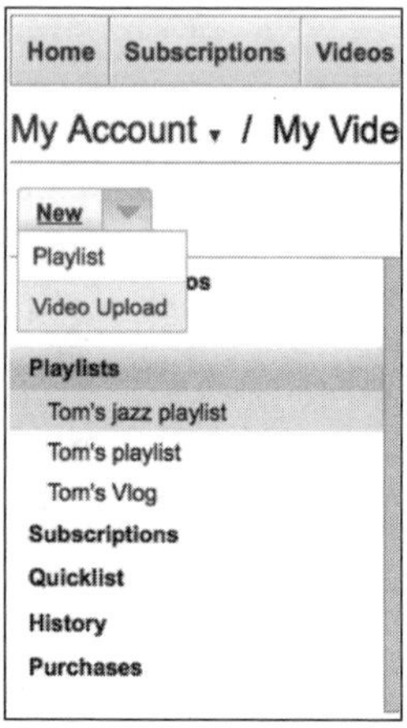

Fig. 2.15
Selecting a Playlist

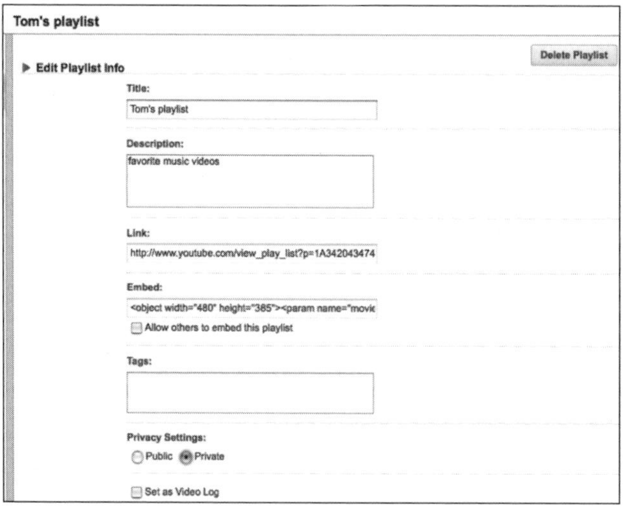

Fig. 2.16
Creating a Playlist

4. Enter a Description.

5. Decide whether to allow other users to embed the playlist. *Embedding* refers to copying the Web location of the Playlist and placing it into another website, such as a blog.

6. Enter tags. *Tags* are descriptive words about a playlist that can be used by others when searching for videos. Be sure to separate each tag by a space. For example, if you are creating a jazz playlist, you might add some of the names of the performers, the styles included, and any other information as separate words.

7. The Privacy Setting is very important. This is most helpful when creating a playlist for your students or others that you don't want to be shared with the entire YouTube community.

8. Check or leave unchecked the "Save as Video Log" button. Video logs, or *vlogs*, are typically a video of a person talking into a camera about their thoughts on a particular subject matter. Vlogs are generally frequent postings of videos that are personal in nature, in keeping with the idea of a "log" or diary.

9. Click Save Changes to create your playlist. Now, you can add selected videos to your playlist and edit the list as needed. The playlist will remain active until you delete it.

TIP   If you want to copy a playlist and embed it in your school website or blog, follow these steps:

    1. Go to the Playlists section of your account.

    2. Select the playlist you'd like to embed.

    3. Copy the embed code from the upper right corner.

    4. Paste the code into your website or blog.

Adding to Your Playlist While Viewing a Video

Now that you have a playlist, you can add videos to it at any time. While viewing a video, click the Playlist icon below the video window (see Fig. 2.17).

Since you have created one or more playlists, you can save the video to one of your lists. You can also create a new playlist from this link.

Creating a Playlist from a QuickList

You worked with QuickLists earlier in this chapter. The difference between a QuickList and a Playlist is that a QuickList only lasts for the current YouTube session. When you quit out of your Web browser or sign

Fig. 2.17
Adding to an existing playlist

off from YouTube, the QuickList information is deleted. A Playlist remains after your session ends. QuickLists are one of the quickest ways to create a permanent playlist.

1. Open your current QuickList by clicking the QuickList link in the upper right-hand corner of the YouTube window (see Fig. 2.18).

Fig. 2.18
QuickList link

2. To remove the videos you do not want added to your playlist, select their related check boxes and click the Delete Selected button.

3. Click the check box next to each video to select the videos that you want to add to your Playlist.

4. When you have selected all the desired videos from your QuickList, click on the Add To button and select Playlist from the drop-down menu.

5. Your playlist(s) will appear. Choose the playlist you want, and all the selected videos on your QuickList will be added to the playlist. Remember: A Playlist is permanent; a QuickList will be deleted when you close your Web browser.

Flagging Inappropriate Videos

YouTube does a good job of removing videos with inappropriate content. The YouTube team reviews uploaded videos, but with so many new videos being added to the site, they also allow users to identify videos with questionable content. This is called *flagging* a video. You can flag a video, and it will be reported to YouTube, and if it agrees, the video will be removed from the site. YouTube defines the following as inappropriate content:

- Graphic sexual activity

- Nudity

- Suggestive, but without nudity

- Shocking or disgusting content

- Promoting hatred or violence against a protected group

- Harmful dangerous acts

If you feel that a video contains any of the inappropriate content above, then you can click on the Flag link at the bottom of that video.

When you click the Flag link, you will then be asked to select a reason (see Fig. 2.19). Reasons include Sexual Content, Violent or Repulsive Content, Hateful or Abusive Content, Harmful Dangerous Acts, Spam, or Infringes My Rights. When you flag a video, YouTube reviews it to see if it does, in fact, violate one or more of its community guidelines. If it does deem the video as inappropriate, the user will be notified and told why the video was taken down from the site.

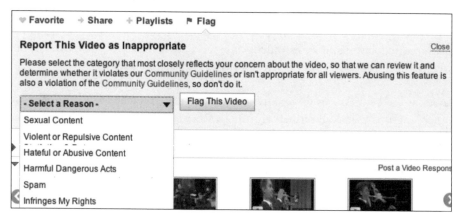

Fig. 2.19

Flagging inappropriate videos

Account Options

Clicking on the Account link in the upper right-hand corner of the YouTube window (see Fig. 2.20) brings you to a list of links organized into three categories: My Videos, My Network, and More.

My Videos	My Network	More
Uploaded Videos	Inbox	Groups
Favorites	Address Book	Active Sharing
Playlists	Subscribers	Edit Channel
Subscriptions	Video Comments	Custom Video Players
QuickList	Video Responses	Change Password
History		
Purchases		

Fig. 2.20
Account options

My Videos

This chapter reviewed most of the links in the My Videos area. The Uploaded Videos link displays all the videos you have uploaded to YouTube (see chapter 10). The History link is helpful if you viewed a video in the recent past and would like to search your viewed videos. There is also a button for clearing the history of the videos you have watched. The Purchases link lists the items you have purchased. Most videos on YouTube are free to view. However, some offer links to download audio and some videos for a fee.

My Network

YouTube is designed to be more than just a place to view videos. It can also be a community for you and your students. Chapter 3 will detail how you can use the My Network functions to facilitate your educational applications.

Inbox is where messages to you are located. Address Book is where you can list other YouTube users. Subscribers are YouTubers who clicked the Subscribe button while viewing one of your videos. Video Comments are comments on your videos from other users, which could be your students, if you wish. Video Responses are your responses to posted comments.

More

The More options are detailed in chapter 3. The most important feature in this category is the Groups option, which allows you to create a private or public group for use with your students.

YouTube Help

One area of YouTube you will want to explore is YouTube Help, which you can access by clicking the Help link in the upper right-hand corner of the YouTube window (see Fig. 2.21).

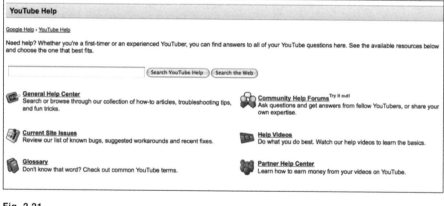

Fig. 2.21
YouTube Help

The Glossary is a comprehensive listing of the terms you will encounter on the YouTube site. If you are a new user, these new terms can be confusing, so the Glossary can help you understand them.

Community Help Forums is where you can ask questions of fellow YouTube users.

General Help Center is the place to go for common and not so common questions about how YouTube works or how others are using YouTube. The Help Center is moderated by YouTube employees.

Video Weblog (Vlog)

Are you familiar with blogs? A *blog* is short for weblog, which is an ongoing list of posts about a topic or subject. Typically, blogs are text-oriented. But there is a cousin of the blog called a *vlog*, which is an abbreviation for video weblog. A vlog typically consists of a series of videos about a topic that is usually informal. If you search for "music vlog" on YouTube, you will be able to view some of the vlogs that have been created.

YouTube offers a handy way to create your own vlog:

1. Sign in to your YouTube account.

2. In the right-hand corner of the screen, click on Account.

3. Under My Videos, click the Playlists link.

4. Under My Account, Click on the New button, and then select Playlist from the drop-down menu. See the steps above for creating a new Playlist.

5. Check the box next to "Set as Video Blog," and the videos from this list will automatically appear on your Video Blog page.

6. You can add videos to your vlog by saving to that playlist or transferring videos from other playlists or your Favorites.

Within your vlog, you can alter the title and description of the videos by clicking on the "Edit Playlist Info" link at the top of the vlog playlist window and then entering the required fields. Typically, users create their own vlogs by videotaping themselves. See chapter 10 for tips on recording and saving videos.

TestTube

TestTube is where YouTube engineers and developers test new ideas and features that are not yet fully implemented into the YouTube site. You can review these new ideas and give feedback to the development team. The TestTube link is at the bottom of the YouTube website under the "Discover" area. Some of your students may be interested in TestTube, which could be a way to explore YouTube from a creative, "under the hood" viewpoint.

Summary

YouTube is a robust community, and joining it will enable you to interact with people who share your interests. YouTube does not necessarily take time to learn. You can jump in immediately, and hone your skills over time. There are four main ways to navigate the site, including browsing by video, category, and channels. In addition, YouTube provides a host of ways to organize the videos you select, including creating QuickLists, Playlists, and Favorites. You can also create your very own vlog, and check out the unique TestTube area for engineers and developers. Take some time to get familiar with these navigational, organizational, and other tools. Your YouTube viewing experience will be greatly improved.

Chapter Three # Creating a YouTube Account

In this chapter, the following topics will be addressed:

- ▸ What is a YouTube account, channel, group, and community
- ▸ How to create a YouTube account
- ▸ Creating a unique screen name
- ▸ Selecting a username and password
- ▸ The difference between a public and private account
- ▸ Setting preferences
- ▸ How to create a group
- ▸ How to create a channel
- ▸ Tips for creating an account for use with your students

Chapter 2 covered the basic functions of YouTube and how to navigate around the site. This chapter will take you step by step through the process of creating your own YouTube account, with tips on the best approach for educators. But first, let's define some terms.

TIP Bear in mind that you should always get administrative approval before you create an environment for your students on a public website such as YouTube.

YouTube Account: A YouTube account allows you to log in to the site. Once logged in, you can customize your homepage, upload videos, comment on videos, join and create groups, and join and create communities. As stated in chapter 2, while it is not necessary to create a YouTube account to view videos, it is necessary to create an account to take advantage of YouTube's many features.

YouTube Channel: When you create a YouTube account, you also create a YouTube channel. A channel is defined as "a centralized location where other users can see your public videos, favorites, comments, subscribers, video log, bulletin status, and recent activity. Users can also see stats about you, like how long you've been a YouTube member, how old you are, and how many videos you've watched."[1] Creating a channel provides students with an easy (and safe) place to connect with you, send you messages, share videos, and comment on videos.

YouTube Group: A YouTube group is defined on the site as follows: "If you've got a topic or group of topics that calls for a discussion with a larger group of people, you may want to consider creating a Group. Groups allow multiple people to discuss things publicly, and post multiple videos that apply to the discussion. As a creator or member of a Group, you can choose to add videos, invite other members, begin conversations, and offer comments to the videos and topics that other members have added."[2]

YouTube Community: The YouTube Community is defined as the collective user base for the website. From time to time, YouTube runs contests and events for its users. As an account holder you cannot create events for the entire YouTube audience, nor can you create your own community. YouTube posts guidelines for the community in terms of the type of content that is acceptable and that which is prohibited. For a full list of community guidelines, visit: www.youtube.com/t/community_guidelines.

Creating a YouTube Account

The first step in creating a YouTube account (also known as a channel) is to click on Sign Up in the upper right-hand corner of the homepage (see Fig. 3.1). It is

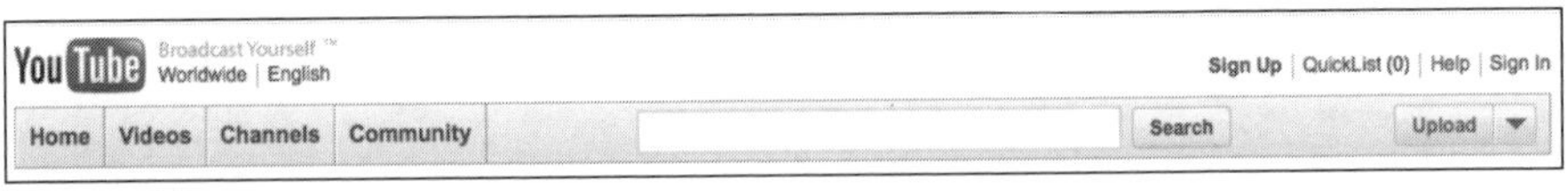

Fig. 3.1
Sign Up on top toolbar

a good idea to have both a username and a password in mind before doing so. Avoid using a username from any other Internet accounts you might have (such as e-mail, online banking, etc.). Teachers might consider using something simple, such as "Ms. Smith" or "ParkAveElemMusic," to make it clear that this is an account used for educational purposes. You should also be aware that YouTube does not limit the number of accounts for an individual e-mail address. You can create as many accounts as you like, which can be helpful if you plan on creating separate YouTube accounts for each school year or class.

TIP If you already have an account with Google, you can use the username and password from your Google account to set up an account with YouTube. However, if it is a personal Google account, you should consider creating a separate YouTube account for use with your students.

Once you click on Sign Up, you will see a new screen, where you will create your YouTube account (see Fig. 3.2). Here, you will be asked to input the following information:

▸ **E-mail Address** — It is recommended that you use your school e-mail account to avoid sharing your personal e-mail address with your students (and the rest of the world).

▸ **Password** — It is wise to create a password that has numbers as well as upper- and lowercase letters. YouTube suggests you make your password at least eight characters. Do not share this password with your students.

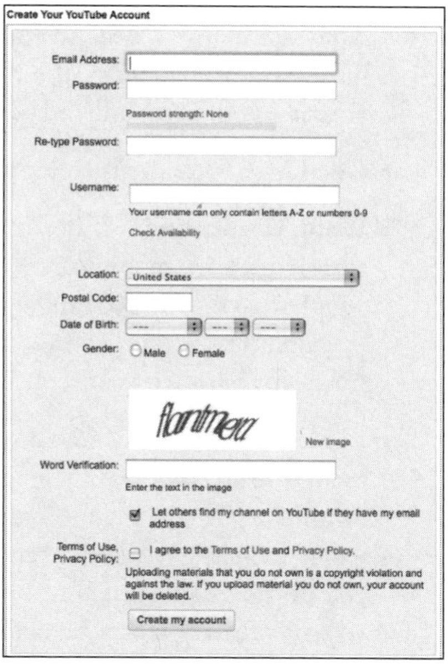

Fig. 3.2
Create your YouTube account

TIP Keep in mind that it is up to you to keep your password secure. You should *never* share your password with others. Also keep in mind that YouTube will never ask you for your password.

▸ **Username**—When choosing a username, use an educationally relevant name (as mentioned above). Do not use a username that you use with other online accounts. For example, for the companion YouTube channel that we created for this book, we chose the username MusicClassroom, rather than our personal usernames.

> **TIP** To maintain your personal privacy, create a username and password that is unique to your teaching position, and use your school e-mail address.

▸ **Location**—The default location is the United States, but you may choose a different location if you live in a different country. If you are in the United States, you do not need to choose the location.

▸ **Postal Code**—Enter the ZIP code for your school.

▸ **Date of Birth**—When selecting your date of birth, you can enter any date—you do not need to enter your actual birthday. YouTube collects this information to identify the demographics of its users. If you don't mind entering your actual birthday, go right ahead!

▸ **Gender**—YouTube is collecting demographic information.

▸ **Word Verification**—Enter the word that appears in the box. The reason why it appears to be warped is so that YouTube can ensure that actual people are creating accounts rather than automated software programs used by spammers. If you cannot read the text in the box, you may click New Image for another word.

▸ **Let Others Find My Channel checkbox**—The default setting for this is to allow those who have your e-mail address to find your YouTube account. As an educator, it is a good idea to leave this box checked so that students, parents, colleagues, and administrators can find your YouTube channel. If you do not want others to find your channel, simply uncheck the box. If you are creating a totally private channel for just your students, then leave this option unchecked.

▸ **Terms of Use Privacy Policy**—In order to create a YouTube account, you must check this box. The details of this policy are discussed later in this chapter.

When you have entered all of the required information, click the Create My Account button.

After you click on Create My Account, you will be directed to check your e-mail (the address that you entered in the form). You need to log in to your e-mail account. You should see an e-mail from YouTube Service welcoming you to YouTube. The e-mail will contain a confirmation button (see Fig. 3.3). Click on the text Confirm Your E-mail Address.

You **Tube** Broadcast Yourself ™   help center | e-mail options | report spam

Confirm your email address to start participating in the YouTube community!

Fig. 3.3
E-mail confirmation

When you click on Confirm Your E-mail Address, you will be routed back to the YouTube site to sign in (log in) to your YouTube account (see Fig. 3.4). Enter your username and password and click Sign In to complete setting up your YouTube account. As stated previously, if you already have a personal Google account, you do not need to create a separate YouTube account, but you should create a separate account when using the site with your students.

You **Tube** Go gle™

Sign in to YouTube with your
YouTube OR Google Account

Username: |
Password:
☑ Remember me on this computer.
Sign in

I cannot access my account

Fig. 3.4
YouTube account login screen

You will notice a check mark next to the text Remember Me on This Computer. If students have access to the computer that you use in school, it is best to uncheck this box. Otherwise your password may be stored by your Web browser, and anyone who uses that computer in the future would be able to log in to your YouTube account.

TIP   If students have the opportunity to use your school computer, it is always best *not* to save your passwords with *any* online accounts. If you save them, anyone can access your private account information.

If you ever forget your username and/or password, you can click on I Cannot Access My Account. This will allow you to enter some of your user information (e-mail address, birthday, postal code, etc.) to try to locate your username and/or password.

Navigating Your YouTube Account

Once you have logged into your account, you should see a shaded box across the top of the YouTube page that reads Your E-mail Has Been Confirmed. You should also see your username on the left side of the toolbar at the top of the page (see Fig. 3.5). There are a number of tabs that relate to your account. Each one is described below.

Fig. 3.5
Account toolbar

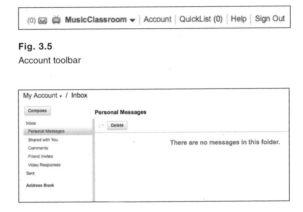

Fig. 3.6
E-mail inbox

E-mail Inbox: YouTube users can send messages directly to your account. These messages can be found in your inbox (see Fig. 3.6). You will know whether you have e-mail in one of two ways: 1) a message will be sent to the e-mail address you entered when you set up your account; or 2) the envelope icon on the Account toolbar will have a star on it when there are new messages. The number in parentheses to the left of the envelope shows the number of new messages. As a YouTube account holder, you can compose messages to other YouTube members as well as receive messages from them. Your e-mail inbox also includes a list of the videos that have been shared with you by other YouTube members, a Comments section that shows comments from other YouTube members about your posted videos, and a Friends Invites section, where friend invitations from other YouTube members are stored.

Active Sharing: The miniature television icon to the right of the envelope on the Account toolbar indicates whether you have chosen to turn on Active Sharing. Active sharing settings are part of the privacy aspect of your account. This will be discussed later in this chapter.

Shortcuts Menu: The next menu option to the right of the Active Sharing icon is a list of shortcuts that can be found by clicking on the drop-down menu arrow to the right of your username. These shortcuts (see Fig. 3.7) include:

Fig. 3.7
Shortcuts menu

- ▶ My Videos—a list of the videos you have uploaded to YouTube

- ▶ Favorites—a list of the videos you have selected as a favorite (see chapter 2)

- ▶ Playlists—a list of the playlists you have created

- ▶ Subscriptions—a list of the channels you have subscribed to (see chapter 2)

- ▶ Inbox—a shortcut to your YouTube inbox

- ▶ More—a button that takes you to the Account Settings page

Account: This menu option brings you to the Account Settings section of your account, described below in further detail.

QuickList: As described in chapter 2, this menu option allows you to mark videos while you are browsing the site. You may add a video to your QuickList by clicking on the small plus sign in the bottom left corner of a video (see Fig. 3.8). This plus sign is only available when you are browsing videos on the site (when they appear as thumbnails). When you view a video, the plus sign disappears. Once you have added videos to your QuickList, you will find them organized in the QuickList section of your account (see Fig. 3.9).

Fig. 3.8
Adding videos to QuickList

Help: Click this menu option if you have questions about any aspect of the YouTube website.

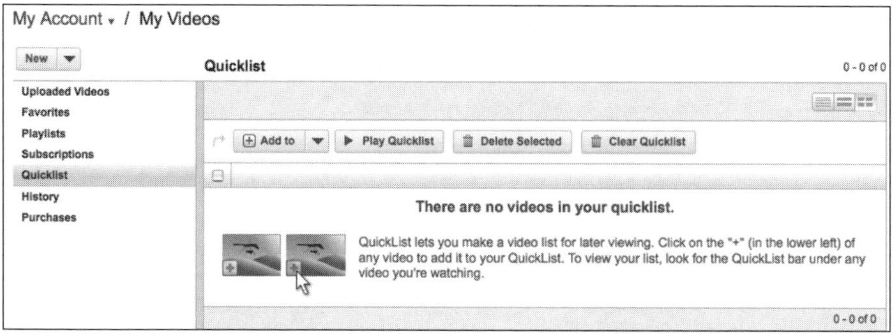

My Account ▾ / **My Videos**

| New ▾ | **Quicklist** | 0 - 0 of 0 |

Uploaded Videos
Favorites
Playlists
Subscriptions
Quicklist
History
Purchases

⊕ Add to ▾ | ▶ Play Quicklist | 🗑 Delete Selected | 🗑 Clear Quicklist

There are no videos in your quicklist.

QuickList lets you make a video list for later viewing. Click on the "+" (in the lower left) of any video to add it to your QuickList. To view your list, look for the QuickList bar under any video you're watching.

0 - 0 of 0

Fig. 3.9
QuickList section

Sign Out: This menu option will sign you out of your YouTube account. This is always a good idea if there is a possibility of someone else using the same computer. Quitting your Web browser will also sign you out of YouTube.

Account Settings

After creating an account for use with your students (or for your own personal use), you should select your account settings. To open your Account Settings page, click on the Account menu option from the toolbar (see Fig. 3.5). The Account Settings section of YouTube (see Fig. 3.10) includes the following:

- ▸ Account Overview
- ▸ My Videos
- ▸ My Network
- ▸ More
- ▸ Profile Setup
- ▸ Customize Homepage
- ▸ Playback Setup
- ▸ E-mail Options

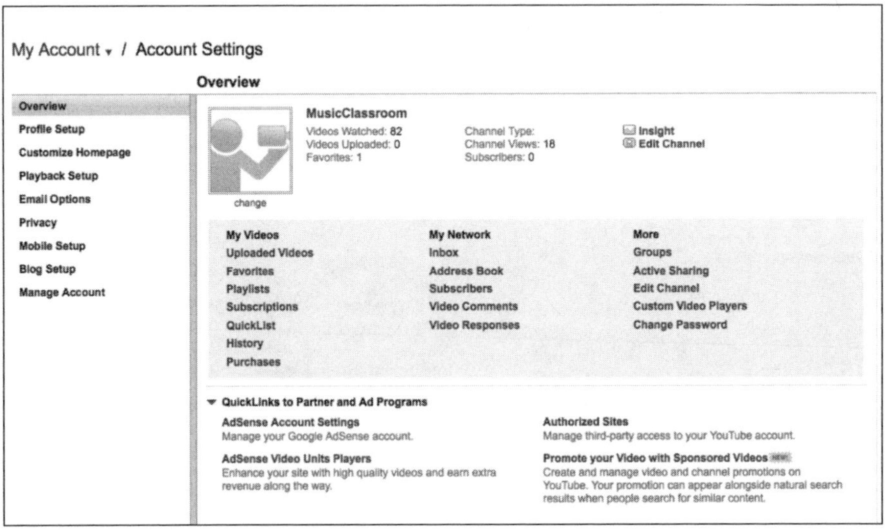

Fig. 3.10
Account Settings page

- ▸ Privacy

- ▸ Mobile Setup

- ▸ Blog Setup

- ▸ Manage Account

Below we will provide step-by-step instructions for setting your account preferences, with a focus on how to best set up an account for use with students of all ages.

Account Overview

When you click on the Account tab in the toolbar, you open up your Account Overview page (see Fig. 3.10). On the left-hand side of the page, you will see a menu for each of the account settings. The main section of the page shows your picture (discussed in the profile settings section later in this chapter), some statistical data about your site usage, and links to your videos, network, and more. The following is a detailed guide to each of these links.

My Videos

The My Videos menu includes your Uploaded Videos, Favorites, Playlists, Subscriptions, QuickList, History, and Purchases. Clicking on each of these menu items opens a new page that displays the related information. If you click any of the items from the My Videos menu, the menu on the left-hand side of each page is the same as the My Videos menu.

When you click on Uploaded Videos, you will see a list of all the videos you have uploaded (see Fig. 3.11). When you first open your account, there won't be any videos listed on this page. As you upload videos, this page is an excellent way to

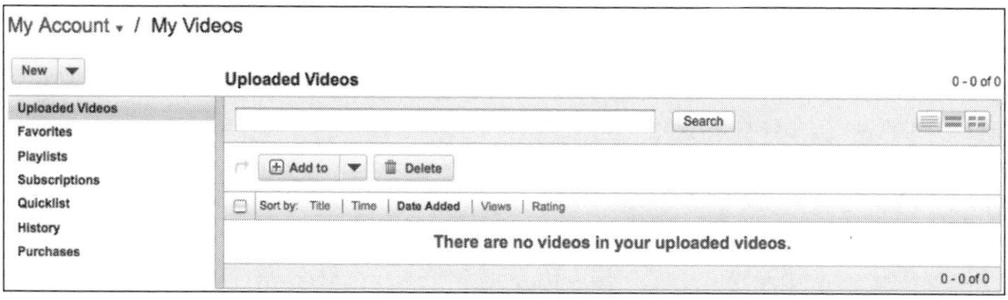

Fig. 3.11
Uploaded videos

manage them, especially if you upload a large number. You can also search for your videos in this section.

The Favorites section is a list of the videos you have added to your favorites list (see chapter 2).

Playlists are lists of videos that you create, usually in some sort of category (see chapter 2). For example, you can create a playlist of videos relating to a specific topic or musical instrument. You can also share your playlists with other YouTube users. When you first open the Playlist section of your Account Settings, you will be asked whether you'd like to "give it a try." By clicking on Give It a Try, you will open the Create/Edit Playlist page (see Fig. 3.12). Here you will be asked to name your playlist; whether you would like the playlist to be the main video log shown on your profile page (a video log—also known as a video blog, or *vlog*—is a form of blogging where the creator videotapes their comments rather than writing them); give a description of your playlist; create *tags* (words that help others find your playlist when they use the YouTube search feature); set privacy settings (you can either make your video public or private); and indicate whether you want to allow others to embed (post) your video on other websites. Ideas for how you can use playlists with your students are covered in chapters 6 and 7.

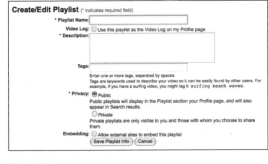

Fig. 3.12
Create/Edit Playlist

If you find a video that you like on YouTube, you can subscribe (see chapter 2) to it. The Subscriptions section of your Account Settings allows you to manage your subscriptions, including add subscribed videos to your playlists, favorites, and QuickList. It is also a convenient place to store all of your subscribed videos.

The QuickList section of the Account Settings page (see Fig. 3.10) allows you to manage your QuickList, such as add videos to your playlists or favorites, delete videos, or clear your entire list at once.

The History section of the Account Settings page includes a listing of all the videos that you have watched while logged in to your account. You can clear your viewing history at any time by clicking on the Clear History button on the page. Some might feel that the history section is an invasion of privacy; after all, do you really want your students to know all the videos that you have watched on YouTube? However, it can be useful if you forget the name of a particular video that you want to locate quickly. If you are not logged in to your account, there is no accessible record of your specific viewing choices.

Some videos on YouTube are available for purchase. For example, many of the music videos that have been legally posted to YouTube by Universal Music Group are available for users to download through either Amazon.com or the iTunes Music Store. The Purchases section of the Account Settings page keeps track of all the videos you have downloaded.

My Network Menu

The My Network menu includes your Inbox, Address Book, Subscribers, Video Comments, and Video Responses. Clicking on any of these menu items opens a new page that displays the related information. Again, if you click on any of the items from the My Network menu, the menu on the left-hand side of each page will be the same as the My Network menu.

The Inbox is similar to your YouTube e-mail inbox (see Fig. 3.6) with the addition of Video Responses, which are videos that other YouTube users have posted in response to a video that you posted. The Inbox also keeps track of messages you have sent to other YouTube account holders.

The Address Book page (see Fig. 3.13) allows you to add friends to your contacts list, delete friends, block users, and compose e-mails. You can also create labels to attach to your contacts. The Address Book can be very useful for educators as it allows you to label who your students are as well as block students from the site if they act in an inappropriate manner. Furthermore, if students create YouTube accounts, you can send messages to them directly through YouTube to draw their attention to a certain video.

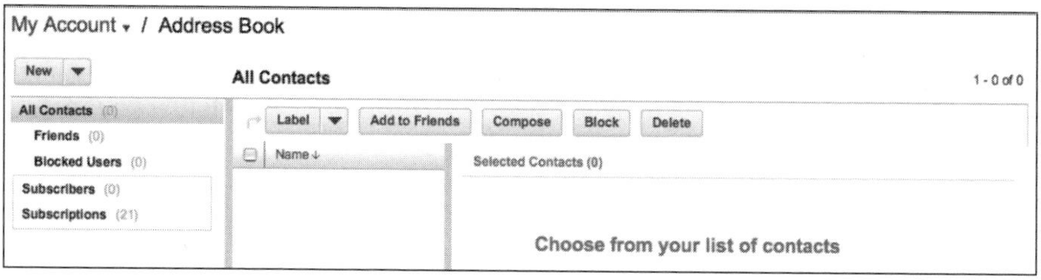

Fig. 3.13
Address Book

The Subscribers page lists all the YouTube users who have subscribed to your videos. You can add subscribers to your address book if you wish. This page also lets you unsubscribe anyone from your account (channel).

TIP   Requiring every student to subscribe to your YouTube channel provides an easy and convenient way to communicate with them.

The last two items in the My Network menu are Video Comments and Video Responses. These pages list comments that other YouTube account holders have made about your videos and video responses to the specific videos you have posted. Comments occur frequently, and can be an integral part of how your students interact with the videos that you post for them. For example, if you post a video of a performance, your students can use the comment feature to post their critiques of the performance. The Video Comments page can serve as a convenient way for you to keep track of all the comments generated by your students. Similarly, the Video Responses menu lists the videos that were posted in reaction to a video that you posted. If someone posts a video response, this page lists it.

More Menu

The More menu option includes your Groups, Active Sharing, Edit Channel, Custom Video Players, and Change Password preferences. Like the My Videos and My Network menus, clicking on each of these menu items opens a new page that displays the related information. Unlike the My Videos and My Network menus, when you click on any of the items from the More menu, the menu on the left-hand side is different for each page.

The Groups page allows users to create groups (as discussed in chapter 2). There are a wide variety of groups on YouTube, usually made up of friends or users who share a common interest. The Groups page also displays the groups that you belong to and the groups you own. The process for creating a group is detailed later in this chapter. Groups can be the easiest way for teachers to keep track of their students. By creating a specific group for your class, you can create a private space on YouTube that only your students can access.

TIP   Consider creating a private group on YouTube for your students. This will help protect their privacy by allowing only approved students to access the private space.

Active Sharing gives you the ability to share your viewing experience with other YouTube members. By turning Active Sharing on, other members will be able to see what video you are viewing as you view it. The default setting for YouTube is to turn Active Sharing off. Educators should keep Active Sharing off *at all times*, as students who know your username would be able to see what videos you view while you view them. They could also see a list of every video that you viewed on your channel homepage (the page that YouTube users see when they click on your username in a video that you have posted). To turn Active Sharing on, simply click Enable Active Sharing and select your preferences. Again — Active Sharing is *not* recommended for educators who are using the site with their students.

Edit Channel

The Edit Channel page (see Fig. 3.14) allows you to set your channel preferences. At the top of the Edit Channel page your unique YouTube channel URL (Universal Resource Locator), or Web address, is listed. The URL for the companion channel to this book (MusicClassroom) is: www.youtube.com/MusicClassroom. The channel URL is always the same as the username you selected when you created

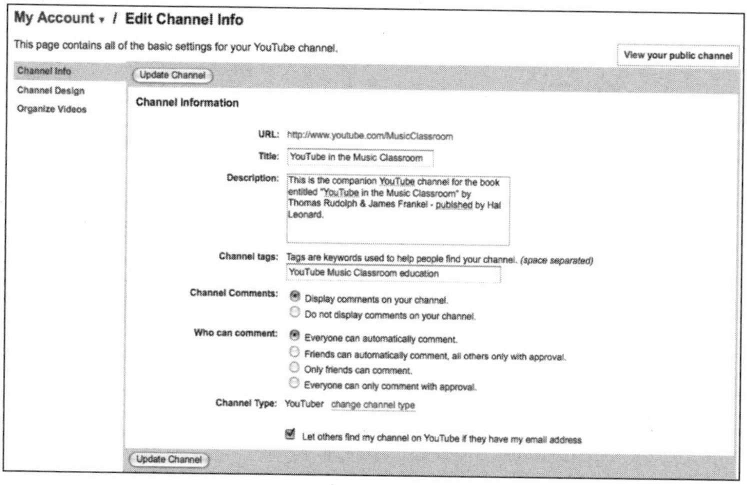

Fig. 3.14
Edit Channel Info

your account. For example, if your username is "ParkAveElemMusic," your channel URL would be http://www.youtube.com/ParkAveElemMusic. The next window down asks you to create a title for your channel. You can enter anything you like, for example: "Park Elementary School Music Department." The title you create will appear at the top of your Internet browser window. Once you have created a title for your channel, you will be asked to type in a brief description of it. For the Park Avenue Elementary School channel, you might type in something like: "This site is intended solely for use by students in the Music Department at the Park Avenue Elementary School." To ensure student privacy, you may not want to identify the city and state where the school is located. Channel tags are optional. If you would like your channel to be searchable, enter in as many tags as you wish, each separated by a space. A music teacher at the Park Avenue Elementary School might enter such tags as: *music, education, Park Avenue, elementary,* and *school.* If you plan on making this channel private, you do not need to enter any tags.

For educators, the next three options in the Edit Channel page are very important. First, the Channel Comments option asks whether you want to display comments on your channel. You need to consider whether you want your students to be able to post comments on posted videos. One reason for allowing comments is if you want your students to critique videos. One reason to not allow comments is to prevent students from writing inappropriate comments (although this can be managed and is discussed later in his chapter). If you enable comments, the next options are very important. You will be asked: Who Can Comment. The options are:

- ▶ Everyone can automatically comment

- ▶ Friends can automatically comment; all others only with approval

- ▶ Only friends can comment

- ▶ Everyone can only comment with approval

The first option, "Everyone can automatically comment," is the least desirable. By allowing everyone to comment, you are allowing any user of YouTube to make comments. This is not a good option for educators because if you were to post a video of one of your students singing an original song, it would be open to comments from the entire YouTube community. Not all comments are kind on YouTube, and it could have a negative effect. This option also means comments can be posted without any type of approval. Once a user types in a comment, it instantly appears in the comments under the video. It should also be noted that comments can easily contain expletives. While comments can be deleted later, this is certainly not an advisable setting for educators.

By selecting the second option, "Friends can automatically comment; all others only with approval," you are giving blanket approval to any comment from a friend. Any other YouTube user comment would require your approval before it is posted to the video comments. A "friend" on YouTube is defined as someone you have personally invited to be a friend (or a member of your group). Typically, your friends would be your students. By selecting this option, your students would be able to post comments automatically without first getting your approval. While this is certainly a better option than the first, you would have the issue of not being able to approve the comments before they are posted, and have to contend with comments from other YouTube users. The third option, "Only friends can comment," is better than the first two, but you would still have the issue of not being able to approve comments before they are posted. Therefore, the last option, "Everyone can only comment with approval," is the best choice for educators. If you are concerned about what students might write in their comments, this is the best way to keep inappropriate comments from being posted. However, you will also get comments (pending approval) from other YouTube users (unless your group is private — see later in this chapter for details).

The next option on the Edit Channel page is to choose the Channel Type. The default setting for this option is YouTuber — a generic categorization. By clicking on Change Channel Type, you can select from the following options:

- ▶ Director
- ▶ Musician
- ▶ Comedian
- ▶ Guru
- ▶ Reporter

You do not need to select any of these, or you might consider them a way to better identify your channel. If you select any of these choices, it will appear on your channel. For example, if you are creating a personal channel to promote yourself as a musician, you would select "Musician" to identify yourself to other YouTube users. Currently there is no option for educators, but this may change in the future. Lastly, at the bottom of the Edit Channel page is a checkbox to indicate whether you would like your channel to be searchable by other users who have your e-mail address. For increased anonymity, uncheck the box.

Once you have entered in your information, be sure to click on the Update Channel button at the bottom left of the page to save your information. If you fail to click this button, all of the information that you entered will be erased if you navigate away from the page.

Channel Design

After you have selected your channel settings, you can select Channel Design from the menu on the left (see Fig. 3.14) to customize the way your channel looks. The Channel Design page has many different options to choose from. The first option is Select a Theme (see Fig. 3.15). Here you can choose the basic color theme for your channel. Try out different color themes by clicking on the appropriate color and then clicking on Update Channel. You will see the colors change in the Channel Preview window on the Channel Design page (see Fig. 3.16). Once you have found a color theme that you prefer, click the Update Channel button to save your selection. Next, you can customize your channel layout preferences, selecting the type of content and features that will appear on your channel (see Figs. 3.17 and 3.18). These layout properties are self-explanatory, and include:

Fig. 3.15
Select a Theme

- ▸ Featured videos
- ▸ Subscriptions
- ▸ Playlists
- ▸ Recent activity
- ▸ Subscribers
- ▸ Friends

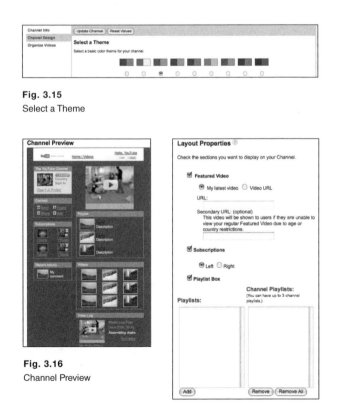

Fig. 3.16
Channel Preview

Fig. 3.17
Layout Properties top

The default layout for any channel is adequate for educators. If you'd like to customize the look and feel of your channel, try experimenting with some of the available options. By selecting any of the layout choices, you can see how it affects the design by looking at the Channel Preview window (see Fig. 3.16). If you are comfortable with Web design languages, try utilizing some of the options in the Advanced Design Customization section of the Layout Properties window (see Fig. 3.19). These options include using custom colors for all aspects of the channel, as well as adding background images. You might consider adding a background image to your channel—perhaps a picture of your school. To do so, follow these simple steps:

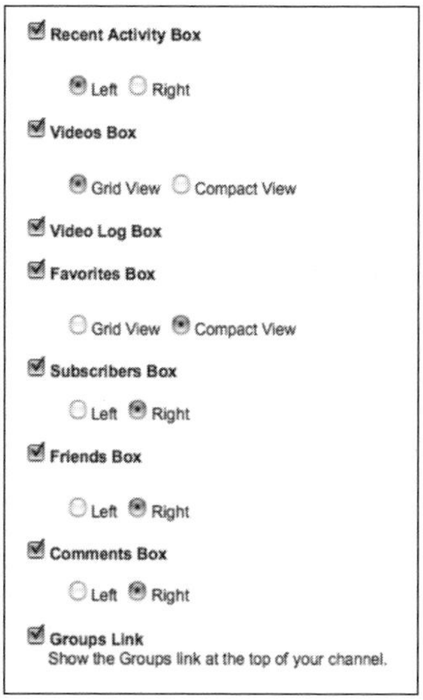

1. In the Background Image box (see Fig. 3.19), click the Browse button and locate the image you would like to use.

2. Click Open.

3. Click Update Channel.

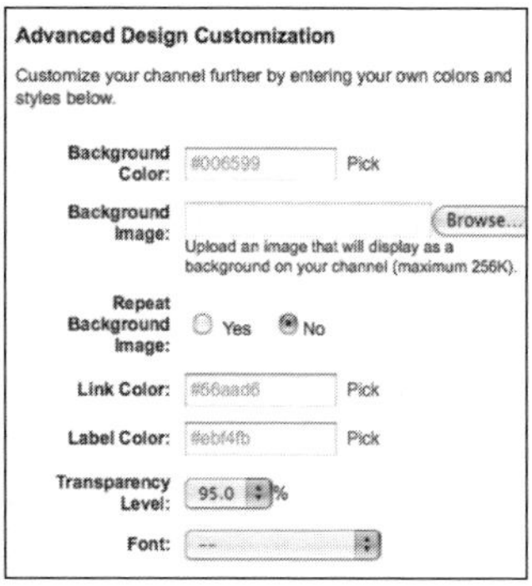

You can also choose whether to tile the image by selecting Repeat Background Image. You might decide after adding a background image that it makes your page look too cluttered. To delete the image, click Delete.

Fig. 3.18
Layout Properties bottom

Fig. 3.19
Advanced Design Customization

Organize Videos

The last menu option on the Edit Channel page is Organize Videos. On this page (see Fig. 3.20) you can arrange how the first nine videos appear on your channel. You are presented with a grid where you can drag and drop videos. These videos will appear on your channel on the lower right-hand side of the page. If you have less than nine videos, an empty space will appear in each of the unused slots until a new video is added. Once you have arranged your videos, click Update Channel to save.

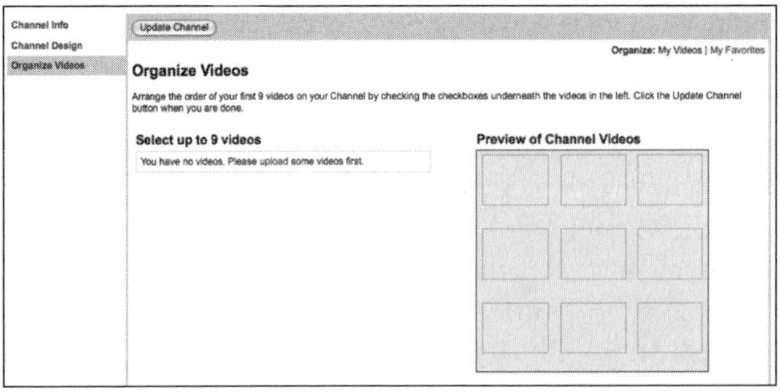

Fig. 3.20
Organize Videos

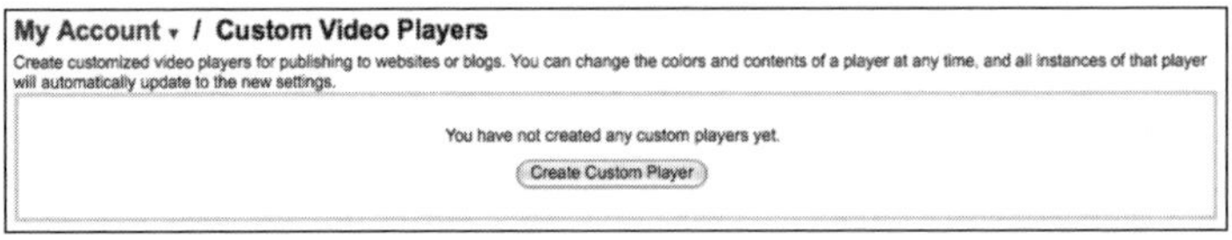

Fig. 3.21
Custom Video Players

Custom Video Players

The next option in the More menu is the Custom Video Players page (see Fig. 3.21). On this page you can create a custom video player that you can then use on other websites (including a school website). Simply click the Create Custom Player button in the center of the screen to begin.

Creating a new custom player is not as difficult as it might sound. To begin customizing your player, follow these steps:

1. Under Player Name, type in the name (title) that you would like to call your custom player (see Fig. 3.22) and a description of the player. For example, you might choose: "My New Player" as the title and "This is a test custom player" for the description.

2. Select the Theme color for your player.

3. Select the Layout for your player.

4. Select the Content that you would like to appear in your player (favorites, playlists, etc.) (see Fig. 3.23).

5. Click the Generate Code button to save your custom player.

While you are customizing your player you will be able to see any changes instantly in the Player Preview window.

After you click the Generate Code button, your page will refresh and you will get an alert message that reads: *Player 'My New Player' was successfully created and the generated code is below.* The code appears at the bottom of the page, and looks pretty strange at first glance. So what is this code and how can you use it? The code is programming language (HTML—hypertext markup language) that

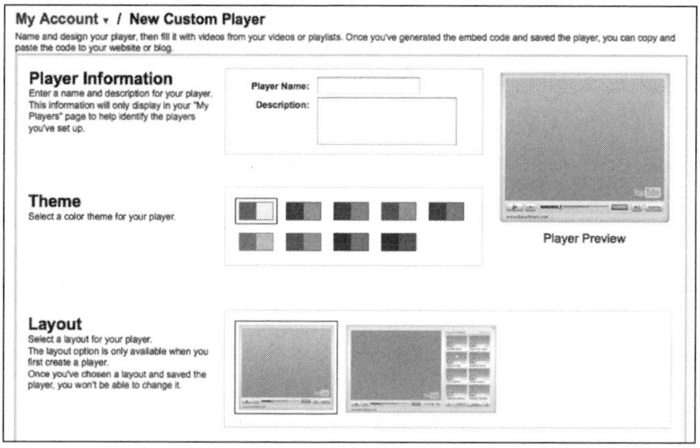

Fig. 3.22
New Custom Player (top of page)

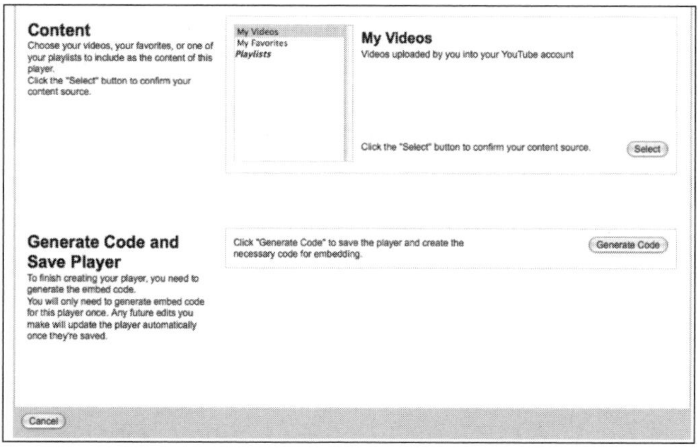

Fig. 3.23
New Custom Player (Bottom of Page)

you can copy and then paste into another website, such as a music department homepage on your school website. This code is known as an *embed code*, which simply means that you can add the new custom video player that you created on YouTube to any other website, and that player will appear on that website exactly as it appears in YouTube. It is important to note that the embed code simply creates a link to YouTube to retrieve the video, but it plays through the video player on your website. You can create as many custom video players as you like, and you can manage them from the Custom Video Players page.

TIP   If your school blocks YouTube (see chapter 8), you will not be able to use this embed code while you are in school. The code will work on any Internet connection where YouTube is not blocked.

If you are not familiar with how to edit the HTML code on your website, you can ask your school's computer teacher or the district technology coordinator. There are also numerous tutorials available online on how to edit HTML code.

The final option under the More menu is Change Password. Use this option to change your account password at any time. You must first type in the old password and then type in a new password (which you will have to retype to verify).

Insight

There is one last button on the Account Overview page that provides some very interesting information. In the upper right-hand corner of the page you will see a small map icon next to a button labeled Insight (see Fig. 3.10). The Insight page (see Fig. 3.24) provides you with statistics about how often your videos are

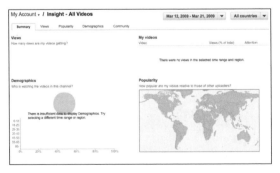

Fig. 3.24
Insight page

being viewed, demographic information about the users who are viewing them, and a map of the world that identifies where the viewers of your videos live. This information can be very enlightening, and you might consider sharing it with your students to illustrate how the Internet is used by people around the world and that show the content that you have posted has worldwide appeal.

Profile Setup

Now that you have taken a tour of the menu options available in the Account Overview page, look at each menu item in the navigation menu on the left side of the page (see Fig. 3.10). The first option is Profile Setup. On this page (see Fig. 3.25) you can enter your personal information so that other users can find out more about you. This information includes:

- Your photo
- A description of yourself
- Your related website
- Personal details including name, gender, relationship status, and age
- Hometown location
- Jobs
- Education
- Interests

Fig. 3.25
Profile Setup

All of this information is completely optional. When using a YouTube account with your students, keep this information to a minimum. You might consider adding your photo, name, a description of yourself, and a related website. To save any changes that you make to your profile, click Save Changes.

Fig. 3.26
Change Picture

To upload a photo to your profile, follow these steps:

1. Click Change Picture (see Fig. 3.26).

2. Click the Upload an Image radio button.

3. Click the Browse button.

4. Locate the photo you would like to upload.

5. Click Open.

6. Click Save Changes.

You can select a still frame from one of your videos as your profile picture and default image. Also, you can change your profile picture from the Account Overview page by clicking the Change button underneath your photo — then follow the steps above.

It is up to you to decide whether you want to include your photo in your profile, although including your picture will help students identify the channel as yours. Also, as mentioned previously, including your name, description, and a related website (such as a music department website or school website) will help others learn a little about you and your school.

Customize Homepage

In the Customize Homepage section of your account (see Fig. 3.27) you can select the modules that appear on your homepage whenever you are logged into your YouTube account. This is only for customizing your view of YouTube. Settings on this page do not affect how others view YouTube. They are your personal preferences. The default modules include: Recommended for You (videos that

Fig. 3.27
Customize Homepage

your friends have recommended you view); Latest from Subscriptions (a list of the newest videos available from those channels you have subscribed to); Featured Videos (the videos that you have chosen to feature); Rising Videos (videos on YouTube that are quickly gaining popularity); Friend Activity (what videos your friends are watching); and Inbox (your YouTube e-mails). Optional modules include: Insight Map (a map of where your videos are being watched); Insight Chart (a statistical chart with data about your videos); Videos Near You (a list of videos that have been created by YouTube users from your hometown); and About You (your profile information).

You can also decide whether you would like to enable The Feed, which is a setting where all of your modules from the left-hand column are combined into one long listing on the homepage. The default setting is the way YouTube normally looks when you view the site (see Fig. 2.1 in chapter 2). By clicking on The Feed, you will dramatically change the way YouTube looks when you view it. This is a matter of personal taste. Try it and then go back to the main page by clicking Home in the upper left-hand corner of the site. If you want to change it back, click Account, and then Customize Homepage, and uncheck The Feed. Remember to always click on Save Changes before navigating away from a page in order to save your preferences.

At the bottom of the Customize Homepage section you will see Friend Activity. This refers to the Channel Design preferences you selected (described above — see Fig. 3.18). If you would like to monitor what your friends are doing on YouTube, this information will show up at the bottom of your YouTube homepage.

Playback Setup

The Playback Setup page (see Fig. 3.28) allows you to select the type of Internet connection you have, which will improve the playback of videos on YouTube with your chosen connection speed. The three settings include:

1. Choose my video quality dynamically based on the current connection speed.

2. I have a slow connection. Never play higher-quality video.

3. I have a fast connection. Always play higher-quality video when it's available.

The default setting is the first option, and it is recommended that you leave it unchanged. This option will automatically determine what type of connection you have and optimize the performance of YouTube accordingly. If you use YouTube on different computers, this option is best because the speed of your connection might vary between computers. If you only use a slow connection, it is best to select the slow connection option, and vice versa.

The Annotations option allows you to disable the annotations that others have included in their videos. Annotations are small text boxes that appear in videos during playback. These annotations are created by the user who uploaded the video. The default setting will show all annotations. If annotations don't bother you, leave the box checked.

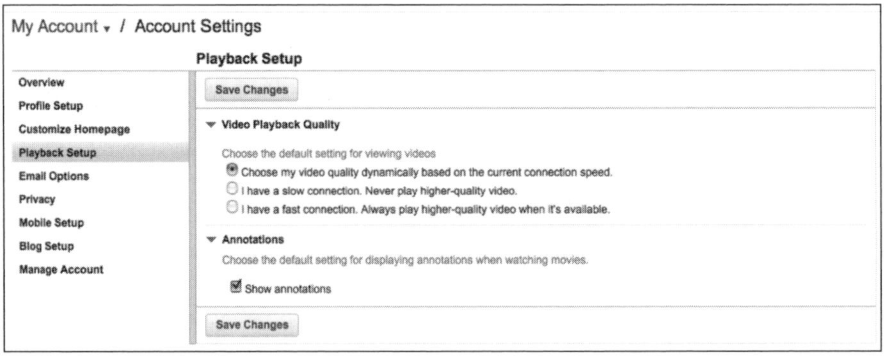

Fig. 3.28
Playback Setup

E-mail Options

The E-mail Options page (see Fig. 3.29) controls what e-mail address your YouTube-related messages are sent to, as well as the type of e-mails you agree to receive. To change the e-mail address where your YouTube e-mail is sent, type in a new e-mail address in the box labeled New E-mail Address, and then retype it to confirm. Once you have entered in the new e-mail address, click Send Confirmation. Then check your e-mail for a message from YouTube Service and click "Confirm your e-mail address" (see Fig. 3.3) to save the change.

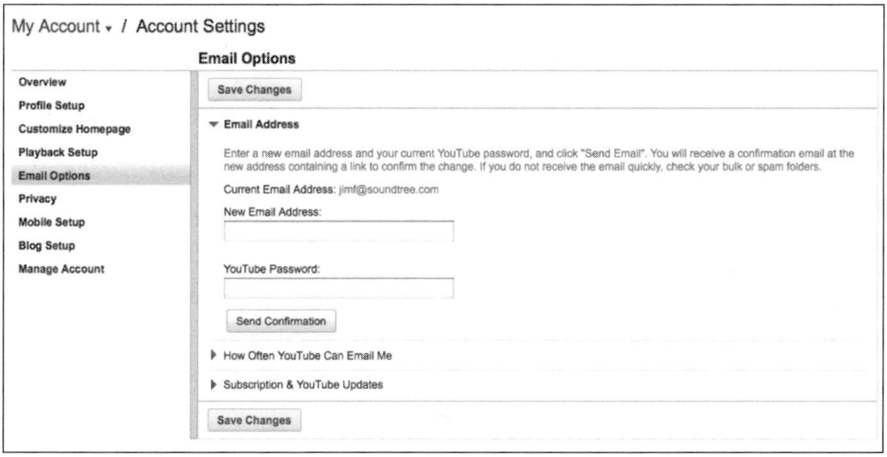

Fig. 3.29
E-mail Options

The next menu option is How Often YouTube Can E-mail Me. Click on the arrow to expand the menu (see Fig. 3.30). In this list you choose whether YouTube sends you an e-mail when:

▸ One of your videos receives a comment or a video response

▸ Someone leaves a comment on your channel

▸ You receive a private message or shared video

Fig. 3.30
How Often YouTube Can E-mail Me page

- ▸ You receive a message from a channel you've subscribed to

- ▸ You receive a friend invite

- ▸ Someone subscribes to your channel

You can also choose not to receive any e-mails from YouTube by selecting "Don't send any e-mails for the above events." Yet you should always select the first option so that you can monitor any activity on your channel. Without e-mail alerts, you run the risk of having inappropriate comments and video responses from students appear on the site without your knowledge.

The last item on the E-mail Options page allows you to choose whether to receive weekly e-mails from the channels you've subscribed to and whether you'd like to receive periodic update e-mails from YouTube. This is basically your junk mail filter for YouTube. The default settings do not allow these types of e-mails. As with all of the other settings, be sure to click Save Changes before navigating away from the page.

Privacy

The settings on the Privacy page (see Fig. 3.31) relate only to you as an account holder. However, if you decide to have your students create their own YouTube accounts, review common Internet safety tips with them (including not divulging their real name, age, picture, location, or any other identifying personal information in their individual account settings or their profile). The privacy settings allow you to decide whether to: allow friends to send messages and share videos with you; let others find your channel if they have your e-mail address; enable Active Sharing; share your recent activity with others; and make your information available to advertisers. If you plan to use YouTube with your students, the following settings are recommended:

1. Leave the Search and Contact Restrictions settings unchanged—this will allow other YouTube users to contact you and find you.

2. Disable Active Sharing—this will keep your viewing history private.

3. Select Uncheck All on the Recent Activity page—this will keep your activity on YouTube private.

4. Uncheck the advertising box in the Advertising Settings menu to cut down on junk e-mail.

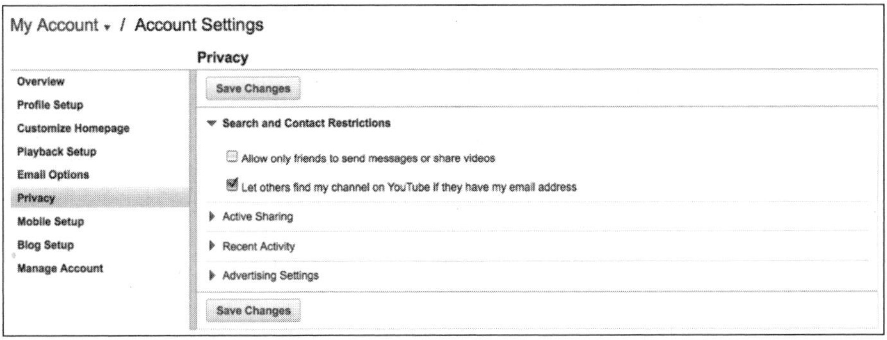

My Account ▾ / Account Settings

Privacy

Overview
Profile Setup
Customize Homepage
Playback Setup
Email Options
Privacy
Mobile Setup
Blog Setup
Manage Account

Save Changes

▾ Search and Contact Restrictions

☐ Allow only friends to send messages or share videos

☑ Let others find my channel on YouTube if they have my email address

▶ Active Sharing

▶ Recent Activity

▶ Advertising Settings

Save Changes

Fig. 3.31
Privacy settings

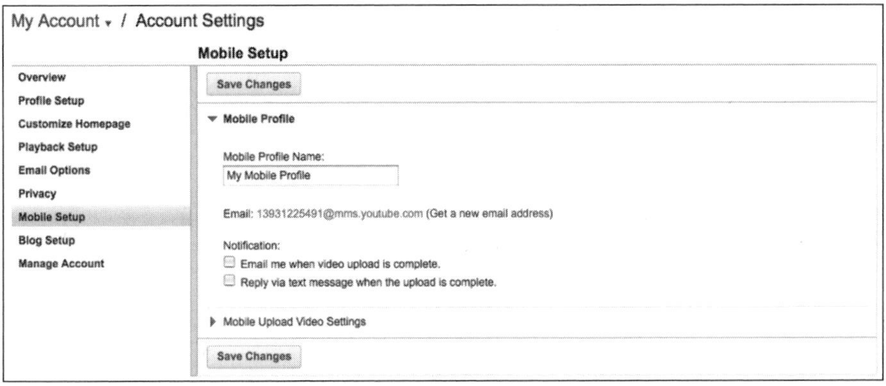

My Account ▾ / Account Settings

Mobile Setup

Overview
Profile Setup
Customize Homepage
Playback Setup
Email Options
Privacy
Mobile Setup
Blog Setup
Manage Account

Save Changes

▾ Mobile Profile

Mobile Profile Name:
My Mobile Profile

Email: 13931225491@mms.youtube.com (Get a new email address)

Notification:
☐ Email me when video upload is complete.
☐ Reply via text message when the upload is complete.

▶ Mobile Upload Video Settings

Save Changes

Fig. 3.32
Mobile Setup

Mobile Setup

If you have wireless access, the Mobile Setup page (see Fig. 3.32) allows you to enter your mobile phone number so you can upload videos directly from your phone. While incredibly convenient, this functionality also makes it possible for students to upload videos that they take with their camera-enabled mobile phones — even while they are in school. There are a number of examples of students secretly videotaping their teachers during class and posting the videos on YouTube. Other students then comment on the videos. Not only is this an invasion of privacy, but it can be embarrassing for you and your school. You must be sure to monitor the activity of the students in your classes with regard to mobile devices. While you cannot control what they do outside of the school environment, you can try to control what they do in the classroom.

To set up your mobile profile, simply enter a name for the profile in the Mobile Profile window, for example: My Mobile Profile. Beneath the window you will see an automatically generated e-mail address. This is the address that you will e-mail videos to from your mobile phone. The address should look something like this: 12345678912@mms.youtube.com. Next, you can choose how you will be alerted that your video upload is complete. Select either E-mail or Text. If you choose e-mail, an alert will be sent to the e-mail address associated with your account. If you choose text, YouTube will send a text message to the same e-mail address associated with your mobile account (12345678912@mms.youtube.com). Be sure to click the Save Changes button when finished.

Once you have created a Mobile Profile, you should select the Mobile Upload Video Settings to choose the default settings for when you upload a video from your mobile device (see Fig. 3.33). The default settings will most likely be adequate for your uploading needs, but you can create a standard title for when you upload a video (the default is "Video from My Phone"), add a short description, and indicate how you would like to append the files—either by filename or by date. For example, if you were to take a video with your iPhone, the device will create a file name for the video (usually something like DSC00024.mov). If you decide to upload that video to your YouTube account, you would send that video file

Fig. 3.33
Mobile Upload Video Settings

to the e-mail address 12345678912@mms.youtube.com (or whatever YouTube assigned your account). If you selected the filename option, YouTube will label the file "Video from My Phone DSC00024." If you selected the date option, YouTube will label the file "Video from My Phone 03/21/09." This is a good way to organize any video content that you upload from your mobile device.

In addition to the title, description, and options for appending your mobile uploaded files, you can select whether to make your mobile uploads private or public, create tags for your videos, select a category for your video, and add the e-mail addresses of users that you wish to share your video with. You can create a new profile for each video you upload, or you can save your preferences for all the videos you upload with a mobile device.

From an educational standpoint, unless you are going to be on a trip without access to a computer and you'd like to upload videos from your phone, you should skip the Mobile Upload video settings altogether, while being aware that students use this function quite often. The most common use of the Mobile Upload function of YouTube is when concertgoers take short videos of their favorite band or musician performing and then upload and share those videos with other YouTube users — including their friends. If you search for any band or musician on YouTube, you will likely find examples of his practice. If you do decide to use this function, remember to save your changes once you have entered all of your preferences.

Blog Setup

A *blog* is a web-based journal where a user writes text posts and readers comment on them. There are numerous examples of educational blogs on the Internet. If you already have a blog using a service such as WordPress.com or LiveJournal .com, you can add your blog to your YouTube account. This allows you to post videos that you view on YouTube directly to your blog by clicking the Share button underneath each video (see chapter 2).

To add your blog to your YouTube account, simply click the Add a Blog button on the Blog Setup page (see Fig. 3.34). You will then be asked to select the service that your blog is hosted on, as well as enter your username and password. If your blog is self-hosted using WordPress, you will need to know your API key (which can be found on your WordPress user profile page) to make this work. Once you enter the correct information, you should see a message that states that your blog was successfully added to your account.

Fig. 3.34
Blog Setup

Manage Account

The final menu option on your Account Settings page is the Manage Account page. On this page (see Fig. 3.35) you can view your account standing, change your password, or delete your account altogether. Your account standing should always be good, unless you have uploaded content that violates the terms of service set forth by YouTube (video that violates copyright law, or videos that have been flagged by other YouTube users as inappropriate—see chapter 2 for details on how to flag videos). YouTube generally issues warnings to users who violate the terms of service, but has the discretion to cancel your account at any time. To change your account password, type in the old password and enter your new password twice for verification. Follow the steps from the Change Password option under the More menu covered earlier in this chapter. If you wish to delete your account completely, enter your password, provide a reason for why you are deleting your account (optional) and click on the Delete Account button. You will then be asked to confirm that you really want to delete your account. Be aware that if you click Delete Account a second time, you will not be able to create another account with the same name (i.e., ParkAveElemMusic) again.

Creating a Group

After you have set up your YouTube account for use with your students, you can create a YouTube Group specifically for them. Creating a group is the safest way to use YouTube with your students. It provides controls to ensure a private space on the website that can only be accessed by you and your students. This privacy is a crucial component of Internet safety, and it is strongly recommended that you set up your group as described below.

My Account ▾ / Account Settings

Manage Account

Overview	▾ **Account Status**
Profile Setup	Your account is in good standing.
Customize Homepage	
Playback Setup	▾ **Change Password**
Email Options	Username: MusicClassroom
Privacy	Verify Old Password:
Mobile Setup	New Password:
Blog Setup	Retype New Password:
Manage Account	Change Password
	▾ **Delete Account**
	Password:
	Reason for Deleting Account:
	Please take a moment to tell us why you are deleting your account.
	Delete Account

Fig. 3.35
Manage Account

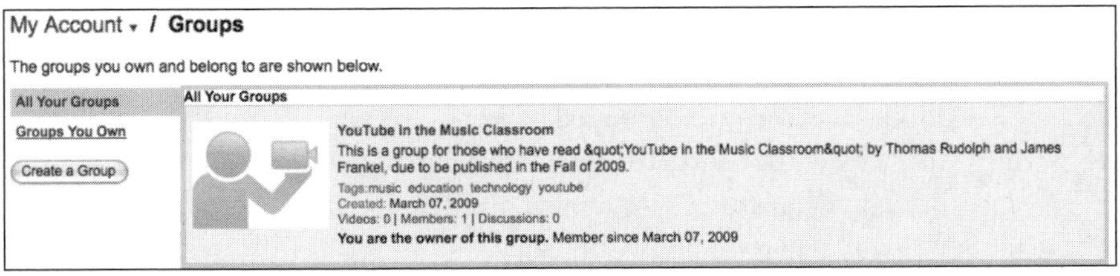

My Account ▾ / Groups

The groups you own and belong to are shown below.

All Your Groups

All Your Groups	
Groups You Own	**YouTube In the Music Classroom**
Create a Group	This is a group for those who have read "YouTube In the Music Classroom" by Thomas Rudolph and James Frankel, due to be published in the Fall of 2009.
	Tags:music education technology youtube
	Created: March 07, 2009
	Videos: 0	Members: 1	Discussions: 0
	You are the owner of this group. Member since March 07, 2009

Fig. 3.36
Groups menu

To create a new group, click on Account on the toolbar in the upper right corner of the YouTube website (see Fig. 3.5). Then click on Groups under the More menu (see Fig. 3.10). On the Groups page (see Fig. 3.36) you can see the groups you belong to and the groups you own, and you can create a group. To create a group, click the Create a Group button. You will then fill out a form (see Fig. 3.37) about your group and its purpose.

The following is an example of how an educator might fill out the Create a Group form:

Group Name: Park Avenue Elementary Music Department

Tags: Music, education, park, avenue, elementary school

Description: This is the YouTube Group for students in the Park Avenue Elementary School Music Department, and is intended for use solely by those students. Enjoy your visit to our Group Page!

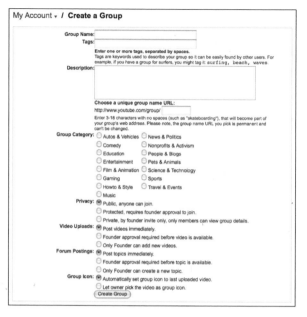

Fig. 3.37
Create a Group page

Choose a unique group name URL: http://www.youtube.com/group/ ParkAveElemMusic

Group Category [*you can only choose one group category*]: Education

Privacy: Private; by Founder invite only; only members can view group details

Video Uploads: Only Founder can add new videos

Forum Postings: Only Founder can create a new topic

Group Icon: Automatically set group icon to last uploaded video

Once you have filled out the form to suit your specific needs, click the Create Group button.

While most of the choices above are self-explanatory, some require further explanation. Privacy is perhaps the most important setting for your group. You have only two recommended choices for the privacy setting for your group: Protected or Private. Do not set your group privacy setting to Public, as any YouTube user will then be able to join the group, view the group details, view the videos associated with the group, and make comments on the videos. Choose Protected if you plan on using YouTube with older students (high school or college), want the group to be viewed by other users, and don't mind non-class members asking to join the group (which will then give them the ability to comment on videos). You should select Private with elementary and middle school students, as it gives you the most protection.

Once you have created your group, then set your preferences for your Group Homepage by clicking on the name of your group (the text color is blue) on the Groups page (see Fig. 3.36). This will bring you to the Group Preferences page (see Fig. 3.38).

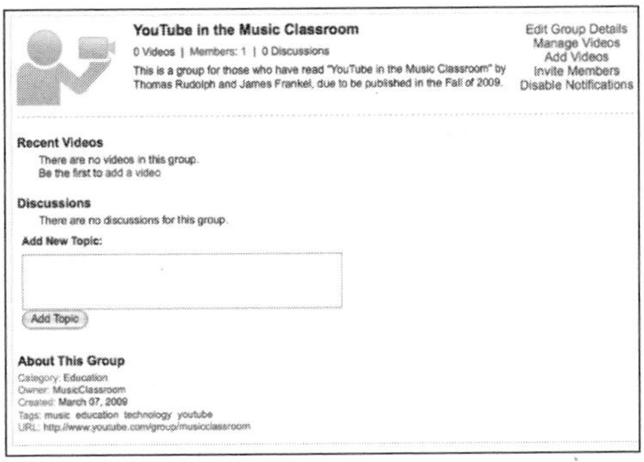

In the upper right-hand corner of the page you will see five menu items: Edit Group Details, Manage Videos, Add Videos, Invite Members, and Disable Notifications. These menus will help you set up an educationally friendly environment for your students.

Fig. 3.38
Group Preferences page

Edit Group Details

If you would like to change any of your group details after you create the group, you can do so by clicking on Edit Group Details. This page is the same as the Create a Group page (see Fig. 3.37). If you decide to make any changes, you must save them by clicking the Update Group button. You can also transfer ownership of your group if you need to by clicking on where it says "Click here to transfer ownership of this group to another user."

Add Videos

To add videos to your Group Homepage, click the Add Videos button. You will see the Add Videos page (see Fig. 3.39). Here you can either add videos that you have already uploaded, upload a new video, or add videos that you have selected as favorites. To add a video that you have already uploaded, select the video by clicking on it and then click the Add to Group button. Once you have finished adding videos to your group, click Done. To add one of your favorite videos, click on My Favorites, select your video by clicking on it, and then click the Add to Group button. When finished, click Done. To upload a new video, click the Upload a Video button and follow the steps mentioned above for uploading a video. When finished, click Done.

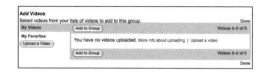

Fig. 3.39
Add Videos

Manage Videos

Once you have added some of your own videos to the group, you can manage them by clicking on the Manage Videos button. You will then see the Manage Videos page (see Fig. 3.40). On this page you can select videos to remove from the group, select videos to serve as the group image, add videos, and approve videos that have been submitted by group members.

To remove a video from the group, click on the check box next to the video that you wish to remove. Then click on the Select an Action drop-down menu, and select Remove from Group. Finally, click on the Go button. Your video will instantly be removed from the group.

Fig. 3.40
Manage Videos

To select a video to serve as the group image, click on the check box next to the video that you wish to use as your group image, click on the Select an Action drop-down menu, and choose Select Video to serve as the group image. Next, click on the Go button. The first frame of your video will then appear as your group image.

To add a video to your group, click on the Upload Video button and follow the steps mentioned previously.

To remove or approve a video that another group member has submitted, click on the check box next to the submitted video and select either Remove from Group or Approve for Viewing from the Select an Action drop-down menu.

Invite Members

You should consider creating student accounts for your students (especially those in elementary and middle school) for use in the classroom. You can create YouTube accounts for your students using usernames such as ParkAveElemMusicStud1, ParkAveElemMusicStud2, ParkAveElemMusicStud3, etc., as well as create unique passwords for them (perhaps using the names of famous composers or musicians). By creating accounts for your students you can ensure that all aspects of a student's identity are protected. For example, when you assign each student in your class a unique username and password, you can control their profile picture (you can use the same one for each student if you wish), the e-mail address linked to their account (you can select your own school e-mail address to filter messages), and you can access their account information at any time to make changes, if necessary. You can also use the same account names from year to year, creating new passwords so previous students cannot access the account. While it might seem like a great deal of work to set this up, it is the safest way to use YouTube with your students. It is up to you to determine whether you want to allow older students to create their own accounts. Certainly at the college level, students should be able to create their own YouTube accounts to participate in group activities.

TIP   To ensure student anonymity while using YouTube Groups, create accounts for your students.

To add students to your YouTube group, click on the Invite Members button. On this page (see Fig. 3.41) you can invite YouTube members (called "friends") to your group, and remove friends from your group. To invite new friends to your group, enter their usernames in the box labeled Invite New Friends. If you are going to add multiple friends at once, make sure to separate each username with a comma. You can add a message to your invitation by typing text into the Your Message box. Before sending out the invitation, you are required to verify your invitation by typing in the text that appears in the image next to the Verification box. If you have created all of the usernames yourself and linked each username to your school e-mail address, you can set all of this up on your own to ensure that each student is added to the group.

Disable Notifications

If you do not wish to receive e-mail about activity on your Group page, you can click the Disable Notifications button. To activate notifications, click on Enable

Notifications. For educators, it is not recommended that you click the Disable Notifications option, as you will no longer receive e-mail alerts about group activity, which is an important way to monitor how your students are using the group.

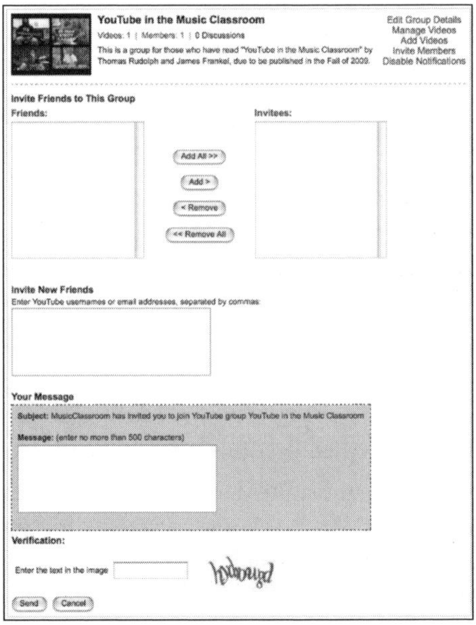

Group Discussions

One feature of Groups is the ability to create discussion topics. To add a new topic, go to the Group Preferences page (see Fig. 3.38), enter a question or topic in the Add a New Topic window, and click Add Topic. Your topic will then be posted as a discussion on your group page (see Fig. 3.42).

Fig. 3.41
Invite Members

You can manage your topics from the Group Preferences page by clicking on the check box next to each topic and selecting either Approve Selections or Delete Topic from the Select Action drop-down menu and clicking Submit. You can also see the number of responses to any given topic and manage those responses (approve or delete). In Fig. 3.42 a topic titled "What did you learn from the video titled 'Tuba Lesson'?" was created. This topic will appear on the Group Homepage. Friends are able to post responses to your discussion topic as well as to responses from other group members. This gives your students an opportunity to critique the videos that you have shared with them. You need to determine whether to allow students to post new topics. In the Forum Postings option of the Create a Group page (see Fig. 3.37) you can set the preference for this to: Post topics immediately (which allows students to post new topics without your approval);

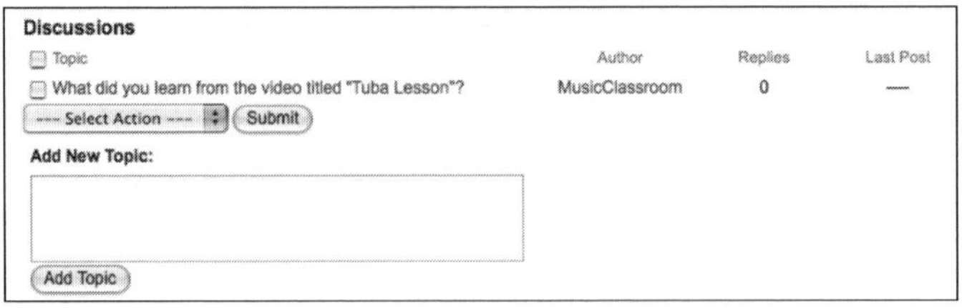

Fig. 3.42
Discussion Topics

Founder approval required before topic is available (students can submit new topics, but you need to approve them before they are available); or Only Founder can create a new topic. Educators might consider using the second option with their students, but should avoid the first option, as students would be able to post topics without any type of approval.

Summary

This chapter provided a detailed overview of all aspects of creating a YouTube account for use in an educational environment. You should carefully consider the tips and suggestions given before using YouTube with your students. Because YouTube is such an incredibly popular site, drawing users of all ages from all over the world, it is important for you to recognize the inherent dangers associated with using a website with your students. By creating specific usernames and passwords for your students and a private group to provide a safe space for using YouTube in the classroom, you can help ensure a safe and successful experience for you and your students.

Playback, Sound Quality, and Display

Chapter Four

Now that you have an understanding of how YouTube works and how to view videos on the site, you should explore getting the best-quality video playback with the equipment you have. This chapter will cover the following topics:

- Playback volume level.

- External speakers and amplifiers

- External audio interfaces

- Display options

- Connecting to a classroom TV, computer projector, or interactive whiteboard

- YouTube screen formats

- Viewing YouTube videos on Apple TV or iPhone

- Downloading files to play on a computer or other device

- Converting videos to play on an iPod

Playback Volume Level

The playback volume of YouTube videos is controlled by several factors. One thing to consider is that the user who uploaded the video can set the volume level, so you may find yourself making volume changes when playing back videos for your class or ensemble. You can also control playback volume through your computer's volume controls and the volume control of the speakers or amplifier to which the computer is connected.

The first place to go to adjust the volume is the YouTube volume control. Just click on the speaker icon at the bottom of the video window to raise or lower the volume (see Fig. 4.1).

Fig. 4.1
YouTube volume control

Also, your computer can control the output volume. If you raise the volume on the YouTube video and it isn't loud enough, you can adjust the system volume on your computer.

Macintosh Volume Settings

The Mac keyboard provides function keys to raise, lower, and mute the system sound. These are the keys with speaker icons on them. When you press these keys, the Mac displays a volume control icon (see Fig. 4.2). Make sure the volume is not muted. It is a good idea to set the Mac volume to maximum and then make adjustments as needed when playing specific videos. This is the most expedient way to control volume.

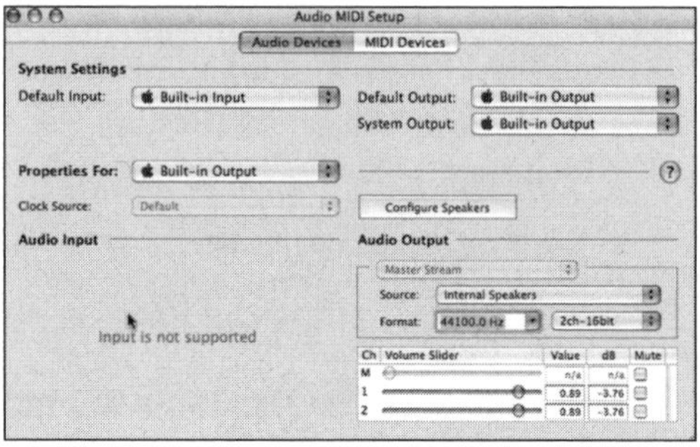

Fig. 4.2
Mac volume control

If controlling the Mac volume level from the keyboard is not resolving your issue, you can go "under the hood" and check the audio settings at the system level:

Fig. 4.3
Mac Audio/MIDI Setup

1. Go to the Finder and choose Go > Utilities > Audio MIDI Setup (see Fig. 4.3).

2. Click on the Audio Devices tab.

3. Next to "Properties For," select "Built-in Output."

4. In the Audio Output area under Audio Devices, make sure "Source" is set to the correct speakers (in most cases this will be "internal speakers") and "Format" is set to 44.1 kHz.

PC Volume Settings

On a PC, the system volume control is slightly different. On the left side of the Start menu you will see a small speaker icon (see Fig. 4.4). Click this to adjust the playback volume.

Fig. 4.4
Windows volume control

You can also go to the Control Panel to adjust the volume. On a PC running Windows XP, follow these steps to adjust the volume (see Fig. 4.5):

1. Click the Start button.

2. Click on Control Panel.

3. Click on Sounds, Speech, and Audio Devices.

4. In the Sounds and Audio Devices, click on the Volume tab.

5. Check the system volume setting.

6. Adjust the volume level.

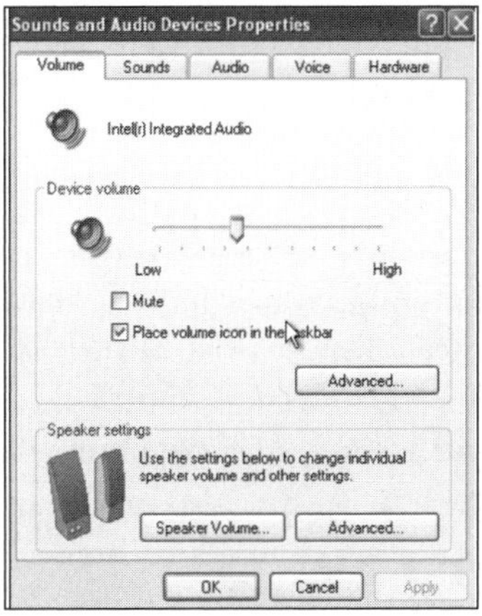

In Windows Vista, you also access the volume control via the Control Panel:

Fig. 4.5
Windows XP volume control

1. Click the Start button.

2. Select Control Panel > Hardware and Sound.

3. Under Sound, click on Adjust System Volume.

4. Set the speaker output to maximum volume.

Adobe Flash Player

Videos on YouTube are streamed using Adobe's Flash Player. If you're still having trouble with your sound, it could be a Flash issue. Check to see if your system meets the following requirements for running the YouTube video player:

- Macromedia Flash Player 7.0 or higher plug-in
- Windows 2000 or higher with latest updates installed

▸ Mac OS X 10.3 or higher

▸ Firefox 1.1, Internet Explorer 5.0, or Safari 1.0 or higher

▸ 500 Kbps or higher broadband connection

You should install the latest version of Adobe Flash after removing (uninstalling) any old versions. For help installing Flash, check out the Adobe website at: www.adobe.com/support/flashplayer.

If your system meets all of the above requirements, but the video player still isn't working properly, try troubleshooting using a different Internet browser. The main browsers for Mac are Firefox and Safari, and for Windows are Firefox and Internet Explorer.

Volume Issues from the Source Video

Another variable with playback is the volume level that was set by the person who created and uploaded the video. This you cannot control. If the person creating the video set the volume excessively high or low you will find yourself adjusting the volume when you press Play.

TIP   Always check the volume before playing back a video. Turn down the volume of the external device and then raise it as needed. A high volume can damage both your speakers and your ears.

External Speakers

Playback quality is determined by two factors: the audio quality of the video, and the quality of the speakers connected to your computer. The only aspect you can control is the quality of the speakers connected to your computer.

For personal listening, computer speakers are okay. These are typically stereo speakers connected to your computer's headphone jack. Computer speakers sometimes include a third speaker, such as a subwoofer, to enhance the bass frequencies, or multiple speakers for surround sound. Reputable speaker manufacturers include Logitech, Harman Kardon, and Bose. You can check reviews online to help you with your purchase. A good place to start is http://reviews.cnet.com/best-pc-speakers.

Classroom Sound Playback Options

To hear YouTube videos in your classes, you will typically need more power than is supplied with desktop speakers. In order to get more power, you have the following choices:

- ▶ Connecting to your classroom's stereo system (if available)
- ▶ Using an amplifier
- ▶ Purchasing powered monitors

Many music classrooms have a stereo system already in place. If your classroom has a stereo or amplifier, check to see if the system has an auxiliary input available. If it does, then you can use a cable to route the headphone output of your computer to the auxiliary input of the amplifier or stereo system.

Audio Cables

You will need an audio adapter cable to connect your computer to a power amplifier or stereo unit. Companies such as Radio Shack sell these adapters in various lengths. Be sure to purchase a long enough cable to go from your computer to the power amp or stereo system. When connecting to an auxiliary input, you will need to set your amplifier to Aux (auxiliary input) and then adjust the volume as needed.

The connector that plugs into the computer headphone jack is a stereo mini plug (see Fig. 4.6). The typical adapter for a sound system is a phono plug, also called an RCA plug (see Fig. 4.7). Check the unit for the specific type of connectors that are required. Stereo amplifiers usually have two RCA plugs, one for the right speaker (colored red) and one for the left speaker (colored white).

Purchase a cable that has a stereo mini connector on one end and two RCA phono plugs on the other (see Fig. 4.8). If you tell the store clerk in a Radio Shack or other audio store that you need to

Fig. 4.6
Stereo mini plug

Fig. 4.7
RCA phono plug

Fig. 4.8
Stereo mini to dual RCA phono cable

go from your computer to a stereo system, they should know exactly what you need. (By the way, this is the same cable that you use to connect an MP3 player such as an iPod to your sound system for playback.) The cost of this cable is typically under $20. The longer the cable length, the higher the cost, and cables typically come in 3-, 6-, or 9-foot lengths. Be careful not to make the cable length too long, such as more than 50 feet.

> **TIP**   As audio cables can be damaged, it's a good idea to purchase an extra audio cable.

Keyboard and Guitar Amplifiers

Some schools may have a guitar or electronic keyboard amplifier for performances. While these amps can be used to amplify the computer audio signal, they are not recommended because they are not designed to be used for computer amplification. Yet if you are in a pinch and the school already owns an amp, then this is certainly an option. In this case, however, you will need a different adapter. The stereo mini plug on the computer end is the same, but guitar and electronic keyboard amplifiers typically have a 1/4" phone plug input (see Fig. 4.9). You could also purchase a Y-adapter to convert two RCA mono plugs to one mono 1/4" plug. Consult with an audio specialist at your school or at a local audio store for advice.

Fig. 4.9
1/4" mono cable (1 ring)

Stereo and Mono Audio Plugs

You can tell if a plug is mono or stereo by the number of rings on the tip. If there are two rings, then it is a stereo plug (see Fig. 4.10). If there is only one ring, it is a mono cable. Mono cables are used for amplifiers. There are adapters that can convert these cables, but you should purchase the proper cable for your needs.

Fig. 4.10
1/4" stereo cable (2 rings)

AV Accessories

If you are like many music teachers who need to move from room to room, a mobile cart for transporting your computer and audio equipment is a useful accessory. Companies like SoundTree (www.soundtree.com) and Wenger (www. wengercorp.com) offer high-end portable workstations for use in music classrooms, with space for a computer, speakers, electronic keyboard, and more. Choosing a good mobile cart is important if you are going to be moving your computer from room to room or if you want to have additional equipment on the cart. Yet if you are on a tight budget, you can make a typical AV cart work.

TIP   Whatever cart you choose, take time to secure the components so they will not fall off and become damaged or cause injury. It is also possible to lock components. Consult with your technology department to review your options for securing your equipment before putting your mobile music cart to use.

Powered Monitor Speakers

Self-powered monitor speakers, also called "active monitors," have built-in amplification and independent volume controls. Speakers that require an outside source of power are called "passive monitors." If you use an AV cart, you will want to purchase active monitors. Then you simply plug in the cables, turn on the speakers, and you are ready to play YouTube videos for classes and large ensembles. M-Audio makes an AV line of monitors that will do a great job on a mobile cart. The AV 40 Desktop Speaker System (see Fig. 4.11) delivers enough power for most classrooms and rehearsal halls.

Fig. 4.11
M-Audio AV 40 Desktop Speaker System

Monitor speaker power is measured in watts. The AV 40 is 20 watts, which is enough power for the average classroom or rehearsal hall. If you are looking for a portable monitor/speaker powerful enough for use in an auditorium, you should purchase monitors that output 35 watts or more. The JBL Control 2P (see Fig. 4.12) is a good choice, with 35 watts of power per speaker. Expect to pay in the $200 to $300 range for a pair of active monitors.

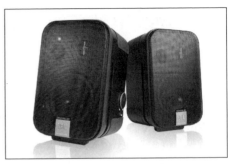

Fig. 4.12

JBL Control 2P Active Reference Monitors

Using an External Audio Interface

Another option for getting high-quality sound is to use an external audio interface, also referred to as a *sound card*. These interfaces, discussed in chapter 9, allow for high-quality microphones to be connected to your computer. They can also enhance the playback quality of videos, and provide a wide range of output and input connectors. You don't need to purchase an external audio interface solely for sound playback, but if you are planning to record high-quality audio for your YouTube videos, then an external audio interface is a good choice.

External audio interfaces typically connect to a USB or FireWire port. The fastest and most accurate transfer protocol is FireWire. Most Apple computers come equipped with FireWire. On Windows machines, FireWire is sometimes called IEEE 1394. If you have a Windows computer, a FireWire card can usually be added for under $50.

M-Audio makes a line of audio interfaces that range from $150 to several thousand dollars. For most school situations, you don't need to spend more than $150 to $400 for a quality audio interface. An excellent option is the M-Audio Fast Track Pro. This interface plugs into a USB port and offers many options for output. See Fig. 4.13 for a look at the back panel of the Fast Track Pro.

When you add an external audio interface to your system, you typically need to install a driver. A *driver* is a small file that helps the computer to communicate with a specific hardware device. This file allows your computer to communicate

Fig. 4.13
Back panel of the M-Audio Fast Track Pro

with external hardware. Once a device is connected and the driver is installed, you need to tell your computer where to route the sound output. By default, a computer will route audio to the built-in hardware—the headphone or audio output on the computer. When using an audio interface, you need to change the settings so the interface will be used for input and output.

On a Mac this is done by going to the Finder and then choosing Go > Utilities > Audio MIDI Setup. Under Audio Devices you can select the audio interface for input/output using the drop-down menu. The interface must be connected and/ or powered on to be listed as an option.

On a PC, click the Start button, click Control Panel, click on Sounds, Speech, and Audio Devices, click the Audio tab, and choose the output device from the pull-down menu.

Classroom Display Options

Now that you have your sound configured and working properly, you will want to show your YouTube videos to your class or ensemble. This will require connecting your computer to a larger monitor.

Connecting to a TV Monitor

If you have access to a large TV monitor connected to a DVD/VCR device, you can also connect the computer to it. Unfortunately, large-screen TVs can have a variety of different inputs. In some cases, it can be an easy connection. If both the TV and the computer have a VGA connector, then connecting a VGA cable is all you need to do. However, in some cases you will need a special converter to get the computer signal to display on the TV. If there is an AV technician at the school, ask for their help. You can also check out the YouTube video on how to connect your computer to a TV: www.youtube.com/watch?v=YpfnmnS5_WQ.

Connecting to a Computer Projector

Computer projectors are becoming ubiquitous in most schools and classrooms (see Fig. 4.14). Also called LCD (liquid crystal display) projectors, they can be placed on the AV cart with your computer and speakers and be easily moved from room to room. The cost of most projectors is under $1,000, and they are relatively easy to connect to a computer. Most use a VGA connector cable. Be sure to turn on the projector and connect the cable before starting up the computer. The projector should recognize the computer when it starts up.

Fig. 4.14
InFocus Computer Projector

There are many projector models to choose from. An excellent company is InFocus (www.infocus.com), which has a section for classroom and auditorium units on its website. When choosing a projector, try to get the most lumens possible—2,500 or more. The more lumens the projector has, the brighter the image.

TIP Typically, schools will have several projectors, which can be signed out and used by staff members. Consult with your school technology department to see if this is an option. Borrowing a projector can also be a cost savings until you are able to purchase your own unit.

Screen Resolution

When using a computer projector it is sometimes necessary to adjust the screen resolution of the computer. This can make the image easier for the class or ensemble to see. First connect the computer projector and see how the image looks. If it is too small or too large, you can adjust the resolution settings of the computer. Try reducing the resolution to 800 × 600 so the screen images are larger and therefore easier to see by the students. Experiment with the settings until you find a good match that works for you.

To adjust the screen resolution on a PC, go to the Control Panel and select Displays. Then click on Settings (see Fig. 4.15). You can adjust the screen resolution as needed.

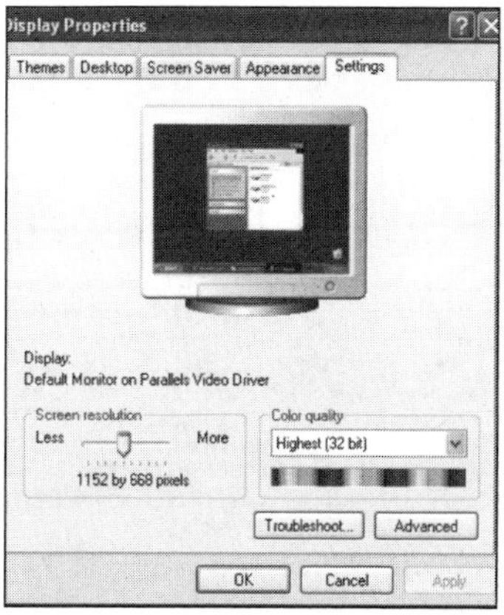

To adjust the screen resolution on a Mac, go to the Apple menu, select System Preferences, and then click on Displays (see Fig. 4.16). You can then adjust the screen resolution to complement the computer projector.

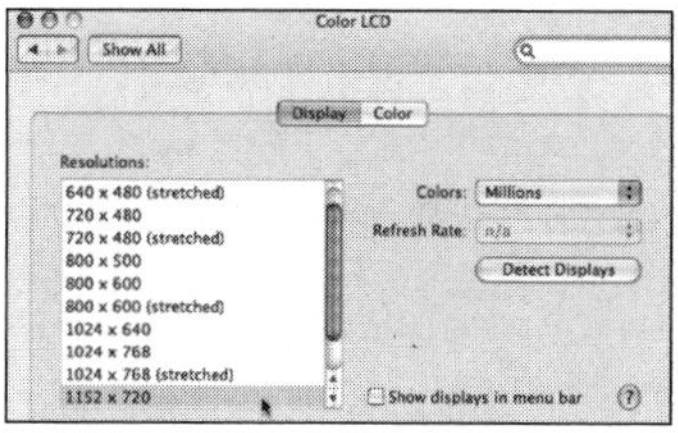

Projecting with an Interactive Whiteboard

An interactive whiteboard, which looks at first glance like a typical whiteboard, is a large interactive display that teachers and students can touch with a pen, finger, or other device to control a computer. Interactive whiteboards (like the ones made by Smart Technologies, Promethean, Panasonic, and 3M) are finding their way into more and more music classrooms.

Fig. 4.15
Windows display settings

Fig. 4.16
Mac display settings

TIP   If you want to find out more about interactive digital whiteboards, go to YouTube and enter the words "Smart Board in the classroom" in the Search box.

An interactive digital whiteboard requires a computer projector, described earlier in this chapter, and needs to be calibrated before use. Be prepared to spend a few hours getting your interactive whiteboard working when it is initially installed. Asking for help from the school's technology support staff is a good idea when getting started with an interactive whiteboard in the classroom.

Using an interactive whiteboard to show YouTube videos to a music class or rehearsal ensemble is not much different than using a computer projector.

However, you can use the whiteboard to start, stop, fast forward, and rewind the YouTube videos you are displaying for the class.

YouTube Screen Formats

YouTube currently offers three screen resolutions: 320 × 240, 480 × 360, and HD. The higher the resolution, the clearer the image. YouTube uses a codec scheme to convert its videos to a smaller file size. *Codec* stands for "compression/decompression," and various codecs are available to reduce the file size of video and music files.

The standard and original YouTube format and the most common is 320 × 240 resolution, which uses the Sorenson Spark codec, with mono MP3 audio. The Sorenson Spark Codec was developed by Sorenson Media and is used in Apple QuickTime and Adobe Flash files.

In March 2008, YouTube introduced a higher-quality video resolution of 480 × 360 with mono MP3 sound. These videos can be viewed with the H.264 codec, which is a standard for video compression. You can also add stereo sound, a huge improvement for music applications.

In November 2008, YouTube began supporting HD, or high-definition television (sometimes referred to as HDTV). The YouTube player can also be expanded to a widescreen format.

Watching YouTube Videos on Apple TV

In 1998, Apple introduced Apple TV, a digital media receiver designed to play digital content such as movies. Apple TV can connect to YouTube, the iTunes store, and other digital services. Some school districts are purchasing Apple TV units for use in the classroom. The advantage of Apple TV to the music educator is its enhanced stereo sound capabilities. As of this writing, YouTube is in the process of converting all its videos to the H.264 codec. If a video is not in this format it will not be able to be viewed on Apple TV.

Watching YouTube on an iPhone

While you won't want to show videos to your classes using an iPhone because the display area is so small, you may find it to be handy for planning which YouTube videos to show to your students (this will be explored in detail in chapters 6, 7, and 8).

On the iPhone there is a YouTube button on the main user interface. Only videos converted to the H.264 format will be viewable on the iPhone. As mentioned above, YouTube is in the process of converting all its videos to this format.

Downloading Files to Play on Your Computer or iPod

It is possible and permissible to download some YouTube videos to your computer's hard drive. Once downloaded, they can then be played offline on your computer or a device such as an iPod. Some YouTube partners allow for videos to be downloaded in MP4 format. MP4, or MPEG-4, is a popular compression method for audio and visual digital data.

TIP   Legally downloading YouTube files to your computer's hard drive will allow you to show videos offline when you are not connected to YouTube.

There are two reasons for this method to be applied to the music curriculum. First, you may not have access to YouTube in your school, as some schools block it from being displayed. Second, you may not have a direct connection to the Internet in your music classroom or rehearsal area. By downloading the files to your computer's hard drive, you can then play the YouTube videos offline for your class.

To do this, first find the video you want to download. Some YouTube videos require that you purchase them from an online store such as Amazon.com or iTunes before downloading them to your computer. If the YouTube partner's file is available for download, you'll see a Download button below the video's Play bar in the lower left-hand corner. Click the Download button to indicate that you'd like to download the video and/or purchase it through the third-party store you are directed to. If you do not see a Download button below a video, it means downloading is not yet enabled for that video.

Once a video is downloaded, you can play the file on your computer using one of the following video players:

1. QuickTime Player (Windows and Mac). This is a free download from www.apple.com/quicktime.

2. VLC media player (Windows, Mac, Linux, and others). This can be downloaded at www.videolan.org/vlc/.

Converting Downloaded Files to Play on an iPod

If you own an iPod or other mobile device that is capable of playing back videos, then you can download some of the content on YouTube to play offline on your iPod. This can be helpful for reviewing videos for your music class or rehearsal or for downloading student performances for evaluation (these applications will be covered in chapters 6, 7, and 8).

Once you have downloaded an MP4 version of a YouTube video as described above, then you can convert it to play on your iPod. The following steps to do this are given in the YouTube Help section:

1. Start iTunes. If iTunes is not on your computer you can download it for free by visiting www.apple.com/itunes.

2. From the File menu, select Add File to Library.

3. Select the MP4 video file on your computer.

4. This video will now appear in your iTunes Library under the Movies section.

5. Connect your iPhone or iPod to your computer; it should appear under the Devices section of iTunes.

6. Click your device name (e.g., "XXX's iPhone").

7. Go to the Video tab on the right-hand side of the page.

8. Scroll down to the Movies section, enable Sync Movies, and then enable the check box in front of the name of the video file.

9. Click the Apply (or Sync) button.

Summary

This chapter focused on the various options for sound and video playback when viewing YouTube videos. Sound options covered included adjusting computer playback volume; amplifying playback for a classroom or ensemble through a stereo system, amplifier, or external speakers; and purchasing the proper audio cables. Video options covered included increasing the display size for viewing by class/ensemble members by connecting the computer to a TV monitor, computer projector, or interactive whiteboard; and adjusting the computer's screen resolution for imcreased sharpness. Other topics covered in this chapter included legally downloading available YouTube videos to a computer hard drive for viewing when you are offline or not connected to YouTube; and video conversion for playback on portable video players such as iPods.

Chapter Five

Copyright and Copywrong

This chapter will cover the following topics:

- ▶ Copyright issues and how they apply to YouTube
- ▶ The Takedown Notice
- ▶ Copyright infringement cases involving YouTube
- ▶ How to determine what qualifies as fair use
- ▶ How to determine what is considered an infringement
- ▶ How to determine what is legal to upload
- ▶ How to find YouTube's copyright policies
- ▶ Downloading videos from YouTube
- ▶ Using copyright-free music and video from YouTube and other sources

One of the most common concerns that teachers and administrators have is how copyright law applies to the videos that are posted on YouTube. Educators have many questions about what is legal and what is considered an infringement. The most common questions include:

- ▶ Is it legal to post videos that contain copyright-protected music or video on YouTube?
- ▶ Is it an infringement to post clips of copyright-protected videos on YouTube for use with students—even if the video is private?

- ▸ Is it an infringement for a user to view videos on the site that contain copyright-protected material?

- ▸ Is it legal to show students an episode of a program on PBS that has been posted to YouTube?

- ▸ Is it a copyright infringement to embed YouTube videos that contain copyrighted materials on a school website?

- ▸ What are the possible legal ramifications if a teacher posts videos that are an infringement of copyrights?

- ▸ How can an educator use YouTube without violating copyright law?

In order to properly answer these questions, it is necessary to gain a basic understanding of what copyright is, what it protects, what is fair use, how to determine whether a use is considered fair, and what is infringement.

A Copyright Primer

Copyright literally means the right to copy or reproduce an original work. An original work can be a literary work, a work of art, a musical composition, an audio recording, or a movie. In order for a work to be eligible for copyright protection, it must meet two criteria: 1) the work must be original; and 2) the work must be fixed in a tangible form. A *tangible form* (which can be in a variety of media formats) is a form that can be read, viewed, or heard, either directly or with the aid of a machine.

For a work to be considered original, it must show a "minimal spark of creativity." The more creative the work is, the easier it is to show originality. Once an original work is in a fixed and tangible form it is inherently granted copyright protection, regardless of whether it is published or not. This means that the minute you record a short video, copyright law protects you. This protection affords you the right to sell your original work to an individual or to a company that can then reproduce and distribute that work. It also protects you from individuals or companies that might use the original work without compensating you. Fundamentally, copyright is about being fair to both the creators and the distributors of original works, and providing financial incentive.[1]

What Copyright Protects

Provided that a work meets the criteria stated above, copyright grants the owner six exclusive rights. These include:

- The right to reproduce a work
- The right to prepare derivative works of the work
- The right to distribute copies of the work
- The right to perform the work publicly (excluding sound recordings)
- The right to display the work publicly
- The right to publicly perform a sound recording by digital audio transmission[2]

What Does Copyright Law Cover?

There are eight categories of original works that fall under copyright protection. They include:

- Literary works
- Musical works, including any accompanying words
- Dramatic works, including any accompanying music
- Pantomimes and choreographic works
- Pictorial, graphic, and sculptural works
- Motion pictures and other audiovisual works
- Sound recordings
- Architectural works[3]

What Does Copyright Law Not Cover?

There are eight categories of works that do not fall under copyright protection. They include:

- Works that are in the public domain
- Works of the United States Government
- Works that are not in a fixed, tangible form
- Titles, names, short phrases, and slogans
- Familiar symbols or designs
- Type fonts, lettering, or coloring

- Ideas, facts, procedures, methods, systems, processes, concepts, principles, discoveries, or devices

- Works consisting entirely of information that is common property and containing no original authorship[4]

What Is Fair Use?

Fair use of copyright-protected materials is permitted for purposes such as criticism, comment, news reporting, teaching, scholarship, and research. *Fair use* erroneously causes many teachers to feel that *any* use of copyright-protected materials in the classroom is permitted, but that is not the intention of fair use. Fair uses are limited.

The Fair Use provision of the Copyright Act of 1976 (17 USC §107) is stated as follows:

> Notwithstanding the provisions of sections and the fair use of a copyrighted work, including such use by reproduction in copies or phono records or by any other means specified by that section, for purposes such as criticism, comment, news reporting, teaching (including multiple copies for classroom use), scholarship, or research, is not an infringement of copyright. In determining whether the use made of a work in any particular case is a fair use the factors to be considered shall include:
>
> 1. The purpose and character of the use, including whether such use is of a commercial nature or is for nonprofit educational purposes;
>
> 2. The nature of the copyrighted work;
>
> 3. The amount and substantiality of the portion used in relation to the copyrighted work as a whole; and
>
> 4. The effect of the use upon the potential market for or value of the copyrighted work.
>
> The fact that a work is unpublished shall not itself bar a finding of fair use if such finding is made upon consideration of all the above factors.[5]

These fair use guidelines provide educators with criteria for what they are permitted to do with copyright-protected materials in their classroom. To boil all of this down, teachers are permitted to use limited portions of copyrighted works with their students for educational purposes. YouTube poses many challenges to the fair use provision because of the very nature of the technology upon which it is based. By providing users with access to videos that contain copyrighted material, the possibility for the unlawful reproduction of that material is as easy as clicking a mouse.

An example of a fair use of video materials would be if a teacher took a short 30-second clip of a feature film and had students create a new film score to it. For example, if an educator purchases a copy of Disney's *Fantasia*, then uses a software program to import the DVD into their computer so that they can cut a scene from the movie into several short segments for a film scoring lesson, it would most likely be considered a fair use. What teachers do with the final product is where they might run into trouble. For example, if they then take those finished student versions of *Fantasia* and post them on YouTube for the rest of the world to view, then the use may not be fair. As a rule of thumb, there is almost never a problem using copyrighted materials in your classroom provided that copies of those materials never leave your classroom. When you post things online, the game changes dramatically.

What Is Copyright Infringement?

Copyright infringement is defined as any violation of the exclusive rights of the copyright holder. This includes the unlawful reproduction, distribution, and creation of derivative works, public performance, or public display without the permission of the copyright owner. Online music piracy, the illegal downloading of music from peer-to-peer file sharing services, is a glaring example of copyright infringement. Other examples of copyright infringement include:

- ▶ Copying and distributing copies of promotional DVDs of movies on YouTube without permission

- ▶ Recording and then posting content from a television program on YouTube without permission

- ▶ Making a video of a copyright-protected musical and posting it on YouTube without permission[6]

Nearly every use of YouTube therefore could be considered an infringement of copyright. For example, the following actions clearly violate copyright protection:

- ▶ Capturing, downloading, or recording a video on YouTube (the right to reproduce a work) without permission

▸ Making a remix or mash-up using videos from YouTube (the right to make derivative works) without permission

▸ Embedding videos from YouTube that contain copyrighted material on another website (the right to distribute copies of the work and the right to display the work publicly) without permission

Each of these practices is quite common on YouTube, and each could be considered an infringement. When an educator uses YouTube in this way, fair use may apply, but currently the law is unclear. The reason for this is that many of these actions would be considered a fair use (as described above) within the walls of a classroom, but because these videos can be accessed by potentially millions of users, copyright owners might have a legitimate argument about the financial impact of these practices — even if it was done for educational purposes and even if the site where the videos are posted is password-protected.

The Takedown Notice

So what happens if you knowingly (or unknowingly) happen to post content on YouTube that contains copyrighted material and the owner complains? Don't worry; you won't be going to jail or paying steep fines — at least not for your first couple of offenses. When Congress passed the Digital Millennium Copyright Act (DMCA) in 1998, it included an instrument known as the *takedown notice*. What this means is that if someone spots a video on a site like YouTube that they believe to contain copyrighted material, they can file a DMCA takedown notice with YouTube. YouTube will remove the video and notify the person who posted it. If the owner believes they are within their rights to post the material, they can file a counter notification and YouTube will investigate. If the video is found to contain no offending material, YouTube must repost the video within 10 to 14 days.[7] The DMCA states that when a website receives a takedown notice it must comply immediately. In return for a website complying with takedown notices, it receives unwritten blanket protection from copyright infringement lawsuits — although this is not always the case, as detailed below. Because a website like YouTube merely provides the tool for users to upload content rather than the content itself, it is the action of the individual user that constitutes the infringement rather than the technology that facilitated it. While there has been recent litigation against YouTube, the site has not been taken down because of its compliance with the DMCA.

Many YouTube users receive takedown notices for possible copyright infringement. When they do, YouTube sends them a message that typically says: "Your video titled

_____ has been removed from the site as a result of a third-party notification by _____ Inc. that your video contained copyright-protected material which they own." The takedown notification usually also includes a warning to stop posting copyright-protected material. Receiving too many of these warnings can result in the termination of your YouTube account.

Copyright Infringement Cases Involving YouTube

There are many well-known stories about YouTube users receiving takedown notifications. Some comply and others fight back. One such case involved a woman named Stephanie Lenz, who posted a 29-second video showing her young child walking around the kitchen with a walker while a song by Prince, "Let's Go Crazy," played in the background. Ms. Lenz received a takedown notice from Universal claiming that the recording infringed on its copyrights. The video was promptly removed from the site (it has since been reposted). Stunned by the action, Ms. Lenz then filed a lawsuit against Universal, which as of this writing is still in the courts.[8] In a similar action, a young aspiring artist named Juliet Weybret posted a video of herself singing the song "Winter Wonderland." She received a takedown notice from YouTube stating that Warner Music Group requested that the video be removed as it infringed on its copyrights. What makes this case different than the Lenz case is that the video was of Ms. Weybret's version of the song rather than the actual sound recording. Copyright law clearly protects this practice, but some view issuing takedown notices for videos containing amateur versions of copyright-protected music as draconian. The Electronic Frontier Foundation (an organization dedicated to defending the rights of citizens in the digital world) is actively fighting this practice, though it certainly faces an uphill battle.[9] There are countless other examples of corporations issuing takedown notices for similar types of copyright infringement. When talks over a music licensing deal between YouTube and Warner Music Group failed, Warner Music Group demanded the takedown of thousands of videos that contained music that it owned the copyrights to. In some cases, YouTube actually removes the audio from videos instead of taking down the video completely—often without the knowledge of the user who uploaded the video.

Perhaps the most well-publicized copyright infringement case is the lawsuit filed on behalf of Viacom in March 2007 claiming that Google (which owns YouTube) was responsible for the rampant copyright infringement that existed on its website. The lawsuit, which seeks $1 billion in damages, contends that over 160,000 unauthorized clips of Viacom's programming (which were subsequently viewed over 1.5 billion times by YouTube users) were available on the site, causing a huge financial loss for the company. In an additional lawsuit in support of its infringement claim, Viacom sued Google to release the account information of every YouTube user in an effort to prove which videos users watch on the site. In July 2008, Google and Viacom reached a compromise whereby Google agreed to provide Viacom with the usernames and IP addresses of all of its account holders, but not the personal information behind the accounts. The lawsuit is still in the courts and will likely be settled in 2009 or 2010. The result of this lawsuit will most certainly have widespread implications not only for YouTube, but also for copyright in general.

YouTube and Copyright

For many appropriate reasons, YouTube is vigilant about preventing its users from infringing on copyright law and educating them about what qualifies as fair use and what qualifies as copyright infringement. In addition to posting warnings on various sections of the site (see Fig. 5.1), YouTube also employs unique software, called the Video Identification Tool, to help identify videos that contain copyrighted material. This tool creates what are known as ID files (a database containing thousands of reference videos of copyrighted content such as

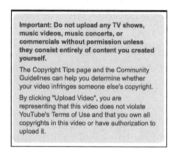

Important: Do not upload any TV shows, music videos, music concerts, or commercials without permission unless they consist entirely of content you created yourself.

The Copyright Tips page and the Community Guidelines can help you determine whether your video infringes someone else's copyright.

By clicking "Upload Video", you are representing that this video does not violate YouTube's Terms of Use and that you own all copyrights in this video or have authorization to upload it.

Fig. 5.1
YouTube copyright warning

movies and television programs), which are then compared with every video that users upload to the site. When a match occurs, the copyright holder's preference policy is applied to the video. To create your own copyright preferences, search for "Content ID" in the YouTube Help Center or visit www.youtube.com/content_id_signup. When you get to the Content Identification Signup page (see Fig. 5.2), you will need to fill out the form and select from one of three options concerning your permissions (see Fig. 5.3). These options include Block, Track, or Monetize. Below is a more detailed description of each option:

▸ **Block:** *I want to block unauthorized distribution of my content on YouTube.* This option is the strongest protection against the use of your content.

▸ **Track:** *I don't mind others uploading my content, but would like to track upload activity and views.* This option allows users to use the content in your videos without restriction, and provides you with statistical information about how often the videos are viewed.

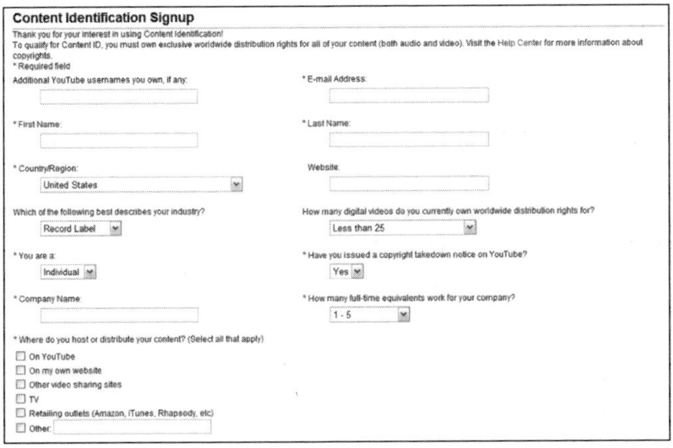

Content Identification Signup

Thank you for your interest in using Content Identification!
To qualify for Content ID, you must own exclusive worldwide distribution rights for all of your content (both audio and video). Visit the Help Center for more information about copyrights.
* Required field

Additional YouTube usernames you own, if any:

* E-mail Address:

* First Name:

* Last Name:

* Country/Region:
United States

Website:

Which of the following best describes your industry?
Record Label

How many digital videos do you currently own worldwide distribution rights for?
Less than 25

* You are a:
Individual

* Have you issued a copyright takedown notice on YouTube?
Yes

* Company Name:

* How many full-time equivalents work for your company?
1 - 5

* Where do you host or distribute your content? (Select all that apply)
☐ On YouTube
☐ On my own website
☐ Other video sharing sites
☐ TV
☐ Retailing outlets (Amazon, iTunes, Rhapsody, etc)
☐ Other:

Fig. 5.2
Content Identification page

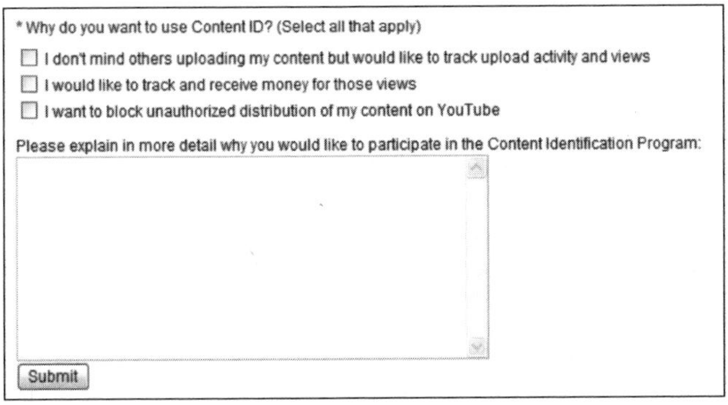

* Why do you want to use Content ID? (Select all that apply)
☐ I don't mind others uploading my content but would like to track upload activity and views
☐ I would like to track and receive money for those views
☐ I want to block unauthorized distribution of my content on YouTube

Please explain in more detail why you would like to participate in the Content Identification Program:

[Submit]

Fig. 5.3
Content Preferences options

▶ **Monetize:** *I would like to track and receive money for those views.* This option requires that users obtain permission and pay for the right to use your content. Content creators who wish to make money from their posted videos can join the YouTube Partner Program by visiting: www .youtube.com/partners.

After selecting one of the above options, explaining why you are using the tool, and submitting your preferences, you will be asked to upload videos of the content that you would like to protect.

This extraordinary technology illustrates part of YouTube's efforts to control copyright infringement. Here is YouTube's statement about this system:

Since its launch in 2005, YouTube has been committed to giving copyright owners the ability to maximize their choice in how their content is made available on the site. Video identification is the latest in a series of the tools that YouTube offers content owners to more easily identify and manage the use of their content on the site.[10]

In addition to the Video Identification Tool, creators can also use the Audio Identification Tool, which can also be found on the Content Identification page. This tool matches protected audio files by searching for matches in the audio contained in the uploaded videos.

So what happens if a video or audio file that you post gets matched to one that has been uploaded through the Content Identification Tool? If a match is identified, the video ID tool will automatically apply whatever preference the copyright owner selected. The audio ID tool can find audio within a video and identify just the audio. If something that you have uploaded is matched, you will receive a notification next to your video on the My Videos page. If the copyright holder has chosen the Block option, your video or video's audio will be immediately deleted from the site. If you feel that your video was pulled in error, you can fill out a short form listing the reason for your dispute. This dispute form is linked to the "Video ID Matches" page when you receive the notification on your video. It is very simple to fill out, and is sent to the content owner whose video reference file was matched to your video. The content owner reviews the match, and if he or she believes that his/her copyright has been infringed by your video, s/he can submit an official takedown notice. The takedown notice will result in the disabling of your video and/or penalties against your account.

If you feel that your copyrights have been infringed on, you have a number of options. First, you should read what the US copyright law defines as infringement and determine whether the use of your content is in fact infringement (covered previously in this chapter). You can also inform YouTube using the company's Copyright Complaint Form, located at: www.youtube.com/copyright_complaint_form (see Fig. 5.4). Once you have selected your country on the first page, you will be required to fill out a form providing your personal information as well as information about the infringement. You should ensure that the suspected infringement you are reporting is, in fact, an infringement, as YouTube states that false claims might result in the termination of your account.

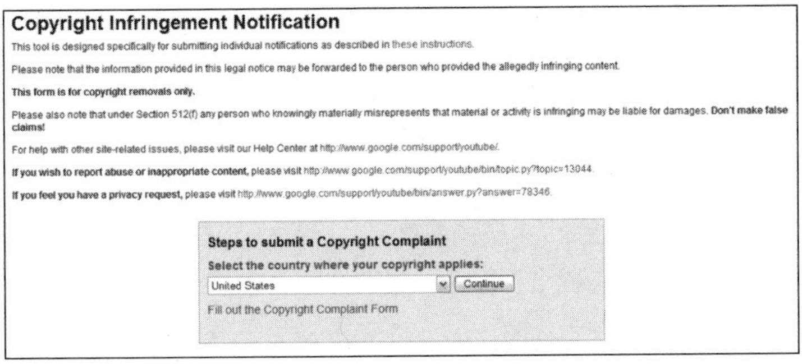

Copyright Infringement Notification

This tool is designed specifically for submitting individual notifications as described in these instructions.

Please note that the information provided in this legal notice may be forwarded to the person who provided the allegedly infringing content.

This form is for copyright removals only.

Please also note that under Section 512(f) any person who knowingly materially misrepresents that material or activity is infringing may be liable for damages. **Don't make false claims!**

For help with other site-related issues, please visit our Help Center at http://www.google.com/support/youtube/.

If you wish to report abuse or inappropriate content, please visit http://www.google.com/support/youtube/bin/topic.py?topic=13044.

If you feel you have a privacy request, please visit http://www.google.com/support/youtube/bin/answer.py?answer=78346.

Steps to submit a Copyright Complaint

Select the country where your copyright applies:

United States ▾ [Continue]

Fill out the Copyright Complaint Form

Fig. 5.4
Copyright Infringement form

Here are the instructions that YouTube provides along with the complaint form:

To file a copyright infringement notification with us, you will need to send a written communication that includes substantially the following (please consult your legal counsel or see Section 512(c)(3) of the Digital Millennium Copyright Act to confirm these requirements):

i. A physical or electronic signature of a person authorized to act on behalf of the owner of an exclusive right that is allegedly infringed.

ii. Identification of the copyrighted work claimed to have been infringed, or, if multiple copyrighted works at a single online site are covered by a single notification, a representative list of such works at that site.

iii. Identification of the material that is claimed to be infringing or to be the subject of infringing activity and that is to be removed or access to which is to be disabled, and information reasonably sufficient to permit the service provider to locate the material. Providing URLs in the body of an e-mail is the best way to help us locate content quickly.

iv. Information reasonably sufficient to permit the service provider to contact the complaining party, such as an address, telephone number, and, if available, an electronic mail address at which the complaining party may be contacted.

v. A statement that the complaining party has a good faith belief that use of the material in the manner complained of is not authorized by the copyright owner, its agent, or the law.

vi. A statement that the information in the notification is accurate, and under penalty of perjury, that the complaining party is authorized to act on behalf of the owner of an exclusive right that is allegedly infringed.[11]

If you prefer to contact YouTube via mail, e-mail, or fax, use the following address:

DMCA Complaints
YouTube, Inc.
901 Cherry Ave.
Second Floor
San Bruno, CA 94066
Fax: 650-872-8513
E-mail: copyright@youtube.com

Once you have submitted your complaint, the user who uploaded the infringing material will be informed that you have submitted a complaint, and the infringing content will be disabled and replaced by a message that contains the claimant information you provided when you filled out the form. For example:

The video you have requested has been disabled due to a claim of copyright infringement made by "Ms. Music Teacher."

What Can You Legally Post on YouTube?

In an effort to inform YouTube users of its copyright policies, YouTube has included a copyright link at the bottom of the main page (or the Help Center page). You will find in-depth information about YouTube's copyright policies as well as a set of guiding principles on what you can and can't post to YouTube. The following text is posted on the YouTube site:

> YouTube respects the rights of all creators, and hope you will work with us to keep our community a creative, legal, and positive experience for everyone, including all creators. Posting copyright-infringing content can lead to your video being blocked from the site, the termination of your account, and possibly monetary damages if a copyright owner decides to take legal action. Below are some guidelines to help you determine whether your video may infringe someone else's copyright. You can also find copyright entries within our Help Center.

▶ If you taped it off cable, videotaped your TV screen, or downloaded it from some other website, it is copyrighted and requires the copyright owner's permission to distribute or can only be used within the limits of legal exceptions to copyright.

▶ If you give credit to the owner/author/songwriter, it is still copyrighted.

▶ If you are not selling the video for money, it is still copyrighted.

▶ If similar videos appear on our site, it is still copyrighted.

▶ If the video contains a copyright notice, it is still copyrighted.

▶ If you created a video made of short clips of copyrighted content, even though you edited it together, the content is still copyrighted.

Please note, this material is provided for informational purposes only. It is not, nor is it intended to be, legal advice, or a substitute for legal advice.[12]

YouTube also includes these helpful copyright tips:

The way to ensure that your video doesn't infringe someone else's copyright is to use your skills and imagination to create something completely original. It could be as simple as taping some of your friends goofing around, and as complicated as filming your own short movie with a script, actors, and the whole works. If it's all yours, you never have to worry about the copyright — you own it!

Be sure that all components of your video are your original creation — even the audio portion. For example, if you use an audio track of a sound recording owned by a record label without that record label's permission, your video may be infringing the copyrights of others, and may be subject to removal. YouTube offers a library of authorized music to liven up your video [called AudioSwap — discussed below]."[13]

What happens to you when your video is found to be an infringement?

There are really two answers to this question. First, what actions does YouTube take; and second, what consequences are you subject to according to US copyright law? When YouTube becomes aware that a video or any part of a video that you posted to the site using your account infringes on the copyrights of a third party, they immediately take it down as required by the Digital Millennium Copyright Act. Accounts determined to be repeat infringers may be subject to termination.

Users with suspended or terminated accounts are prohibited from creating new accounts or accessing YouTube's community features.

If, however, you believe that your video was removed in error and that either you have permission to post the content or that you are in fact the copyright owner of the content in the video, you can file a counter claim with the US copyright office by filling out the form located at www.copyright.gov/legislation/dmca.pdf, or by sending the following information to YouTube:

1. Identify the specific URLs of material that YouTube has removed or to which YouTube has disabled access;

2. Provide your full name, address, telephone number, and e-mail address, and the username of your YouTube account;

3. Provide a statement that you consent to the jurisdiction of Federal District Court for the judicial district in which your address is located (or San Francisco County, California, if your address is outside of the United States), and that you will accept service of process from the person who provided notification under subsection (c)(1)(C) or an agent of such person;

4. Include the following statement: "I swear, under penalty of perjury, that I have a good faith belief that the material was removed or disabled as a result of a mistake or misidentification of the material to be removed or disabled"

5. Sign the notice. If you are providing notice by e-mail, a scanned physical signature or a valid electronic signature will be accepted.

Send the written communication to the following address:

YouTube, LLC
Attn: YouTube DMCA Counter-Notification
901 Cherry Ave.
Second Floor
San Bruno, CA 94066
Fax: 650-872-8513
E-mail: copyright@youtube.com

or fax to:

650-872-8513, Attn: YouTube DMCA. Counter-Notification[14]

Copyright, YouTube, and You

Now that you have a better understanding of copyright law and how it applies to videos and audio on YouTube, it is easy to understand the types of problems that can arise. Because all videos on the site are inherently in a fixed, tangible form, copyright law protects them all. For example, if you create a video of yourself riding a bicycle around your driveway, it is protected by copyright. If you make a video of yourself playing a scale on your instrument, it is protected by copyright. While it might not seem like these activities would qualify as showing a minimal spark of creativity, they do according to law because of the fact that the thought process involved in creating the video as well as the location of the camera, lighting, and any editing is considered creative. If you post a video on YouTube that contains original content, copyright law protects that video and you have the right to control how others use it.

But what if you create a video that contains copyright-protected content? For example, if you make a video of a copyright-protected musical without permission, it is a clear infringement of copyright to post that video on YouTube. Many schools do this. If you search for "*The Wizard of Oz*" on YouTube, you will receive tens of thousands of matches. Not only will you find many segments of the original film; you will also find countless videos of the musical version performed by high school drama clubs, videos of all-state ensembles performing musical highlights from the movie, and many different versions of the movie set to different music—specifically Pink Floyd's *Dark Side of the Moon*. Every one of these videos qualifies as an infringement of copyright if the user who posted the videos did not receive permission to do so, and most have not.

On the flip side of the coin, you might ask why anyone who wanted to protect his or her original work would post it on YouTube in the first place. If you are concerned about others stealing your work, why share it with the world? One possibility could be that the majority of users who post videos of themselves on YouTube want their video to be viewed and shared by as many people as possible. Others post them simply to share with other family members. However, when those videos are captured (by a third-party software title or website—see chapter 8) and then used in another video without the permission of the creator, does that qualify as infringement? Yes, it does. There are many of these types of questions that will come up when using YouTube with your students.

As chapter 9 notes, when you upload any video to YouTube, you can select whether other viewers can view, share, and embed your videos on other websites. Most videos on YouTube allow users to share, view, and embed them. Some sponsored videos are available for download. If you allow others to view, share, and embed your video(s), does that mean that you are relinquishing your copyrights? No, it does not.

Copyright Q&A

At the beginning of the chapter a number of questions were posed about common uses of YouTube. Here are the answers:

Is it legal to post videos that contain copyright-protected music or video on YouTube?

Without permission from the copyright owner, it is not permissible to post copyrighted music or video on YouTube. Although fair use guidelines allow educators to use small segments of video and audio in multimedia projects, it is not clear whether it is considered a fair use when you then post those projects on a site such as YouTube. While it may in fact be a fair use, it is not recommended that you include copyrighted material in videos that you post to YouTube. Educators should encourage students to create original content for their projects.

Online content can include images, text, sound recordings, software, and videos. There is a major difference between showing students a video during class and posting that video on a website. When a teacher shows a video in class, it is a temporal experience, meaning that the students do not walk out of the classroom with a personal copy of the video, only the memory of viewing it. When a video is posted online, it can be downloaded, reproduced, and distributed. Before posting any copyrighted material online, a teacher needs to obtain permission to do so.

Is it an infringement to post clips of copyright-protected videos on YouTube for use with students—even if the video is private?

As stated above, fair use guidelines are unclear as to whether it is an infringement to post copyrighted material solely for educational use. But what if you set the uploaded content to "private" so that only your invited students can view it? Copyright law is clear on this. Even if the video is private or password protected, it is a violation of copyright law to post someone else's material without their permission and/or paying a licensing fee. The only time that it is considered a fair use is when the course that the videos are being used for is part of a distance-learning program where the students never meet in person.

Is it an infringement for a user to view videos on the site that contain copyright-protected material?

It is not considered an infringement to actually view videos from YouTube that contain copyrighted material. Here the user who actually uploaded the content commits the infringement. However, if you then use software or another type of capturing tool to save that content, you are then committing an infringement.

Is it a fair use to show students an episode of a program on PBS that has been posted to YouTube?

The answer to this question is similar to the one above. It is not considered an infringement to simply view the video with your students. It's almost a case of "finders, keepers" when it comes to finding videos on YouTube. In some cases, networks such as PBS may have actually posted the content on YouTube. You can usually identify when a network has sponsored a posted clip if an advertisement appears next to the video, or in some cases in the beginning of the video. It should be noted that PBS posts a great deal of content on YouTube. A recent search for "PBS" yielded over 100,000 videos.

Is it an infringement to embed videos from YouTube on a school website if they contain copyrighted materials?

Yes. Plain and simple. It is considered an infringement of copyright law and not a fair use when you embed videos that contain copyrighted material on any website, including a school website. There are two types of links: links and deep links. A *link* is simply a link to a URL: www.youtube.com, for example. A *deep link* links directly to specific content on the site; for example, a specific video on YouTube. Deep linking to a file on YouTube can either be done by copying the address that appears in the URL window of your Internet browser, or copying the embed code that accompanies most videos on YouTube. The embed code can be found in the box that appears to the right of most videos (see Fig. 5.5). In terms of infringement, when linking to an outside website—for example, YouTube—if the website contains infringing material, it might be considered an infringement to merely link to it. When deep link-

Fig. 5.5

Embed code box

ing—for example, to a specific video on YouTube—if the video itself is copyright protected (and posted without permission), it would be an infringement to link to it.[15]

What can happen if a teacher posts videos that are an infringement of copyrights?

As described above, the first thing that will happen to you if you are caught posting a video that contains copyrighted materials (either by the original copyright owner or the Video Identification Tool), your video will be disabled and removed from the site. When this happens you will also receive an e-mail from YouTube that informs you that a claim has been filed against your video. YouTube will also make a note of the complaint on your account, and if you receive a number of these complaints, your account will be permanently canceled. That is usually all that will happen as far as YouTube is concerned. The copyright owner also has the right to pursue litigation against your infringement. The penalties for infringement can be up to $250,000 in fines and up to five years in prison—though no teachers have been sued for copyright infringement in the classroom.[16]

How can an educator use YouTube without violating copyright law?

There are many ways that an educator can use YouTube in the classroom without violating copyright law. Actually, the applications mentioned in this book do not violate copyright. As described earlier in this chapter, you are permitted to show YouTube videos in your classroom, even if they contain copyrighted material. You can upload videos of student work that contain original material. You can videotape your lessons and post them. Chapters 6 and 7 will provide numerous other ways for you to incorporate YouTube into your music curriculum.

Downloading Videos from YouTube

Many school districts block YouTube completely (see chapter 8 for more information). One of the most common ways that music teachers circumvent this issue is by downloading videos from YouTube to their computer hard drive at home, saving them to a USB drive, and then bringing the USB drive to school to show the videos to their students without having to log on to YouTube. While this is certainly a convenient method of circumventing school district policy (which might not be such a good thing to do if your district blocks the site), and many music teachers admit to doing this, it is a clear violation of both the YouTube Terms of Service and copyright law. Downloading a video is the same as making a duplicate copy of the video, which is one of the protections afforded by copyright.

If you search for "Downloading Videos from YouTube" in the YouTube search window, you will find thousands of videos that explain how to do so. Most provide links to third-party software titles that allow you to download any video directly from YouTube by entering either the URL of the video or the embed code and converting the video to a selected video format (see chapter 8). Other video screen-capture software allows you to draw a box around the video and record it from your screen. As described in chapter 9, Firefox has a Download Manager plug-in that allows you to download videos as well as content from other websites. Do note that some websites, such as TeacherTube.com, allow for downloading, which is discussed in chapter 8. However, the copyright laws still apply for these videos.

While each of these third-party software solutions is legal, their use on YouTube most likely is not, because there are so many ways to use the software. To be clear, the mere act of downloading or copying video from any site that prohibits this is an infringement of copyright law, and is not likely to be considered a fair use, because the material being copied was not legally acquired.

As detailed in chapter 8, rather than downloading YouTube videos illegally, it is far more advantageous and legal to consider doing the following:

- ▶ Use school-friendly video sites such as TeacherTube or SchoolTube

- ▶ Contact the user who posted the video to see if they will send you a copy (only if it is their original work)

- ▶ Ask your students to search at home for videos you suggest. Simply by telling students to try and find videos about a given musician or topic, you can still use the resource, just outside of your classroom. See chapter 8 for more details on these suggestions

Recently YouTube instituted a feature that allows viewers to download associated media files (mostly songs). When a video offers a "Download This Song" option, viewers can purchase the song (or video) from stores such as iTunes or Amazon. com. At the time of this writing, only songs were available for purchase, though it is highly likely that videos will be available as well, as YouTube is currently working with a series of partners to allow videos to be downloaded. It is assumed that most of these services will require the user to pay a fee.

Using Copyright and Royalty-Free Materials with YouTube

Numerous resources are available to educators that contain copyright- and royalty-free audio and video content that can be used for any purpose. Using these materials is a good way to ensure that the video and audio files that you post to YouTube are not infringing on copyrights.

Sources for copyright- and royalty-free videos include:

▸ **Internet Archives Moving Pictures Library** (www.archive.org/details/movies) This site contains thousands of copyright- and royalty-free videos that can be downloaded in a variety of formats, including .mp4 and .wav. This site also hosts the Prelinger Archives. With over 60,000 films (acquired by the Library of Congress in 2002), this incredible collection, started in 1983 by Rick Prelinger, includes classic television commercials, ephemeral films, and more. Chapter 8 includes a number of teaching strategies that use films from this collection. You can also find a wonderful collection of animated films and cartoons on the site. Educators should not send students directly to the website, as there is also a collection of films that contain nudity. Educators are encouraged to browse the site on their own and download appropriate films for student use.

▸ **The Open Video Project** (www.open-video.org) This site is managed by the Interaction Design Laboratory at the School of Information and Library Science at the University of North Carolina in Chapel Hill. The site contains thousands of copyright- and royalty-free video clips that have been obtained from the collections of US government agencies such as NASA and the American National Archives, as well as videos from the Carnegie Mellon Informedia Project and Johns Hopkins University. The videos are categorized by subject area, duration, and whether they are black and white or color. It is an incredible resource for students and teachers alike who are looking for videos to use in their projects.

▸ **WGBH Sandbox** (http://lab.wgbh.org/sandbox) This collection of nearly 800 copyright- and royalty-free videos has been posted on the WGBH homepage (the public television station for Boston, Massachusetts). They are free for students to use for multimedia projects. The videos are categorized into groups such as beauty, culture, history, and technology. The site also hosts videos that students have created using the materials on the site. All of the videos on the site are licensed through a Creative Commons

Attribution license, which permits others to use the work provided that they properly credit WGBH as the source. For more information about how Creative Commons licensing works, visit www.creativecommons.org.

▸ **The Space Telescope Science Institute** (http://hubblesource.stsci .edu/sources/video/clips) The Astronomy Visualization Lab (AVL) at STScI produces animations and visualizations of celestial phenomena to accompany press releases. In the past, broadcast-resolution copies of these animations were available only on professional Betacam videotape, with lower-resolution digital movie clips posted on STScI's website. Now the clips are available for noncommercial educational use in full video resolution as MPEG-2 video files and in smaller MPEG-1 format.

▸ **Dance Instruction Manuals** (http://memory.loc.gov/ammem/dihtml/ divideos.html) These dance clips were selected from two different videotaping sessions. The first was a public event, "Society Dances and Parlor Amusements in the Great Hall," which took place at the Library of Congress on October 15, 1997. The event, which marked the 100th anniversary of the Library's Jefferson Building, featured late-19th-century dances performed in costume against the backdrop of the Great Hall, with music provided by a wind band using period instruments. The second videotaping session took place in the Library's Coolidge Auditorium on April 14, 1998. The videos from this session feature a pair of dancers demonstrating specific dances or movements from selected manuals in the collection. All time periods are represented in these videos. These videos are relatively short and make wonderful examples for students who are learning to score music to a video or for other projects.

▸ **The Sibelius Education Website** (www.sibeliuseducation.com) The notation software Sibelius comes with several royalty-free videos that can be used for educational projects. Additional movies are posted on the website. You have to be a registered Sibelius user to access these materials.

Sources for copyright- and royalty-free audio include:

▸ Software programs such as GarageBand and Logic for Mac, Mixcraft and Sony Acid for PC, and other digital audio programs, contain copyright- and royalty-free loops that can be used to create audio tracks for use with video. GarageBand includes full-length jingles that can be used. You should go to this type of resource first to allow your students to create their own original music for their video projects.

▸ **The Internet Archives Audio Archive** (www.archive.org/details/audio) Similar to the Moving Pictures Library, this collection contains thousands of copyright- and royalty-free audio files that can be used for video projects such as film scores. There are numerous recordings of well-known bands that permit the taping and distribution of their live shows, including the Grateful Dead, Phish, and Dave Matthews Band. These recordings can be used in the student work that is posted on YouTube.

▸ **AudioSwap** (www.youtube.com/audioswap_main) AudioSwap is a new feature YouTube created to allow users to automatically and easily add music to their uploaded videos. Users can select from the extensive list of songs that have been posted to the AudioSwap page (see Fig. 5.6) by YouTube partners. The service is free, and educators can be confident that when students use AudioSwap songs, the music in their videos will not infringe on copyrights. You can try songs out by clicking Preview and Next, and browse by genre, artist, and track. Once you find the perfect song, click Publish to add the song to your video.

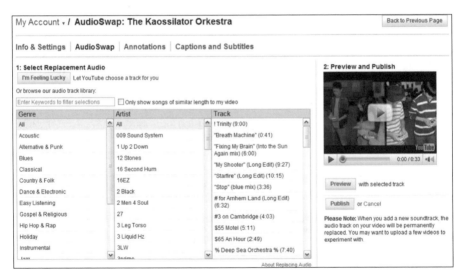

Fig. 5.6
Audio Swap page

Summary

Copyright law and the way it affects the content that appears on websites such as YouTube is a complex issue. Because technology changes so rapidly, the law sometimes struggles to keep up with how people are accessing and using copyrighted content. With every new feature that YouTube adds, it is more and more mindful of its possible effect on copyright, and the company is making extraordinary efforts to inform its users of the law. Aside from the fact that pending litigation looms like a black cloud over the site, the developers are actively trying to find a way for copyright owners and copyright infringers to find a common ground to ensure that use of copyright-protected material does not have a detrimental financial effect on the owners. Through its licensing deals, video and audio ID tools, and partner programs, YouTube is finding legal alternatives to copyright infringement.

For educators, this issue provides some important learning opportunities for students. By addressing copyright rather than ignoring it, and exposing students to how copyright affects the media that they consume and use to create new works, you are providing them with essential information as citizens in a digital world. Until copyright law is reformed or rewritten to properly address the permissible uses of this new way to access content under the "fair use" provision of the law, students and teachers need to tread lightly and look for legal ways to create, use, and capture content—whether completely original or protected by copyright. There are many videos online that deal with copyright and fair use. A search for these terms yields thousands of results. Show them to your students. Watch them yourself. Get your students talking about copyright.

YouTube Teaching Strategy

Ask your students to review copyright law in general and the YouTube copyright guidelines in particular. Ask them to create their own list of do's and don'ts.

This chapter gives you a comprehensive overview of how copyright law affects using YouTube for music education, and provides ways to comply with the law while making the best use of YouTube and other related sites. The legitimate uses of YouTube far outweigh the copyright-infringing ones, and hopefully this will lend support to its value in the classroom.

Chapter Six

YouTube in the Music Classroom

This chapter will address the following areas:

- ▸ How to find videos for your students that focus on listening skills
- ▸ Copyright issues with viewing infringing videos
- ▸ Specific listening examples for various music genres
- ▸ Music channels geared toward education
- ▸ Videos focusing on the music composition process
- ▸ Using videos for student practice
- ▸ Lesson ideas for specific videos

If you search for any musician, composer, performing ensemble, or genre of music, you will find hundreds or even thousands of videos that you can use for instructional purposes in the classroom. For example, if you search for "Johann Sebastian Bach," you'll find more than 7,500 videos, including many videos of compositions by Bach that contain images of the composer while the selected composition plays in the background. Other videos include live performances of professional and amateur musicians and ensembles performing the works of the great composer. If you dig a little deeper, you'll find playlists and channels set up specifically for Bach. If you would like to find a specific work by Bach, type in "J. S. Bach" and the name of the piece; for example, "St. Matthew's Passion." This specific search yielded 215 videos; almost all of which contained performances of the work by various ensembles.[1]

Because of the copyright issues addressed in chapter 5, this book only includes videos that do not infringe on copyright law. Therefore, this chapter will focus on specific channels that have been created by relevant music organizations. Each of the videos mentioned in this chapter was posted to the site with the express permission of the copyright owner, so you can rest assured that showing these videos in your classroom is not an infringement of copyright law.

Classical Music

For the purposes of this book, we will define "classical music" as any music composed for orchestral instruments, as well as opera (videos featuring operas can be found below). A recent search for "classical music" on YouTube yielded over 48,000 results. A search for "opera" yielded 193,000 results.[2] Playing video performances of classical music for students can facilitate opportunities for critique and enhance lessons that focus on specific eras or composers. No longer are you limited to showing students commercial videos such as *Beethoven Lives Upstairs* or *Bach's Fight for Freedom*. If you would like to show your students a performance of Beethoven's *Symphony No. 5*, just search for it and you'll find nearly 600 performances to choose from.

Looking for a specific performance? Simply add the name of the ensemble and/or the conductor, and you will most likely find what you are looking for.

The following section is a listing of some of the available performances. It should be noted that each of the videos listed below is posted on a channel that was created either by the ensemble that is performing the work or the owner of the content. This means that these specific videos can be viewed without fear of copyright infringement.

TIP Each of the videos mentioned below can be found on the YouTube channel created specifically for this book, at www.youtube.com/MusicClassroom. Along with the video and a short description of what it contains, you will find suggested lesson plans that address a wide variety of ages and musical skills.

VAI Music (Video Artist International) has been producing videos of classical music performances for over 25 years. It has created a YouTube channel (www

.youtube.com/vaimusic) that contains nearly 400 videos from its archives. Because these videos are the property of VAI, educators can rest assured that they do not infringe on copyrights. Some of the most interesting performances from their archive include:

Classical Music Example #1: Leopold Stokowski conducting Tchaikovsky's *Romeo and Juliet: Overture-Fantasy*: www.youtube.com/watch?v=8QVKU_izuRY&feature=channel_page.

This short three-minute excerpt (see Fig. 6.1) was recorded in 1969 by the Orchestra Internazionale Giovanile (St. Moritz) and shows the great conductor Leopold Stokowski conducting one of the most well-known pieces from the classical music genre, *Romeo and Juliet: Overture-Fantasy*.

Fig. 6.1
Romeo & Juliet Overture-Fantasy

While the video excerpt does cut off the last few seconds of the piece, the three minutes that are included provide students and teachers with a glimpse of the legendary conductor and a wonderful performance of Tchaikovsky's music.

YouTube Teaching Strategy 1

Ask students to write a critique of the performance, or a critique of the music. To facilitate this activity, the teacher can post the video to a YouTube group specifically set up for the class (as described in chapter 3) as either a Favorite or as part of a Playlist, and have the students post their critiques as comments under the specific video.

YouTube Teaching Strategy 2

Search for other performances on YouTube of the *Romeo and Juliet: Overture-Fantasy* and compare the conducting style as well as the performance.

YouTube Teaching Strategy 3

Search for ballet performances on YouTube that incorporate Tchaikovsky's music, and have students describe how the music relates to the movement, and vice versa.

YouTube Teaching Strategy 4

Compare the music from the version of *Romeo and Juliet* composed by Tchaikovsky to the version composed by Sergei Prokofiev.

YouTube Teaching Strategy 5

Watch a video of the ballet version of Prokofiev's *Romeo and Juliet*, and compare and contrast it with the work of Tchaikovsky. One suggested video of a ballet version of Prokofiev's *Romeo and Juliet* includes an incredible performance by Margot Fonteyn and Rudolph Nureyev. It is posted on the Royal Opera House YouTube Channel (www.youtube.com/RoyalOperaHouse): www.youtube.com/watch?v=uvOFMvwD-CU&feature=channel.

TIP   Never play a video for your students that you have not previewed. You never know what the video might contain, or whether some of the comments about the video include expletives. Play it safe—watch it first and then add it to your classroom channel.

Classical Music Example #2: Pianist Ruth Laredo performs *Prelude in G Major, Opus 32, No. 5*, by Rachmaninoff: www.youtube.com/watch?v=LiCbvKe4sFU.

The late Ruth Laredo was one of the most acclaimed pianists of the 20th century. This video (see Fig. 6.2) of her performance of Rachmaninoff's *Prelude in G Major, Opus 32, No. 5* for solo piano is from a concert called "A Celebration of the Piano:

A Tribute to the Steinway" in 1988. Interestingly, she was introduced by another great pianist, Van Cliburn. The video contains a beautiful performance of this well-known work for piano and truly captures the artistry of Ms. Laredo. The 3:10 clip provides students and teachers with an example of the piano as a solo instrument.

Fig. 6.2
Ruth Laredo performing Rachmaninoff

YouTube Teaching Strategy 6

Ask students to write a critique of Rachmaninoff's *Prelude in G Major*, or a critique of the performance. See lesson plan on page 230 for ideas on how to facilitate this critique using YouTube.

YouTube Teaching Strategy 7

Search for other performances on YouTube of Rachmaninoff's *Prelude in G Major*, and compare them.

YouTube Teaching Strategy 8

Search for other performances by Ruth Laredo of the works of other composers.

YouTube Teaching Strategy 9

Search for other works composed by Rachmaninoff for piano, as well as some of his orchestral works.

YouTube Teaching Strategy 10

Ask students to explore more about Ruth Laredo by visiting www.ruthlaredo .com. Students can then create a podcast about her life and her association with the music of Rachmaninoff.

YouTube Teaching Strategy 11

Use the music as the basis for a movement activity or as the inspiration for a story.

Classical Music Example #3: "Habanera" from *Carmen* by Georges Bizet: www. youtube.com/watch?v=45ks8qcm4C0&feature=channel.

"Habanera" from the opera *Carmen* written by Georges Bizet is certainly one of the most well-known pieces of music from the world of opera. This incredible video features the legendary opera star Geraldine Farrar as Carmen in this silent film from 1914 directed by Cecil B. DeMille (see Fig. 6.3). The soundtrack features a performance by the London Philharmonic conducted by Gillian B. Anderson. The clip is only 1:37 long, but includes the most well-known passage from "Habanera."

Fig. 6.3
"Habanera" from *Carmen*

TIP Never search for videos in front of students. The results might not always be appropriate for the grade level you teach.

YouTube Teaching Strategy 12

Ask students to write a critique of the "Habanera" performance, or a critique of the music.

YouTube Teaching Strategy 13

Search for videos that contain other scenes from *Carmen*, including "Toreador's Song" and "Gypsy Dance."

YouTube Teaching Strategy 14

Search on YouTube for performances of "Habanera" by other opera companies and compare them.

YouTube Teaching Strategy 15

Ask students to locate an English translation of the words from "Habanera" and then create their own scenes—which can then be performed, filmed, and posted to YouTube (see chapter 10 for more information on creating videos and uploading them to YouTube).

YouTube Teaching Strategy 16

Ask students to research Georges Bizet, the history of the opera (http://en.wikipedia.org/wiki/Carmen), or life in 19th-century Spain.

Classical Music Example #4: Luciano Pavarotti sings *L'Elisir d'Amore*: www.youtube.com/watch?v=DhxbM5Mc8gI&feature=channel_page.

Here we see perhaps the most famous operatic tenor of all time singing an excerpt from the beautiful aria "Una Furtiva Lagrima" from the opera *L'Elisir d'Amore*, composed by Gaetano Donizetti and performed by the Metropolitan Opera orchestra (see Fig. 6.4). The entire opera can be viewed by visiting www.metplayer. org, a website that features both free clips and a subscription plan that allows you to view many different arias (also check out the Metropolitan Opera YouTube channel at www. youtube.com/MetropolitanOpera). While this short clip contains less than a minute of Pavarotti singing, it is one of the only videos on YouTube of Pavarotti singing that has been posted with permission; it has been posted by the Metropolitan Opera, which owns the rights to this clip.

Fig. 6.4

Pavarotti singing from *L'Elisir d'Amore*

YouTube Teaching Strategy 17

Ask students to write a critique of the "Una Furtiva Lagrima" performance, or a critique of the music.

YouTube Teaching Strategy 18

Search for videos that contain other scenes from *L'Elisir d'Amore*.

YouTube Teaching Strategy 19

Search for videos of Luciano Pavarotti singing other arias, including "Nessun Dorma," "Ave Maria," and "La Donna e Mobile."

YouTube Teaching Strategy 20

Search for videos that feature "Una Furtiva Lagrima" sung by a different tenor, and ask students to compare and contrast the performances.

YouTube Teaching Strategy 21

Ask students to find out more about the late Luciano Pavarotti by visiting www.lucianopavarotti.com.

Classical Music YouTube Channels

When searching for performances of classical music on YouTube, you will find that the majority of videos are posted by other YouTube account holders. It is always safe to assume that these users do not have permission to post these videos. However, there are quite a few classical music organizations that have created YouTube channels featuring short clips from performances, interviews with musicians, and sneak peeks into their upcoming seasons. See Table 6.1 for a listing of some of these channels. If you would like to find out if a performing organization in your area has its own YouTube channel, simply search for the name of the organization and click on the Channel link. If they do have their own channel, it often appears as the first search result.

Table 6.1: Classical Ensembles with YouTube Channels

ENSEMBLE	YOUTUBE CHANNEL URL
Baltimore Symphony Orchestra	www.youtube.com/user/BSOmusic
Berlin Philharmonic	www.youtube.com/user/BerlinPhil
Boston Symphony Orchestra	www.youtube.com/user/BostonSymphony
Chicago Symphony Orchestra	www.youtube.com/user/csowebmaster
Cleveland Orchestra	www.youtube.com/user/clevelandorchestra
Live From Lincoln Center	www.youtube.com/user/LFLC
London Philharmonic	www.youtube.com/user/londonphilharmonic7
London Symphony Orchestra	www.youtube.com/user/Lso
Los Angeles Opera	www.youtube.com/user/losangelesopera
Lyric Opera of Chicago	www.youtube.com/user/LyricOperaofChicago

Metropolitan Opera	www.youtube.com/user/MetropolitanOpera
New York City Opera	www.youtube.com/user/newyorkcityopera
New York Philharmonic	www.youtube.com/user/NewYorkPhilharmonic
Orpheus Chamber Orchestra	www.youtube.com/user/orpheusnyc
Royal Opera House	www.youtube.com/user/RoyalOperaHouse
Saint Louis Symphony Orchestra	www.youtube.com/user/saintlouissymphony
San Francisco Opera	www.youtube.com/user/sfoperamedia
San Francisco Symphony Orchestra	www.youtube.com/user/sfsymphony
YouTube Symphony Orchestra	www.youtube.com/user/symphony

Some commercial video and music producers and labels also have their own channels (see Table 6.2).

Table 6.2: Music Companies with YouTube Channels

COMPANY	YOUTUBE CHANNEL URL
EMI & Virgin Classics	www.youtube.com/user/emiclassics
Naxos Videos	www.youtube.com/user/NaxosUSA
Universal Music Group	www.youtube.com/user/universalmusicgroup
Video Artists International	www.youtube.com/user/vaimusic

Obviously this is only a partial listing of some of the many classical music channels that are supported on YouTube. For a more complete listing, visit www.youtube.com/MusicClassroom.

American Folk Music

Although folk music is inherently in the public domain and therefore not protected by copyright law, any video recording of someone performing a folk song is protected by copyright unless the creator specifically grants permission for others to use the video, or if the recording is made or produced by the US government.

Every country has its own folk music, but in this chapter we will be referring only to American folk music. World music videos will be addressed later in this chapter. A recent search for "American folk music" on YouTube yielded over 5,000 results. A search for just "folk music" yielded over 303,000 results.[3] Playing video performances of folk music for students can facilitate discussions about the role of folk music in American culture, as well as provide examples of song performances that you might be teaching as a part of your curriculum.

The following is a listing of some of the folk music performances available on YouTube. As mentioned previously, each of the videos listed is posted on a channel that was created either by the musician performing the song, or the owner of the content (in many cases a record company). Therefore, these specific videos can most certainly be viewed without fear of copyright infringement.

TIP Each of the videos mentioned below can be found on the YouTube channel created specifically for this book: www.youtube.com/MusicClassroom. In addition to the listing of the video and a short description of what it contains, suggested learning activities are included, addressing a wide variety of ages and musical skills.

Established in 1846, the Smithsonian Institute in Washington, D.C., oversees the world's largest museum complex. As a part of its network of museums, the Smithsonian Center for Folklife and Cultural Studies (http://www.folkways .si.edu/) houses the well-known Folkways Recordings collection (founded by Moses Asch), which contains thousands of recordings of folk songs from cultures around the world — the most comprehensive collection. Although many of these recordings are available for purchase, the Smithsonian has created a YouTube Channel that features tracks from these recordings that users can listen to and view on YouTube. The following represents some of the best recordings from their channel.

American Folk Music Example #1: Ella Jenkins sings "Go Tell Aunt Rhody": www.youtube.com/watch?v=5lzWcA5NJeg&feature=channel_page.

This recording features the "First Lady of Children's Folk Songs," Ella Jenkins, singing "Go Tell Aunt Rhody." The track featured in this clip originally appeared on the Folkways album *Songs and Rhythms from Near and Far*, released in 1997. On the recording you hear Ms. Jenkins singing one of the most well-known American folk songs, about an old gray goose who has met an untimely demise and the pressing need to tell Aunt Rhody about what has happened. This version features a guitar, Ms. Jenkins singing the melody, and some tight vocal harmonies provided by backup singers. The video only includes still photos of the album cover (see Fig. 6.5). The performance lasts a little less than three minutes and includes quite a few verses that teachers and students might not be too familiar with.

Fig. 6.5
Ella Jenkins singing "Go Tell Aunt Rhody"

YouTube Teaching Strategy 22

Play the "Go Tell Aunt Rhody" video for students to familiarize them with the song before they sing it.

YouTube Teaching Strategy 23

Play the "Go Tell Aunt Rhody" video while students move around the classroom, interpreting the music through creative movement.

YouTube Teaching Strategy 24

Play the "Go Tell Aunt Rhody" video to illustrate major and minor tonalities, focusing on the verses where the song shifts into a minor key.

YouTube Teaching Strategy 25

Split students into cooperative learning groups, assigning one verse of the song to each group, and ask them to create visual images that reflect the story in their verse. Then compile the images and create a video montage using the complete recording.

YouTube Teaching Strategy 26

Have students record their own performance of the song and use it to accompany a video montage created by the teacher. The final product can then be posted on YouTube.

YouTube Teaching Strategy 27

Ask students to explore more about Ella Jenkins by visiting www.ellajenkins .com.

American Folk Music Example #2: Woody Guthrie sings "Red River Valley": www.youtube.com/watch?v=TM54-ZRd-9k&feature=channel_page.

One of the most well-known singer-songwriters, Woody Guthrie not only sang American folk songs, but wrote original songs that are now considered part of the American folk tradition, including his most well-known song, "This Land Is Your Land." A number of Woody's performances are posted on the Smithsonian Folkways YouTube channel, including his version of "Red River Valley." In this clip (see Fig. 6.6), you hear a track from the 1999 Folkways album *Buffalo Skinners: The Asch Recordings, Vol. 4.*, which features Guthrie accompanied by Cisco Houston — just a guitar and two voices singing this well-known cowboy song about the Red River in New Mexico.

Fig. 6.6
Woody Guthrie singing "Red River Valley"

YouTube Teaching Strategy 28

Play the "Red River Valley" video for students to familiarize them with the song before they sing it.

YouTube Teaching Strategy 29

Ask students to move to the beat of the "Red River Valley" video.

YouTube Teaching Strategy 30

Search for other cowboy songs on YouTube (a recent search returned over 44,000) and have students listen to, compare, and critique similar songs, such as "Home on the Range" and "The Streets of Laredo."

YouTube Teaching Strategy 31

Search for other performances by Woody Guthrie and play them for the students.

YouTube Teaching Strategy 32

Ask students to compose and perform their own cowboy songs using the examples from the search results.

YouTube Teaching Strategy 33

Have students explore more about Woody Guthrie by visiting www. woodyguthrie.com.

American Folk Music Example #3: Pete Seeger sings "Sometimes I Feel Like a Motherless Child": www.youtube.com/watch?v=lNHM4NXSKmI&feature= channel_page.

"Sometimes I Feel Like a Motherless Child" is one of the best examples of a spiritual sung by African slaves in the United States during the early history of our country. The lyrics reflect the common practice of selling the children of slaves off to other slave owners, and the phrase "a long way from home" has been interpreted to mean either a long way from the African homeland or even heaven. The song, which has been performed by many musicians, including Richie Havens, is still haunting today. This video clip (see Fig. 6.7) features one of America's most well-known folksingers, Pete Seeger, performing his version of the song from the 2004 Smithsonian Folkways album *American Favorite Ballads, Vol. 3*. The mood of the song is mournful, and the simple guitar accompaniment and slow tempo truly bring the original meaning of the song to the surface.

Fig. 6.7
Pete Seeger singing "Sometimes I Feel Like a Motherless Child"

YouTube Teaching Strategy 34

Play the video "Sometimes I Feel Like a Motherless Child" for students to familiarize them with the song before they sing it.

YouTube Teaching Strategy 35

Search for other versions of "Sometimes I Feel Like a Motherless Child," and compare the performances.

YouTube Teaching Strategy 36

Search for other spirituals to use for listening, movement, or performance exercises.

YouTube Teaching Strategy 37

View the PBS video on YouTube titled *History Detectives: Slave Songbook*, and discuss the role of music in the lives of the slaves: www.youtube.com/watch?v=1JtD_YpyXYU&feature=channel_page.

YouTube Teaching Strategy 38

Share with your students the following three PBS videos on the musical life of Pete Seeger, titled *The Power of Song*:

Part 1: www.youtube.com/watch?v=Qh0elZi0KG4&feature=channel_page

Part 2: www.youtube.com/watch?v=GizfwgCjtfA&feature=related

Part 3: www.youtube.com/watch?v=-RL8ZcmLEB4&feature=related

The Public Broadcasting System (PBS) is one of the treasures of television, broadcasting member-supported programming that often features musical performances. PBS has created a YouTube channel that contains hundreds of clips from its archives, many of which feature American folk music (though you can find quite a few featuring other musical genres), as well as specials about musicians, like the one mentioned above on Pete Seeger. Visit the PBS YouTube channel at www.youtube.com/user/pbs.

American Folk Music Example #4: Lead Belly sings "Let It Shine on Me": www.youtube.com/watch?v=W0_TnrRZeF4&feature=channel_page.

Huddie William Ledbetter, known as Lead Belly, was one of the most popular folk blues musicians of the 20th century, introducing a larger American audience to the music of the African-American experience through the efforts of musicologist Alan Lomax and Folkways Records founder Moses Asch. He influenced

Fig. 6.8
Lead Belly singing "Let It Shine on Me"

many folksingers, including Pete Seeger and Woody Guthrie. This clip (see Fig. 6.8) features Lead Belly performing the song "Let It Shine on Me" from the 1996 Smithsonian Folkways album *Where Did You Sleep Last Night?: Lead Belly Legacy Vol. 1.* The recording captures Lead Belly telling stories about his life, singing spirituals, and performing the song accompanied by his guitar. It provides a vivid picture of this seminal musician.

YouTube Teaching Strategy 39

Play the video "Let It Shine on Me" as an introduction to Lead Belly and his music.

YouTube Teaching Strategy 40

Search for other videos of Lead Belly performances, including "Pick a Bale of Cotton."

YouTube Teaching Strategy 41

Search for other versions of the song "Let It Shine on Me," and have students compare and contrast the performances.

YouTube Teaching Strategy 42

Search for other performers singing the songs of Lead Belly.

YouTube Teaching Strategy 43

Ask students to find out more about Lead Belly and his influence on popular American music by visiting www.leadbelly.org/intro.html.

Most dedicated YouTube channels focusing on American folk music have been created by individual YouTube account holders, and therefore the videos likely qualify as copyright infringement, because all performances are protected by copyright law, regardless of the content within them (see chapter 5). Therefore, while many channels feature exciting videos, they are not listed in this book because of copyright infringement. For example, a recent search for "Oh! Susanna" yielded nearly 1,000 results.[4] Yet some folk musicians have created their own channels. For example, Matthew Sabatella has created the channel Ballad of America (www.youtube.com/user/balladofamerica), which contains more than 20 videos of songs like "Old Joe Clark," "Wabash Cannonball," and "Shenandoah," performed by Sabatella and his Rambling String Band. This is a great resource for teachers as it offers a good sampling of well-known folk songs and shows students the various types of instruments that are used in the folk music tradition. Because folk songs are inherently in the public domain, performances of those songs by musicians do not constitute infringement, but the videos of those performances are still protected. Teachers can be confident that playing videos for students of American folk songs by groups such as Matthew Sabatella and the Rambling String Band is not only a wonderful example of the folk tradition, it is also a fair use of the content.

World Music

A recent search for "world music" on YouTube yielded over 5,000 results. Showing performances of world music for students can facilitate discussions about the role of music in other cultures, the differences and similarities between American folk songs and folk songs from other countries, and provide examples of performances of world music that are part of your music curriculum. Like American folk music, folk music from cultures around the world (also known as "world music") is in the public domain, and video recordings of those performances are protected by US copyright law as well as international copyright law.

Following is a listing of some of the world music performances available on YouTube. As mentioned in previous sections, each of the videos listed below is posted on a channel that was created either by the musician performing the song, or the owner of the content (in many cases a record company). So these videos can be viewed without fear of copyright infringement. Each of the videos mentioned below can be also found on the YouTube channel created specifically for this book: www.youtube.com/MusicClassroom. Also included are suggested learning activities that address a wide variety of ages and musical skills.

World Music Example #1: Javanese gamelan performance from Wesleyan University: www.youtube.com/watch?v=RUQsFou8o-Q.

Wesleyan University is home to one of the most well-respected ethnomusicology departments in the world. Since 2003, the department has hosted an incredible website called the Virtual Instrument Museum (http://learningobjects_devel.wesleyan.edu/vim/), which contains video and audio files of performances on instruments from around the world. In 2006, the university created its own YouTube channel (www.youtube.com/user/wesleyan), posting videos of lectures, events, and aspects of student life. A recent search for music on this channel yielded a few dozen results, one of them being a wonderful video of a performance of a Javanese gamelan by faculty and students. The video shows a large group of musicians playing instruments including the bonang, gender, celempung, and kenong. The clip is less than three minutes long (see Fig. 6.9) and provides teachers and students with a terrific example of the gamelan tradition.

Fig. 6.9
Javanese gamelan at Wesleyan University

YouTube Teaching Strategy 44

Use this video to introduce the gamelan music tradition to your students.

YouTube Teaching Strategy 45

Ask students to write a critique of the Javanese gamelan performance.

YouTube Teaching Strategy 46

Use the video to inspire students to create their own Javanese gamelan–style instruments as part of their own gamelan ensemble.

Visit the Virtual Instrument Museum website to find out more about the individual instruments that make up a gamelan ensemble.

Search YouTube for other gamelan performances, and compare and contrast them.

World Music Example #2: Omiyage 2007 by the Taiko Project: www.youtube .com/watch?v=OIyBP-MvV2w&feature=related.

Japanese taiko drumming is an exciting musical experience, and students will enjoy this performance by the Taiko Project (www.youtube.com/user/taikoproject), a group based in Los Angeles, California. Founded in 2000, the group performs around the world and is dedicated to educating people about this music-making tradition (visit www.taikoproject.com for more information). In this clip (see Fig. 6.10) talented drummers play various types of taiko drums, including the odaiko, nagado-daiko, chu-daiko, and sumo-daiko. The video (which runs a little over 10 minutes) includes a humorous moment when the group brings in a popular video game for the Sony PlayStation 2 titled *Taiko: Drum Master,* and interacts with it. Students will thoroughly appreciate the reference as well as the way the traditional group incorporates the video game into their performance.

Fig. 6.10
Taiko Project

Introduce taiko drumming to your students using the Omiyage 2007 video.

YouTube Teaching Strategy 50

Search YouTube for other taiko drumming ensembles (including the Kodo Drummers) and compare and contrast the performances.

YouTube Teaching Strategy 51

Visit the Taiko Project YouTube channel and watch other videos of their performances and compare and contrast them.

YouTube Teaching Strategy 52

Ask students to create their own taiko drumming ensemble using traditional percussion instruments.

YouTube Teaching Strategy 53

Encourage students who own a Sony PlayStation 2 gaming console to purchase a copy of *Taiko: Drum Master*. Ask them to bring in their console to play the video game in the classroom.

World Music Example #3: Gauthier Aubé playing the didgeridoo: www.youtube .com/watch?v=5bHLa0oJmJc&feature=channel_page.

While this video does not depict an aboriginal person performing this traditional aboriginal instrument, it does include an incredible performance by a well-known didgeridoo player—Gauthier Aubé. The short one-minute clip (see Fig. 6.11) illustrates the many different techniques

Fig. 6.11
Gauthier Aubé playing the didgeridoo

used in didgeridoo playing, including circular breathing, embellishing the sound with voice, and creating rhythmic patterns. The video is part of a YouTube channel called IDIDJUK (www.youtube.com/user/IDIDJUK), created by a London-based company named Aboriginal Arts (www.aboriginalarts.co.uk). Also included on the channel are a number of instructional videos on how to play the didgeridoo, and videos of performances on various instruments. Aubé's performance is exceptional, and students will certainly enjoy watching and listening to it.

YouTube Teaching Strategy 54

Introduce the didgeridoo using the video of Gauthier Aubé playing the instrument.

YouTube Teaching Strategy 55

Search for "didgeridoo" (or "didjeridoo") on YouTube to find other performances featuring the instrument. This video, on a YouTube channel from Australia, is one of the best: www.youtube.com/watch?v=QSXjpWU DvO4&feature=related.

YouTube Teaching Strategy 56

Search for videos on how to make a didgeridoo, and have students build their own instruments. There are a number of websites that provide step-by-step instructions, including: www.kinderart.com/multic/didgeridoo. shtml.

YouTube Teaching Strategy 57

Ask students to search for and watch video tutorials on how to play the didgeridoo.

YouTube Teaching Strategy 58

Videotape student didgeridoo performances, and post the videos on your own YouTube channel.

World Music Example #4: The Silk Road Project—Siamek Aghaei: www .youtube.com/watch?v=dlr2Gc88t8I&feature=channel.

The Silk Road Project is a nonprofit organization that was started by famed cellist Yo-Yo Ma in 1998 as a way to connect musicians from cultures along the "Silk Road," an ancient trade route between Asia and the Middle East, India, and Europe. The Silk Road Ensemble is made up of exceptional musicians from a wide variety of cultures who perform music that blends their individual musical traditions into a new tradition. The Silk Road Project's YouTube channel (www.youtube .com/user/silkroadproject) contains performances by the Silk Road Ensemble and interviews with the individual musicians. One of these videos features an amazing santur player named Siamek Aghaei. The *santur* is a hammered dulcimer that is used in traditional Persian music, in what is now modern-day Iran. In this clip (see Fig. 6.12) Aghaei talks about the instrument, describes how it developed and how it is played, and performs traditional music on it.

Fig. 6.12

Siamek Aghaei playing the santur

YouTube Teaching Strategy 59

Use the Silk Road Project video to introduce Middle Eastern music and the santur.

YouTube Teaching Strategy 60

Search for videos of other performers playing the santur.

YouTube Teaching Strategy 61

Search for Siamek Aghaei and watch some of his other performances.

YouTube Teaching Strategy 62

Search for "hammered dulcimer," widely used in traditional American folk music, and ask students to compare and contrast the way it is used in each culture.

YouTube Teaching Strategy 63

Watch other videos on the Silk Road Project YouTube channel, and describe how the santur is used in the ensemble. A wonderful example is the Silk Road Project's performance at the Summer Olympic Games in Beijing: www.youtube.com/watch?v=GD5rwsfGPTQ.

YouTube Teaching Strategy 64

Listen to the Silk Road Project's recorded version of "The Star-Spangled Banner" (www.youtube.com/watch?v=qOjFyk8p4Ak) and discuss how the instruments affect how the anthem sounds.

For more examples, you can search other YouTube channels that have been created by record labels specializing in world music. Table 6.3 lists some of these channels.

Table 6.3: World Music YouTube Channels

RECORD LABEL/COMPANY	YOUTUBE CHANNEL URL
Afro Tempo	www.youtube.com/user/afrotempo
Cumbancha Records	www.youtube.com/user/Cumbanchamusic
Putamayo Records	www.youtube.com/user/PutumayoWorldMusic
Smithsonian Folkways	www.youtube.com/user/SmithsonianFolkways
World Connection	www.youtube.com/user/WorldConnections
World Music Institute	www.youtube.com/user/worldmusicinstitute

Jazz

The American art form jazz has strong roots in both African and European musical traditions. YouTube contains thousands of videos that feature a wide range of jazz performers—everyone from Kid Ory, Scott Joplin, Louis Armstrong, and Billie Holiday to Charlie Parker, John Coltrane, and Thelonious Monk. Because many of these performers were featured in the 1950s and '60s on television, there are many videos to choose from when teaching about a particular musician or style of jazz. In addition to these videos, you can also find many home videos taken during concerts at famous jazz venues around the world. A recent search for "jazz" on YouTube yielded over 675,000 results.[5] A search for the jazz style "bebop" yielded over 44,000 clips.[6] Searching for a specific jazz musician can also yield some impressive results. For example, if you search for "Miles Davis," you'll find more than 12,000 videos.[7] Search for "Charlie Parker," and you'll find over 2,600 videos.[8] Playing videos of performances by jazz musicians for students can facilitate discussions about the role of jazz in American culture, as well as provide examples of musician performances that you might be teaching as part of your music curriculum.

The following is a listing of some of the jazz performances available on YouTube. As mentioned throughout this chapter, each of the videos listed below is posted on a channel that was created either by the jazz musician or the owner of the content (in many cases a record company).

Jazz Example #1: A Tribute to Ella Fitzgerald: www.youtube.com/watch?v=ftBl D627RDE&feature=channel_page.

Verve Records, a well-known contemporary jazz record label, has created its own YouTube Channel (www.youtube.com/user/VerveRecords), where it has posted a number of videos featuring jazz artists from the label. One of these videos is a tribute to the legendary jazz singer Ella Fitzgerald, featuring performances of such well-known Fitzgerald songs as "A-Tisket, A-Tasket," "Lullaby of Birdland," and "Lady Be Good" by a number of Verve recording artists, including Natalie Cole, Diana Krall, Dianne Reeves, and k.d. lang (see Fig. 6.13). It is a great portrait of the First Lady of Song, and shows the influence that she has had on other singers. While the primary purpose of the video is to promote a Verve record, the interviews and performances are certainly worth showing to students.

Fig. 6.13
Ella Fitzgerald tribute (featuring Diana Krall)

YouTube Teaching Strategy 65

Ask students to critique the different performances on the video *A Tribute to Ella Fitzgerald*.

YouTube Teaching Strategy 66

Play the original versions (on iTunes.com) of the songs sung by Ella Fitzgerald in the video, and ask students to compare her original performances with those featured on the video.

YouTube Teaching Strategy 67

Search for other videos that feature Ella Fitzgerald, and play them for your students.

YouTube Teaching Strategy 68

Ask students to explore more about Ella Fitzgerald by visiting her official homepage at www.ellafitzgerald.com.

YouTube Teaching Strategy 69

Ask students to search the Verve YouTube channel for other videos that feature jazz artists.

Jazz Example #2: Wynton Marsalis performing "Bourbon Street Parade": www.youtube.com/watch?v=wrQ6NW2huic&feature=channel_page.

Wynton Marsalis is one of the most well-known modern jazz artists. The Sony BMG YouTube Channel (www.youtube.com/user/sonybmg) has posted a music video (see Fig. 6.14) featuring Wynton Marsalis performing "Bourbon Street Parade" from his album *Standard Time Vol. 2*, released in 1991. The video shows Marsalis playing trumpet with a traditional New Orleans–style jazz ensemble.

Since the video is being sponsored by a record label, you will notice an advertisement to download the song from Amazon.com directly underneath the video, as well as a pop-up ad that appears at the beginning of the video. Aside from this brief commercial, the video provides teachers with an excellent example of traditional jazz played by one of the greatest trumpet players of our generation.

Fig. 6.14
Wynton Marsalis performing "Bourbon Street Parade"

YouTube Teaching Strategy 70

Play this video as an introduction to a jazz unit.

YouTube Teaching Strategy 71

Ask students to critique Wynton Marsalis's performance.

YouTube Teaching Strategy 72

Search for other performances of "Bourbon Street Parade."

YouTube Teaching Strategy 73

Search for other performances by Wynton Marsalis, and compare and contrast them with the "Bourbon Street Parade" video.

YouTube Teaching Strategy 74

Ask students to search for videos about New Orleans and its influence on jazz.

YouTube Teaching Strategy 75

Search for other famous jazz trumpet players, and watch videos of their performances.

Jazz Example #3: Woody Herman and His Swingin' Herd: www.youtube.com/watch?v=CyoQfatss9I.

Woody Herman was one of the most popular big-band leaders in the 1930s and '40s. A jazz saxophonist, clarinetist, and vocalist, his bands played jazz and blues. The VAI Music YouTube Channel (mentioned above in the classical music section) includes a video of Woody Herman performing "Jazz Me Blues" with his Swingin' Herd during a 1964 TV appearance (see Fig. 6.15). This exciting performance, featuring a 17-piece ensemble and an inspired solo by Woody Herman, epitomizes the big-band era. The video is a little under three minutes, and VAI Music has added some annotations throughout the video asking viewers to visit its homepage, where they can purchase the full 50-minute video of the performance.

Fig. 6.15
Woody Herman and His Swingin' Herd

YouTube Teaching Strategy 76

Use this video as an introduction to a jazz unit on the big-band era.

YouTube Teaching Strategy 77

Ask students to critique the performance of Woody Herman and His Swingin' Herd.

YouTube Teaching Strategy 78

Search for other performances by Woody Herman, and compare and contrast them.

YouTube Teaching Strategy 79

Search for other performances of "Jazz Me Blues," then compare and contrast the different versions of the song.

YouTube Teaching Strategy 80

Compare this video with "Bourbon Street Parade," and discuss the similarities and differences between the two pieces and performances.

YouTube Teaching Strategy 81

Ask students to transcribe Woody Herman's solo.

Jazz Example #4: Producer Orrin Keepnews: www.youtube.com/watch?v=bZ--Xr6ZWrU.

Orrin who, you ask? Orrin Keepnews, founder of Riverside Records and Milestones, is one of the most respected record producers in the jazz world. He worked with such legendary jazz musicians as Bill Evans, Thelonious Monk, John Coltrane, Cannonball Adderley, and McCoy Tyner. His recordings of these artists are counted among the seminal works of jazz. The Concord Music Group, a jazz record label, has created its own YouTube channel (www.youtube.com/user/concordrecords) where it has posted a 20-part video podcast series on Orrin Keepnews, including stories not only about Keepnews's work with these jazz legends, but also about the famous recordings that he made with them. While there are 20 videos in all, it is a good idea to start with the first one in the series (see Fig. 6.16), where we are introduced to Keepnews and hear about his early work with Thelonious Monk. Each video is about 10 minutes long, and includes in-depth interviews with Keepnews, photos documenting his work, and excerpts from many of the recordings that he made. These videos are appropriate for high school and college students who are interested in the history of jazz.

Fig. 6.16
Producer Orrin Keepnews

YouTube Teaching Strategy 82

Ask students to watch each video podcast from the series and write a summary about this important record producer.

YouTube Teaching Strategy 83

Search for videos of the jazz musicians featured in the Orrin Keepnews videos.

YouTube Teaching Strategy 84

Search the iTunes Music Store for the specific recordings mentioned in the Orrin Keepnews videos to hear the finished product.

YouTube Teaching Strategy 85

Search for other videos that feature the work of Orrin Keepnews.

YouTube Teaching Strategy 86

Discuss the role of a record producer in the creative process, and search for videos on other well-known jazz record producers, such as Rudy Van Gelder and Nesuhi Ertegun.

In addition to these video examples, you can search other YouTube channels that have been created by record labels and other companies specializing in jazz (see Table 6.4).

Table 6.4: Commercial Jazz YouTube Channels

RECORD LABEL/COMPANY	YOUTUBE CHANNEL URL
Concord Music Group	www.youtube.com/user/concordrecords
Greenleaf Music	www.youtube.com/user/GreenleafMusicHQ
Ovation TV	www.youtube.com/user/OvationTV
PBS	www.youtube.com/user/PBS
Sony BMG	www.youtube.com/user/sonybmg
VAI Music	www.youtube.com/user/vaimusic
Verve Music Group	www.youtube.com/user/VerveRecords

Summary

While many other musical genres could have been included in this chapter, the videos and genres listed demonstrate that many YouTube videos can be used in the classroom. Other areas not covered in this chapter can be searched on YouTube. Whether you are interested in gospel music, country music, mariachi, bluegrass, hip-hop, rap, rock, blues, heavy metal, or easy listening, you can find relevant videos on YouTube to support your music curriculum. When you search for videos and play them for your students, fair use protects your actions in the classroom. The classroom activities in this chapter offer ways to use YouTube videos with your students.

Chapter Seven # Teaching Music with YouTube

This chapter shows the applications for using YouTube in all facets of music education, including:

- ▶ Classroom music

- ▶ Instructional uses

- ▶ Performance (chorus, band, strings, jazz)

- ▶ Humor: Just for fun

- ▶ Music education-related YouTube channels

- ▶ YouTube channels created by music educators

- ▶ Tips for using YouTube in the music curriculum

This chapter focuses on specific lessons and applications of YouTube in the music classroom, rehearsal room, and for practice and performance. See the chapter 6 videos organized by musical style (jazz, folk, world music, and more).

In early March 2009, co-author James Frankel posted a request on the e-mail discussion board for the Technology Institute for Music Educators (TI:ME), as well as on the Music Technology in Education blog he hosts (http://jamesfrankel. musiced.net), for music educators to submit ideas and strategies on how they use YouTube in their music classroom and rehearsals. He asked teachers to share how they are currently using YouTube with their students, if their schools block YouTube, and how they get around it if they do (chapter 8 addresses what to do if you are blocked from YouTube).

Approximately 30 responses were received from music educators around the world who either use YouTube in their classrooms or are blocked from using it in their classrooms, but would welcome the opportunity to use it in their teaching. Of those teachers who are allowed access to YouTube, many submitted strategies illustrating their use of the site when teaching music (see the additional lesson plan ideas at the end of chapter 10). Teachers also submitted links to some of the numerous videos that they use with their students. This chapter summarizes the responses received from educators who use YouTube in their classrooms, as well as the related teaching applications of the authors.

Chapter 8 includes the responses from respondents who teach in a school district whose school district technology coordinators and/or school board have decided to implement a policy of blocking the YouTube site altogether due to the possibility of exposing students to inappropriate content, both in the videos themselves and in the comments posted by users. Creative suggestions are given on how to get around those firewalls without breaking any copyright laws or getting your district administration upset.

TIP The examples in this chapter can also be found in the companion website to this book, located at www.youtubemusiced.net.

Classroom Music Applications

Chapter 6 included a host of applications for the music classroom, including videos on American folk music, world music, and more. Below are some specific applications in the K-12 and higher education music classroom, including applications by the co-authors and those submitted by other music educators.

amazing grace|	Se
amazing grace bagpipes	Suggestions
amazing grace lyrics	
amazing grace my chains are gone	
amazing grace chris tomlin	
amazing grace with lyrics	
amazing grace leann rimes	
amazing grace karaoke	
amazing grace guitar	
amazing grace piano	

Fig. 7.1
Search results for "Amazing Grace"

YouTube Teaching Strategy 87

Search for YouTube videos to supplement listening examples for college jazz history courses

Dr. Joseph Pisano, a well-known music technology blogger (www.mustech. net) and assistant chairman of music and fine arts at Grove City College in Grove City, Pennsylvania, teaches a college-level jazz history course. Dr. Pisano uses YouTube to find jazz videos to demonstrate performances by particular artists. He also posts videos of himself teaching and performing— something music educators are beginning to do more and more (described later in this chapter).

Dr. Pisano says that YouTube has many hard-to-find and obscure videos, including performances that are no longer commercially available. See chapter 5 for specific information on copyright and how it affects these videos.

YouTube Teaching Strategy 88

Search YouTube for songs with lyrics

Do you teach songs by rote? If so, many songs are available on YouTube with the lyrics included. For example, Joseph Brennan uses YouTube when he teaches a rote song to his students. He searches for songs by title and includes the word "lyrics" in the search. For example, if you are teaching the song "Amazing Grace," enter the words "Amazing Grace with lyrics" (see Fig. 7.1).

Now the song that you are teaching by rote can be listened to while the lyrics are displayed. This can be very helpful in the classroom if you have your computer connected to a projector (see chapter 4). You can then use the YouTube video as you are teaching the rote song to your class or ensemble. And, of course, you can provide your students with the link to the song on your class channel or playlist.

Supplement group piano and music theory lessons with YouTube videos that students can view in class or at home

Co-author Tom Rudolph teaches in a MIDI lab at Haverford Middle School, in Haverford, PA. He searches for YouTube videos that reinforce piano and music theory skills. To do this, enter the words "music theory piano" in the YouTube search area. Then, click on Channels, and select "piano lessons" (www.youtube.com/user/PianoMusicLessons). You can also check out the playlists for relevant videos. Rudolph saves the YouTube URLs and provides them to his students for study at home away from the classroom.

Another strategy Rudolph uses is to search for "Music theory 101." This generated a host of results, including a demonstration on the treble clef:

www.youtube.com/watch?v=3bfl4iAnCEs&feature=PlayList&p=EB3E00 1F43CADAE9&playnext=1&playnext_from=PL&index=44.

TIP   Sites such as www.musictheory.net can be a good supplement to learning after watching music theory videos.

Instructional Applications and Tutorials

Search for videos that demonstrate vocal techniques

Matthew Hill, choir director at Welsh Valley Middle School in the Lower Merion school district in Pennsylvania, showcases elements of music in a "real-world way" via YouTube. Instead of only talking about vocal techniques, he demonstrates them by finding appropriate YouTube videos.

Search for a term such as "falsetto," for example, and you'll find dozens of relevant videos on channels such as ExpertVillage (www.youtube.com/user/expertvillage—one of the best educational channels on the site), with voice teachers explaining how to best use and improve your falsetto.

YouTube Teaching Strategy 91

Search for videos to reinforce instrumental instruction in general and guitar instruction in particular

Jamie Knight, a teacher at Huntington Beach High School in California, uses YouTube in his guitar class. He has students search for the songs they are learning so they have an example to follow. In fact, he has recently installed iPod Touch players at the practice guitar stations so students can watch YouTube videos as they practice. Knight believes that YouTube is one of the most important resources that has ever been made available to educators, and his students make use of it on a daily basis.

Alan Coady, a music educator and blogger from Great Britain (http://edubuzz .org/blogs/alancoady/), has created a page on his blog (http://edubuzz.org/ blogs/alancoady/recommended-guitar-websites/recommended-youtube-performances/) that includes links to guitar videos on YouTube for his students (he also has a General Music links page).

Coady also has his own YouTube channel (www.youtube.com/user/ PuffBartok), and has created his own videos, including tutorials on how to change guitar strings and other guitar techniques (for more information on creating your own videos to post to YouTube, see chapter 10).

YouTube Teaching Strategy 92

Play YouTube videos for your string students that demonstrate string bowing and other performance techniques

Joseph Brennan, a string instructor at Haverford Middle School and High School in Haverford, PA, uses YouTube to demonstrate string techniques to his students. He found a YouTube video of Itzhak Perlman performing the fourth movement of Tchaikosky's *Violin Concerto,* conducted by Eugene Ormandy, legendary conductor of the Philadelphia Orchestra (www.youtube.com/watch?v=ATK_pj2iMqg). Brennan plays this video for his middle school and high school string students to demonstrate the bowings (martele and sautille) and performance techniques (octaves and false harmonics) that are used.

Brennan also references Todd Ehle's string tutorials. Enter "Todd Ehle" in the YouTube search box, and then click on Playlists. Then click on Todd Ehle's list (www.youtube.com/results?search_type=search_playlists&search_ query=Todd+Ehle&uni=1).

YouTube Teaching Strategy 93

Access YouTube videos to enhance flute instruction

Nina Perlove (www.realfluteproject.com) is a well-known, highly accomplished flute player (she was also a member of the YouTube Symphony Orchestra) who has created her own YouTube channel (www.youtube.com/user/ninaflute) (see Fig. 7.2). Here she posts free lessons on a wide variety of topics, from how to produce a basic sound to more advanced techniques such as double tonguing and vibrato.

The channel also includes many performances by Ms. Perlove, as well as interviews with other flautists. While it seems that many of her lessons were filmed using the built-in webcam on her computer rather than a more advanced stand-alone digital video camera (see chapter 8), the content is always well planned and highly informative. Her videos provide an excellent example of why it is important to plan exactly what you are going to cover, such as preparing a script to read rather than speaking extemporaneously. This is covered in more depth in chapter 10.

Fig. 7.2
Nina Perlove's flute channel

Search for instrument lessons on the YouTube channel Expert Village

Expert Village (www.expertvillage.com) posts informative videos on its website as well as YouTube. While the YouTube Expert Village channel (www.youtube.com/user/expertvillage) (see Fig. 7.3) has many videos that have nothing to do with music, you can use the channel's Search box to find dozens of well-produced videos featuring experts on many different instruments.

The Expert Village videos are supported by banner advertisements, which often appear during the videos. This commercial aspect aside, you can find some great lessons on this channel. For example, if you search for "voice lessons," you will find hundreds of videos to choose from. Each one is short (often around 2 minutes in length), and at the end of each video is a link is given to the next lesson(s) that would logically follow. The Expert Village Channel also has hundreds of software tutorials. If you search for your favorite music software program, such as Sibelius or Finale, you'll find dozens of videos, each highlighting various software features. These Expert Village videos provide an excellent example of how you can break your lessons down into effective short segments rather than posting a one-hour lecture that will be a challenge for students to sit through.

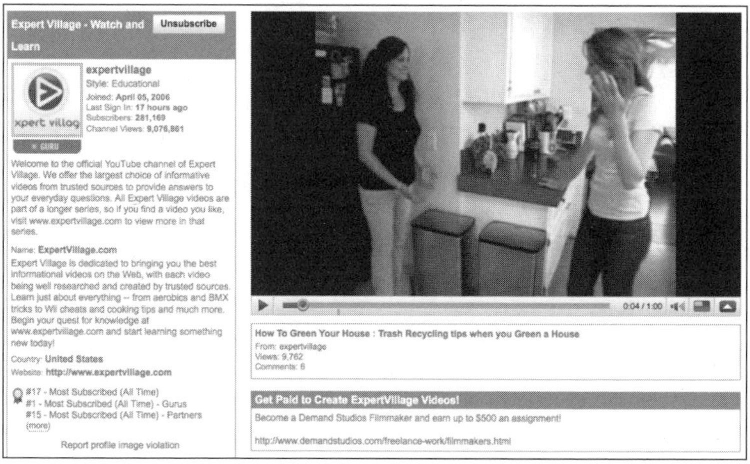

Fig. 7.3
Expert Village channel

YouTube Teaching Strategy 95

Use videos to help students care for their instruments

Use YouTube to demonstrate to your students the proper way to care for their instrument. For example, search for "cleaning a trumpet" or "cleaning a clarinet." You will find informative videos on proper cleaning and other techniques, many hosted by expert repair technicians. Some examples include:

▸ Cleaning a trumpet (www.youtube.com/watch?v=681ENFKO5ek)

▸ Cleaning a clarinet (www.youtube.com/watch?v=T8HLF0VCpVQ)

▸ Installing a violin bridge (www.youtube.com/watch?v=b0peWaEIKLI)

YouTube Teaching Strategy 96

Reference videos for your students on jazz improvisation

You will find many YouTube videos on jazz improvisation. These can be used for demonstration in the classroom or rehearsal room, or you can provide students with links to reference at home. A search for "jazz improvisation" yields results for guitar, trumpet, sax, and other instruments.

For example, Billy Taylor, one of the foremost experts on jazz in general and jazz improvisation in particular, has a YouTube video called "Billy Taylor Explains Jazz Improvisation" (www.youtube.com/watch?v=UQe PLNWQY0c&feature=PlayList&p=AE2D4F322EE78BBF&index=4). Other informative jazz improvisation lessons can also be found. Some of the results include:

▸ Jimmy Bruno's soloing method (www.youtube.com/watch?v=8x XUgfjlgzk)

▸ Aaron Noe's lesson on playing blues trumpet (www.youtube.com/ watch?v=oq3sk6w1n9c&feature=PlayList&p=3087B516AADEB7F5& index=10)

Remember to also click on the channels and playlists to narrow your search, or add more words to the search criteria, such as "jazz improvisation blues trumpet."

Performance Applications (Chorus, Band, Strings, Jazz)

YouTube Teaching Strategy 97

Search YouTube for examples of performing ensembles to share with your students for critique and reflection

Matthew Hill, choir director at Welsh Valley Middle School in the Lower Merion school district in Pennsylvania, uses YouTube as an instructional and motivational tool for his middle school choruses. If you search for the title of a composition that you are performing with your school chorus, you will most likely find dozens of different performances by middle school choirs from around the country, often posted by their music teachers. As discussed in chapter 5, music educators do not have the right to post performances of copyrighted music without the permission of the copyright holder (in most cases the publisher of the arrangement). However, in what may seem like a complete contradiction, it is almost certainly a fair use to watch the videos in your classroom. If you find a performance, you can play it for your students—just don't post your own versions. Playing videos of other middle school choirs performing the same work that your choir is working on is a wonderful educational resource for your ensemble. You can have students critique the performance and compare it to their own performances. Being able to play multiple performances of the same piece that your ensemble is working on opens up possibilities for student critique and reflection.

Joseph Brennan, string instructor for Haverford Middle and High Schools in Haverford, PA, searches for videos to help his students understand the mood or context of a work being rehearsed. He finds this especially helpful if the music is from an opera or ballet.

YouTube Teaching Strategy 98

Ask students to find YouTube videos to enhance their jazz listening skills

Co-author Tom Rudolph teaches instrumental and classroom music at Haverford Middle School in Haverford, PA, and directs the Haverford Middle School Jazz Ensemble. He asks jazz ensemble members to find their favorite jazz artist on YouTube by searching for their instrument along with the word "jazz," for example, "jazz guitar." Rudolph finds that YouTube is a free and easy way for students to begin to develop models they can emulate. Often students do not have experience listening to jazz. YouTube is a great way to get them started. While students are encouraged to purchase jazz audio tracks and CDs, YouTube can provide a host of jazz listening skills.

YouTube Teaching Strategy 99

Post videos of yourself playing individual parts of pieces you are rehearsing in your class

Alan Coady, a music educator and blogger from Great Britain, records and posts videos of himself playing the individual parts to some of the ensemble pieces he is rehearsing with his class. He can then provide the links to these videos on students' own YouTube channels, or post the links on the school website or his blog.

Humor: Just for Fun

One of the first things co-authors Tom Rudolph and James Frankel remember when YouTube arrived on the scene was watching humorous videos. Tom Rudolph's 13-year-old son was showing him videos of people walking into glass doors, and James Frankel had his students sharing videos of people falling off of skateboards and bicycles. You can find many instances of humor on YouTube—some in the music area.

Breaking Bow

Joseph Brennan located a YouTube video of the first movement of De Beriot's *A Minor Violin Concerto*, where a young student breaks his bow: www.youtube.com/watch?v=pnV5BXMrAE8 (you can also search for "Bowbreaking De Beriot"). He shows this to his high school students when they are preparing for district auditions. It is rather amusing, and Brennan finds it helps to calm his students' nerves about auditioning.

Pachelbel Rant

A search for "music humor" yielded a video by a string quartet playing an interesting and funny version of Pachelbel's *Canon*. Do a search for "Pachelbel Rant paganini" or go to: www.youtube.com/watch?v=j_dKCrKJR7Y&feature=PlayList&p=9B24DA08D4D0C94A&index=0.

Marimba Madness

Co-author Tom Rudolph's older brother John is currently the principal percussionist for the Toronto Symphony. He is also an instructor at the University of Toronto, and uses YouTube videos to help his students relax. Do a search for "Marimba Lady" that features a performance at the Miss America pageant. John likes to use this video to point out to his students the interesting technique she uses to change mallets during the performance.

If you find this one funny, do a search for "drumFunny.com" to find other videos that may tickle your funnybone.

Another favorite of John's class is "Reg Kehoe and His Marimba Queens." This is an old black-and-white video that is quite funny indeed. Check out the bass player!

Canadian Brass

Co-author Tom Rudolph's favorite humorous performances include those by the Canadian Brass. Do a search for the group and click on Playlists. One of his favorites is the "Canadian Brass Jazzed Up."

Out-of-Tune Trumpet

Tom is a trumpet player, and he enjoys playing this for his students. The trumpet and video are in slightly different keys. Search for "Star Wars trumpet solo."

Other Artists

You can find a plethora of funny videos by searching for any of the artists who specialize in humor, such as PDQ Bach and Victor Borge. This can provide a break for your students from the stress of practicing and rehearsing, and is just plain musical fun.

YouTube Music Education Channels

In March 2009, YouTube unveiled a new channel that focuses exclusively on educational videos: www.youtube.com/edu. This channel is filled with thousands of videos posted by a wide variety of educational institutions, including colleges and universities from around the world. Each institution has its own channel, many containing hundreds of videos featuring lectures, classes, events, and more. You can browse through all of the institutions that have videos posted to this channel by clicking on the Directory tab from the menu (see Fig. 7.4). At the time of this writing, nearly 200 colleges and universities were represented on the channel, with thousands of videos among them.

Fig. 7.4
YouTube educational channel

Two of the institutions most relevant to music educators are:

Berklee College of Music (www.youtube.com/user/Berkleemusic)

There are quite a few videos on the Berklee College of Music site that feature Berklee teachers giving free lessons, interviews with famous Berklee alumni, software tutorials, and interviews focusing on the music business. This is a fabulous resource for anyone interested in making music in the 21st century.

USC Thornton School of Music (www.youtube.com/user/USCThornton)

This channel is a wonderful example of how a university can use YouTube as a recruitment tool for prospective music education students, both undergraduate and graduate. The channel includes interviews with famous musicians associated with USC Thornton; an introductory video by Dr. Robert Cutietta, dean of the School of Music; student performances; and faculty lectures. It is highly likely that many other music schools will follow this example.

Many other universities feature videos of musical performances and lectures on their respective YouTube channels. Search for your alma mater to see if they have joined this trend. If they haven't, perhaps you could mention it to your former music education professors to encourage them to join the digital age.

Other music education–focused channels include those created by music educator associations and professional organizations. Below are some of the channels from this category.

MENC: The National Association for Music Education (www.youtube.com/user/MusicEducators)

MENC created its own YouTube channel back in June 2008, and has posted more than 20 videos, including interviews with Executive Director John Mahlmann and President Barbara Geer, advocacy materials, and videos of performances from the National Anthem Project that MENC ran in 2008. While the channel has not had much activity since it began, it could certainly become a central location for more advocacy materials and information about the organization, including announcements of upcoming events, calls for proposals, and more.

ACDA: The American Choral Directors Association (www.youtube.com/user/NationalACDA)

The American Choral Directors Association's channel features over 100 videos of choral groups from the United States and around the world. Other videos on the channel include performances and sessions from ACDA conferences, videos of special events, interviews, and warm-up exercises. Every choral educator should subscribe to the site as soon as possible—it is a fantastic resource.

The Midwest Clinic
(www.youtube.com/user/midwestclinic)

The Midwest Clinic, a very popular international band and orchestra conference held annually in Chicago, has its own YouTube channel, with videos of performances from the conference by the school's performing ensembles. It is amazing to note how many times each video has been viewed. Students in these ensembles most likely have seen their performances and have passed them on to family and friends. While the channel only has a little over 100 subscribers, at the time of this writing the videos had been viewed thousands of times. It is a testament to the extent to which YouTube reaches the students in our classrooms.

Children's Music Workshop
(www.youtube.com/user/schoolmusic)

This Los Angeles–based music education organization provides music instruction and curricular support to school districts that do not have instrumental music programs in their schools. This wonderful YouTube channel is filled with music advocacy materials, profiles of music educators, videos of performances by students in their programs, and more. This channel should provide a model for similar types of businesses as well as private music teachers who are looking for a way to market their instructional services.

Music for All (www.youtube.com/user/musicforalltv)

Music for All is one of the largest music education organizations in the United States, focusing on active music making through its music advocacy and activities with Bands of America and Orchestra America. The organization's YouTube channel features videos about its programs, members, performances, and advocacy materials. The channel is also host to one of the most viewed videos concerning music education, "The Case for Music Education" (www.youtube.com/watch?v=wUhylSoaJ1c). This is a wonderful advocacy tool for music educators facing cuts to their school music programs.

YouTube Channels and Videos Created by Music Educators

www.youtube.com/hlgmusicangel

YouTube user and music educator "Miss C" has created a great little video titled "My Elementary Music Classroom," which she posted to the site in August 2008.

It provides a wonderful glimpse into what an elementary school music classroom can look like, and Miss C takes us on a tour of her classroom, from bulletin board displays to musical instruments, class rules, teaching materials, furniture, and the music centers she has set up around her room. Anyone interested in elementary music education should view this video for ideas on how to set up a music classroom. Experienced music educators might want to post comments that include advice on possible changes to the environment. It is a wonderful opportunity for collaborative sharing among music educators.

www.youtube.com/user/pianoteaching

Irina Gorin is a piano teacher in Indiana who has set up a YouTube channel that focuses on her private piano teaching studio. It contains hundreds of videos of her students performing various works for piano in their recitals as well as a few piano lessons given by Ms. Gorin. This is a terrific example of how private music instructors (as well as public school music teachers) can use YouTube to showcase the musical efforts of their students.

www.youtube.com/user/susanappe

Created by San Francisco music educator Susan Appe, this channel showcases her teaching, student performances, and teaching philosophy. It is a great example of what pre-service music educators (as well as seasoned veterans) can do with YouTube to create a powerful depiction of their teaching style and selected student performances. Music education professors should consider including this type of portfolio in their students' resume packets, and in-service music educators should consider this type of portfolio when compiling teaching artifacts for the tenure process.

www.youtube.com/user/haasda01

This channel features a handful of videos of Iowa music educator David Haas conducting his high school choir, and provides viewers with an insight into what is involved in teaching this particular aspect of music. The videos showcase performances of choral works and various warm-up exercises, and there is also a video of a performance of arrangements and transcriptions composed by Haas. The channel illustrates how younger music educators are videotaping their teaching and posting it to YouTube as a way of sharing their ideas with other music educators around the world.

www.youtube.com/user/OakwoodBand

The Oakwood High School Band from Dayton, Ohio, has their own YouTube channel that contains over 60 videos of highlights from their winter and spring concerts and marching band shows. It is an example of how a music department can showcase its performances on the site. There are many other high school bands that have similar channels on YouTube. You need only search for "HS band" and you will find them.

As always, be aware of fair use guidelines (see chapter 5), and decide if a video that you have posted to the site requires permission. In most cases, a simple e-mail to the publisher of the piece being performed in the video is all you need to legally post the video to YouTube. Also, as a reminder, if your use of copyrighted material is deemed an infringement, YouTube will take the video off the site, and you'll be informed of such action.

Tips for Using YouTube in the Music Classroom

Before we move into the final section of the book, let's look at some tips for using YouTube in the music classroom, based on all of the information presented thus far. Hopefully this will provide you with a clearer understanding of what you can and cannot do with YouTube in the classroom. Chapter 8 will focus on what to do if your district blocks YouTube altogether. These tips assume that you can access YouTube in your classroom.

> ▸ **Always preview any videos that you are going to show to your students.** While this may seem like an obvious tip, one can never be too careful when using Internet materials with students. As mentioned in the book, profanity is permitted on the site, as well as material that would be considered inappropriate for use in a school. Be sure to view each video in its entirety—every second—before showing it to your students. It is always better to be safe than sorry.

> ▸ **Never have students search for videos on YouTube—create your own group or channel for use with students, and post videos there.** If you incorporate online research into your music curriculum, do not allow students to surf the Internet freely. Regardless of the firewalls that your district has put into place, if it allows YouTube, it allows every aspect of the site. As you are certainly aware, students can easily get "lost" searching for videos, and end up watching street fights, fatal car crashes, or worse. To avoid these situations, follow the instructions given in chapter 3 for setting up your own group or channel, and have your students only visit that part of the site. Classroom management skills, such as closely monitoring student activity, will also help enforce this rule.

▸ **Embed, embed, embed.** The best possible way to incorporate YouTube videos into your classroom is to embed them into a class website or blog (see chapter 10). This completely avoids having students on YouTube and the possibility of their being exposed to inappropriate content. This also provides the teacher with the ability to control how the video is viewed, as well as provide any contextual information about the video. Embedding is legal, whereas applications that allow you to download YouTube videos to your hard drive are not.

▸ **Always protect student anonymity.** The safety of your students should always be of paramount importance, especially when using websites such as YouTube. School districts have strict acceptable use policies for the Internet, and many state and federal laws protect the identities of minors online. It is not recommended to ever include a student's name with their image on a video that you post to YouTube. Because viewers will most likely be able to ascertain a student's grade level and school location, it is extremely important not to provide any personal information about individual students, as it could lead to the opportunity for contact between viewers and students. Be sure to read and understand your district's policies regarding the placement of student images online before posting videos to YouTube. To be safe, always consult an administrator first.

▸ **Know your copyright law.** As mentioned in chapter 5, there are quite a few ways to infringe on others' copyrights when using YouTube. Fair use guidelines may not absolve you from infringing activities because of the accessibility of the content (anyone can download and watch the videos you post). To be as safe as possible, always privately post those videos that you feel might infringe on copyrights and invite students to the group where the videos are posted. To be as legal as possible, always try to contact the copyright owner of the work included in the video and ask for permission to post.

Summary

This chapter has provided a number of examples of how YouTube is being used in music education and how it can be used as part of the curriculum. The examples given are just that: examples. There are literally thousands of other videos and hundreds of other channels that could have been included in this text. It is highly recommended that you spend some time exploring YouTube and searching for specific keywords that are of interest to you. For example, if you search for "trumpet lessons" or "American folk music," you'll find hundreds of relevant videos to play for your students. If you search for "vocal warm-up exercises," it will take you a couple of days to get through all of them. By far the most useful part of YouTube is the free access to relevant teaching materials at the touch of a button. Smart searching can provide any music educator with incredible resources for use with students. YouTube is the biggest public video library on the planet, and educators need to know how to use it.

What to Do If Your School Blocks YouTube

Chapter Eight

This chapter will address your options if your school district blocks YouTube, as well as provide other Web video options. The areas covered include:

- ▸ Why some schools block YouTube
- ▸ Allowing access to YouTube on specific computers
- ▸ Accessing specific YouTube videos
- ▸ Requesting copies of YouTube videos
- ▸ Accessing YouTube via proxy servers and anonymizers
- ▸ Other video website options for educators: SchoolTube, TeacherTube, and Archive.org
- ▸ Downloading video files when downloading is not supported
- ▸ YouTube download help
- ▸ Manipulating downloaded videos in other programs
- ▸ Adjusting the tempo and/or key of videos
- ▸ Using QuickTime Pro

In response to co-author Jim Frankel's music educator survey discussed in chapter 7, approximately a dozen music teachers said they wanted to use YouTube in their classes, but the site was blocked by their school district. If you find yourself in this predicament or if you want to review other options to YouTube, then read on!

Why Some Schools Block YouTube

There are several reasons why certain school districts block YouTube. Even though YouTube does block nudity and other inappropriate content, the site contains many videos that are not appropriate for use in education. YouTube could expose students to inappropriate content both in the videos themselves and in the comments posted by users. In speaking with a number of district technology coordinators while researching this book, most reported that while they were personally in favor of unblocking YouTube and it's potential for education, their school district and administration was firmly against allowing access to the site due to school board policy regarding the Internet. However, since there is widespread agreement among educators in general and music teachers in particular that YouTube has a plethora of appropriate material it behooves us to find ways to make it available in the classroom.

Allowing Access to YouTube on Specific Computers

If your school blocks YouTube, you can try to gain access to the site by requesting that only your teacher computer be permitted to access it. It may be possible to give you access to the site from a specific computer or from a specific location in the building, such as your teacher station (if you have one) located in the music classroom.

This is typically possible only if school district Internet policy permits it. If you are successful and can gain access, then you can view and display videos for your students (see chapter 4 for information on displaying YouTube videos for an entire class).

TIP This is a repeat of a tip given in chapter 7, but it bears repeating. Be sure to preview *all* your YouTube videos, as well as your YouTube searches, before showing them to students in your classroom.

Be sure to secure your computer so others cannot access it without your permission. This can be achieved by password-protecting your computer — make sure you keep the password private. The main limitation of this option is that it only facilitates classroom demonstration of YouTube videos.

Accessing Specific YouTube Videos

A second option is to ask permission for selected YouTube videos to be made accessible to you and/or your students. Just about every school has a firewall installed that can allow or block specific sites such as YouTube. If your school blocks YouTube, check with the district technology administrator to see if specific YouTube videos can be viewed in your classroom.

If your district blocks YouTube, you will have to access the site at home or away from school. It may also be possible to search YouTube using a computer in the technology administrator's office, which may not be affected by the district firewall. Check with your technology administrator to see if this is possible. If it is, your next step is to search for YouTube videos to share with your students. You will then need to record the specific Web location of each video. Every YouTube video has a unique Web address, sometimes referred to as a URL (Uniform Resource Locator). This address is displayed at the top of the YouTube site in the Web browser address box. It is also located in the Subscribe area to the left of the video once it is loaded. URLs are listed throughout this book, for example: http://www.youtube.com/watch?v=_7Urp6zZHzI.

One way to record URLs is to open a Microsoft Word file and copy and paste the URLs into a document. Once you have copied the URLs, you can share the list with your district technology administrator and ask that they be unblocked by the district firewall. Once they are unblocked, you and your students should be able to access them by entering the specific Web address for each video.

You have several options for sharing with your students the specific URLs of the videos that the district will allow. If you have a teacher website, you can post the URLs there. Or, if you maintain a blog (see chapter 3), you could post them there. Or you could simply paste them into Microsoft Word or other word processing software you are using. Note that Word converts URLs to Web links, so when you click on them they launch your Web browser automatically. Word also has a handy option for saving files in HTML (hypertext markup language), which can be posted on websites. Simply choose File > Save as Web Page.

Another option is to try to find the same video posted on another website. Many times multiple sites host the same video. To find out if a video is available on another site, try entering the exact title of the video in a Google search. You just might find that it is on a different site that is not blocked by your district.

Requesting Copies of YouTube Videos

As mentioned in chapters 5 and 10, another option for gaining access to a specific video is to request that the person who posted it send you a copy. Everyone who uploads a video to YouTube has a user account. When the video loads in the YouTube browser, there is a link to the person's username; for example, in Fig. 8.1 the username is "matta21."

Fig. 8.1
YouTube username

When you click the username, it will open a new window. Here you can choose to send a message to the person who posted the video (see Fig. 8.2). Ask for permission to use the video, and supply your e-mail address. Be sure to mention that you are a teacher, and that the video will be used for educational purposes only.

Accessing YouTube via Proxy Servers and Anonymizers

There may be a way to get around the firewall that school districts use to block YouTube and other sites. For years Internet privacy experts have been using anonymizers, or anonymous proxy servers.

Websites such as YouTube are hosted on computer servers. A proxy server acts as a go-between between you (the client)

Fig. 8.2
Send Message

and the other website, in this case YouTube. There are two reasons to access a proxy server: 1) to hide your identity from spyware as you browse the Internet; and 2) to access sites that are blocked by a firewall.

The typical way proxy and anonymous servers work is you first connect to the proxy website, which then acts as the intermediary between you and the blocked site, such as YouTube. Many school districts are aware of proxy servers and anonymizers, so you may have to try a host of different options, and it might not be possible to gain access if your district firewall is exceptionally strong and blocks some or all proxy servers from being used by staff and students.

Before you look into this option, check with your district administrator and review your school Internet policy to see if this is permissible.

TIP In many cases using proxy servers and anonymizers is a violation of a district's Internet usage policy, so be sure to ask for permission before using a proxy server in your classroom.

Locating a Proxy Server

If you receive permission from your administration to use a proxy server, you can start by using the free Web browser Firefox, which has built-in proxy connection settings. Download Firefox (www.mozilla.com/en-US/firefox/personal.html) and see if it can get around the school firewall. If not, then you need to find a proxy server that works. Most of these services charge a fee for use, but there are some free options, such as Mark 7 (see Fig. 8.3). Mark7 (http://mark7.info/) is currently a free Web service that appears to the school's firewall as if your computer is connecting to the proxy's Web address, not YouTube. If successful, YouTube will load on your computer.

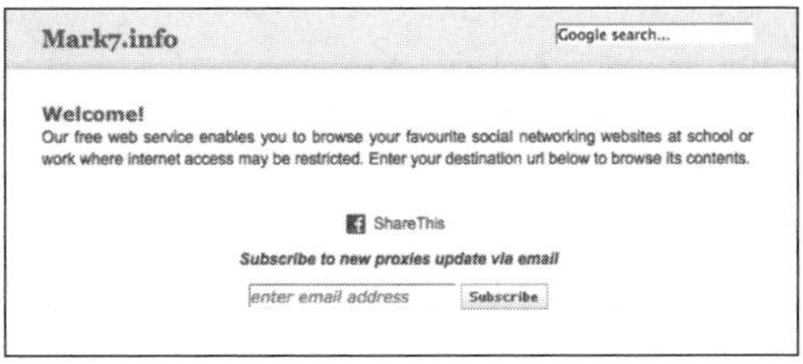

Mark7.info | Google search...

Welcome!
Our free web service enables you to browse your favourite social networking websites at school or work where internet access may be restricted. Enter your destination url below to browse its contents.

ShareThis

Subscribe to new proxies update via email

enter email address | Subscribe

Fig. 8.3
Mark7 website

You can also do a Google search (www.google.com) for the phrase "proxy server." You will see many proxy websites. Once you locate a free proxy server, test it to see if you can access blocked sites such as YouTube. You will want to conduct the test using a school computer.

Other services, such as www.anonymizer.com, offer options for a fee. Yet it also has a free trial period, as do most services that charge fees.

Other Video Website Options for Educators

Since many schools block YouTube, other services designed specifically for education have emerged. Two of the largest services are SchoolTube.com and TeacherTube.com.

TeacherTube.com

One viable option for accessing videos is TeacherTube.com. Officially launched on March 6, 2007, the goal of the site is "to provide an online community for sharing instructional videos. We seek to fill a need for a more educationally focused, safe venue for teachers, schools, and home learners. It is a site to provide anytime, anywhere professional development with teachers teaching teachers. As well, it is a site where teachers can post videos designed for students to view in order to learn a concept or skill" (see www.teachertube.com/staticPage.php?pg=about).

The focus of this site is on instructional videos rather than performances. However, you and your students can post any education-related videos. It is a free service that, like YouTube, only requires that you sign up and create a user account. A search for "music band" yielded four pages of results. The series "Quick Tips for Band" by Michael Goodman, would be appropriate to show to students and share with other staff members (see Fig. 8.4).

Fig. 8.4
TeacherTube video "Quick Tips for Band Posture"

Like YouTube (see chapter 3), with TeacherTube you can create a user account and view and upload your own videos. It also offers channels as well as the ability to comment on posted videos and flag inappropriate ones.

TeacherTube allows for a variety of media to be uploaded and viewed, including videos, audio files, and photographs. When you search the site, choose the type of file that you want, for example videos, by selecting it in the TeacherTube toolbar.

TeacherTube has one unique feature—a co-branded version of the site for K-12 schools and colleges. Once you create an account, you can then customize it through a variety of settings (www.teachertube.com/mysite/). For example, you can customize the look of your "MySite" by choosing from a host of designs, and can add custom backgrounds such as your school colors and school graphic logo. A neat option is to customize the URL of your site with your school name (e.g., http://teachertubemysite.com/YOURSCHOOL).

Features can be added or subtracted as needed. For example, if you don't want students to upload files, this option can be removed. There are no ads on the site, so this is a perfect way to create a customized website that suits your needs and can be changed when you want to. The major downside, however, is that the MySite option is not free. Yet the cost is reasonable, with 20 users for only $99 per year, and you can add more users as needed for an additional fee.

Get started with the free TeacherTube.com site first. Also, be sure to check with your technology administrator to see if they will cover the cost of setting up a MySite account.

SchoolTube.com

SchoolTube.com is another education-oriented website that was formed with many of the features of YouTube in an attempt to create a site that is friendlier to teachers and schools. Its mission is to educate and empower educators and students in the areas of safe, effective video production and Internet publishing. The site states, "The SchoolTube platform allows students to upload media into a 'holding' area that keeps the media inactive. An email is sent to a moderator informing them that the media is available to be viewed for approval. Only after the media has been approved by the moderator is it available for viewing on the site." SchoolTube.com includes channels, categories, and other features that will be familiar to the experienced YouTube user (see Fig. 8.5).

Any current K-12 student, teacher, or administrator who is registered with SchoolTube is eligible to upload videos. However, all videos uploaded to SchoolTube must be teacher approved. During the registration process students are required to pick a moderator to review their videos. SchoolTube is free for basic users, with revenue streams generated from premium school memberships, advertising, product referrals, and affiliate partner programs (www.school-video-news.com/index_files/School_Tube.htm).

SchoolTube has a growing list of partners (www2.schooltube.com/Partners.aspx), including MENC, the National Association for Music Education (www.menc. org). SchoolTube has been featured by MENC in its "MENC News," which is regularly sent via e-mail to its members. Its May 12, 2009, posting included the following text:

> Greetings! It's been a great year seeing the first MENC member videos on SchoolTube! This month, we are featuring a *Behind the Music*-style video about Frenship's Honors Band and the hard work necessary to achieve great success: http://www.schooltube.com/video/30432/FHS-Honors-Band-Behind-the-Music
>
> All videos submitted of your students' performances, including those from parents, are highly valued by your students and local communities and build respect for the music programs that play an essential role in the educational experience.

SchoolTube features many music performances and tutorials. A search for "marching band" yielded 915 videos. And, of course, the number of school videos is increasing rapidly, as teachers can be assured that the content on the site is heavily moderated, much more so than YouTube.

Like TeacherTube, SchoolTube offers a premium service, or channel, for school districts and educational institutions. Its major advantages are that it:

- ▸ Reaches students both in school and beyond the classroom—unlike most commercial sites, which are blocked by school districts
- ▸ Provides masthead space for branding, with custom graphics and links
- ▸ Offers a custom-branded Channel page
- ▸ Offers a customizable video presentation for your channel

For more information on this option, click on the Store link on the SchoolTube website (see Fig. 8.5).

Fig. 8.5
SchoolTube.com

Archive.org

Another Web service to consider is Archive.org, which allows users to upload videos and other media. The site also has many commercial videos that are in the public domain (see chapter 5). Archive.org is not likely to be blocked by school district firewalls, so it could be a viable option for you to upload your educational videos. While it doesn't have as many music education–related videos as YouTube, SchoolTube, and/or TeacherTube, many videos are appropriate for viewing and

downloading. The home page is quite complex, and lists all the files available for viewing, listening, and downloading. By clicking on the Moving Images option on the toolbar, you will be redirected to the video portion of the site (see Fig. 8.6). A recent search for "marching band" yielded 311 posts.

Fig. 8.6
Archive.org video "US Navy Marching Band"

Archive.org offers the least number of YouTube-like features. There are no channels or playlists, but you can upload videos for free.

Downloading Videos for Offline Use

As mentioned in chapter 5, YouTube explicitly prohibits downloading videos for use offline or when you are not connected to the Internet. However, other sites, such as TeacherTube.com and Archive.org, make it quite easy to download files to your computer's hard drive. SchoolTube.com does not specifically prohibit downloading, but does not offer a download link on its site.

Downloading Made Simple

Of the sites mentioned in this chapter, TeacherTube.com and Archive.org provide the easiest downloading options. TeacherTube has a download option in the window when videos load (see Fig. 8.4). When you click the Download button, the video downloads in Flash format. The file extension is .flv. This is the file format that is used by YouTube and SchoolTube.

After the file is downloaded, you may need to download a Flash player to view the video on your computer. There are several Flash players (sometimes referred to as media players) to choose from, with several options for Mac and Windows.

For both Mac and Windows

▸ Adobe Flash Player

▸ Adobe Media Player (AMP)

▸ VideoLAN VLC media player

▸ Wimpy Desktop FLV player

For Mac only

▸ Apple QuickTime Player with Perian component

For Windows only

▸ FLV Player (by Martijn de Visser)

▸ Riva FLV Player

My favorite player is the VideoLAN VLC media player (www.videolan.org/ vlc/). It is a free player for Mac and Windows and will play a host of file formats including flash (.flv).

After you download a flash video (.flv), try launching the downloaded file by double-clicking on it. If it does not open a media player, you may need to install one of the above players. After installing the player, the video can be launched without needing to access a website. The file will be opened in a playback screen that will resemble the online players on YouTube and other sites. You can typically expand the window when showing it to your students.

Archive.org Download Options

Archive.org also features a download option (see Fig. 8.7). When a video is loaded, there is a download window to the left. If you click on one of the links, your Web browser will attempt to play the file in the selected format.

To download one of the three options, right-click on the link (if you have a one-button Mac, hold down the Control key and click on the link). You will be presented with the option to save it to your hard drive. Always remember to save your videos to a location that you will remember.

Fig. 8.7
Archive.org download options

Which file format should you choose? The MPEG-4 file format (abbreviated MP4 with the file extension .mp4) can be played by most media players, such as QuickTime and the VLC media player. QuickTime files can be played by Apple's QuickTime player, which is a free download for Mac and Windows. The advantage of QuickTime files is that they can be opened in other software programs for editing. The Ogg Vorbis file format is an attempt to provide an open standard for more efficient video streaming. The Xiph.Org Foundation put together the specifications for the open standard, hoping to create a patent-free method for encoding media. Most media players will play Ogg Vorbis files on the Archive.org site. Remember that video files can be quite large and take up a significant amount of hard drive space. The longer the video, the larger the file size. Keep this in mind when you are downloading multiple videos. When you are accessing YouTube or other sites, the files are not downloaded to your computer; instead, they are streamed to your computer and played by your Web browser.

Downloading Video Files When Downloading Is Not Supported

SchoolTube.com does not currently have a download option. Yet its terms of use do not prohibit downloading as YouTube does, so with the appropriate software you can download files from SchoolTube.com using third-party software. Several music teachers who responded to co-author James Frankel's survey reported that they use a variety of methods to download videos.

YouTube Teaching Strategy 100

Teachers can download videos from sites that permit it, such as SchoolTube.com, TeacherTube.com, and Archive.org. so they can be accessed offline. Be sure to comply with copyright law (see chapter 5) and the terms of service for specific sites.

Websites for Downloading

An easy way to download videos is to do so through an external website such as www.keepvid.com, www.savetube.com, www.youtubecatcher.com, http://vixy .net, and other similar sites.

The first step is to copy the URL of the video you are viewing on YouTube. Then, go to one of the external websites given above and paste the URL in the appropriate location. The site then does the conversion and makes the file available for you to download. Each of these sites offers different download options. Sites that provide a range of file options are preferable, depending on how you want to use the video once it is downloaded to your hard drive. Once you download the file, you can use a media player to play back the file when you are offline.

Of the many websites offering free download services, http://vixy.net is recommended, as it offers a wide range of file options (see Fig. 8.8).

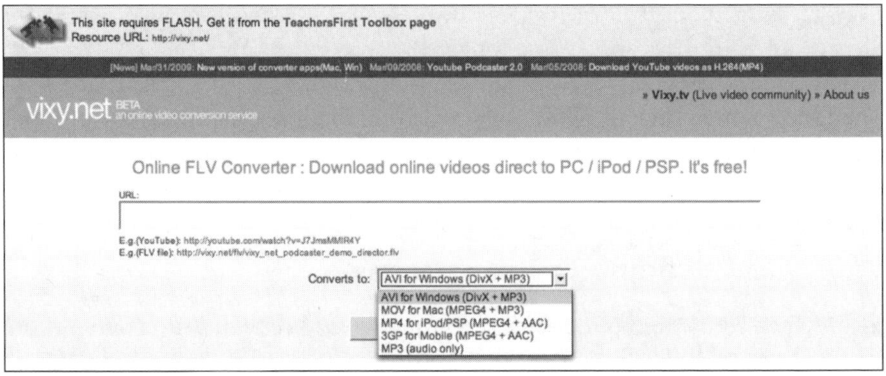

Fig. 8.8
Vixy.net

There are also sites dedicated to downloading YouTube videos, such as www. downloadyoutubevideos.com. This site is similar to the others mentioned above—it converts the video to a format that you can download and play offline.

Downloading Videos Using Your Web Browser

The free Web browser Firefox can be used to download videos that are playing on sites such as SchoolTube and YouTube. Many music teachers mentioned

that they use the free Firefox add-on "Download Helper." Check it out at www
.downloadhelper.net. There are clear instructions on the site for installing the
helper. Once installed, an icon appears
next to the URL in Firefox.

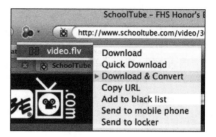

The "Download" and "Quick Download"
options save the video in Flash format
(.flv). The "Download and Convert"
option (see Fig. 8.9) allows you to save
the loaded video in a variety of useful
video formats.

Fig. 8.9
Download Helper options

YouTube Download Help

Interestingly, there are tutorial videos on YouTube with instructions on how
to download videos. Be careful when using these techniques with YouTube,
as downloading files from YouTube is not permitted according to its terms of
service. However, the tutorials will help you to download videos from other sites
mentioned in this chapter.

The fastest way to download YouTube videos in Flash format is to drag a link to
the toolbar of your Firefox Web browser. Then, when you are viewing a YouTube
video, click the toolbar link and the video can be downloaded. The only file
option is .flv (flash format) however. Yet here is a fast way to download a YouTube
video as an MPEG-4 file:

1. Go to http://googlesystem.blogspot.com/2008/04/download-youtube
   -videos-as-mp4-files.html.

2. Navigate down to the "Get YouTube
   Video" link. Click and hold the mouse
   on the "Get YouTube Video" text and
   drag it to your Firefox toolbar at the top
   of the window (see Fig. 8.10).

3. Navigate back to YouTube and load a
   video.

4. Click on the Get YouTube Video icon
   in the Firefox toolbar to download it.
   Done!

Fig. 8.10
Creating a toolbar icon to download
YouTube videos

This option is only applicable to YouTube videos. It will not work with other sites such as SchoolTube or TeacherTube.

Manipulating Downloaded Videos in Other Programs

One of the main reasons for downloading videos in MPEG-4 or QuickTime format is that they can then be opened in video editing programs.

YouTube Teaching Strategy 101

Download videos in MPEG-4 or QuickTime format, and open them in your video editing software.

You can open a video and edit it to keep only the parts you want to show to your class. This can be useful for listening lessons in the classroom. Chapter 10 deals with editing videos in iMovie and Windows Movie Maker, which are both free programs for Mac and Windows, respectively. You can also use other programs such as Final Cut Pro and Pinnacle Studio to open and edit downloaded videos, provided they are in a compatible file format.

YouTube Teaching Strategy 102

Download videos and use them as a source for students to compose music using video-scoring software such as Sibelius and Finale on Mac and Windows, GarageBand and Logic on Mac, or Sonar and Acid on Windows. There are many other software options in this category.

Once a video has been downloaded in MPEG-4 or QuickTime format, it can then be opened in music software programs. Students can then compose music to the video. A complete review of this process is beyond the scope of this book, but there are many resources to help you in the scoring-to-video area. Start with a Google search for "Scoring to video." Also consider contacting music organizations such as TI:ME (Technology Institute for Music Educators; www.ti-me.org) and ATMI (Association for Technology in Music Instruction; http://atmionline.org) for more information on this activity.

Adjusting the Tempo and/or Key of Videos

Joseph Brennan, a secondary-string instructor in the Haverford School District in Havertown, Pennsylvania, downloads YouTube videos, as some of his school's rehearsal areas do not have Internet access. He then converts them to QuickTime format using several of the options mentioned above. Then he opens the file in Apple's QuickTime Player. QuickTime Player is a free download for Mac and Windows, available at www.apple.com/quicktime.

YouTube Teaching Strategy 103

Use QuickTime to change the audio pitch of a video.

Mr. Brennan uses QuickTime to teach rote songs to the students in his sixth-grade string ensemble. This is the process that he follows:

> In rehearsal, I ask the students to play along with the QuickTime version of the song I am teaching by rote; for example, "Trumpet Voluntary." By using [QuickTime's] A/V controls, I slow down the tempo without changing the pitch by adjusting just the playback speed. This proves to be very helpful when learning a rote song. In rehearsal, I ask the students to play along with the QuickTime version, and by using the A/V controls, I can adjust the pitch to the key using the Pitch Shift controls.

Once a video is downloaded and converted to QuickTime format (.mov), open the QuickTime Player and access the A/V (audio/video) controls from the Window menu (see Fig. 8.11). You will see a control to change the playback speed, and a Pitch Shift control to change the key. So it is possible to just change the speed, the key, or a little of both!

Using QuickTime Pro

QuickTime Pro (for Mac and Windows) is one of the cheapest and most powerful video editing programs available. You can purchase it online from Apple for $29.99. Go to www.apple.com/quicktime and click on the link "QuickTime Pro."

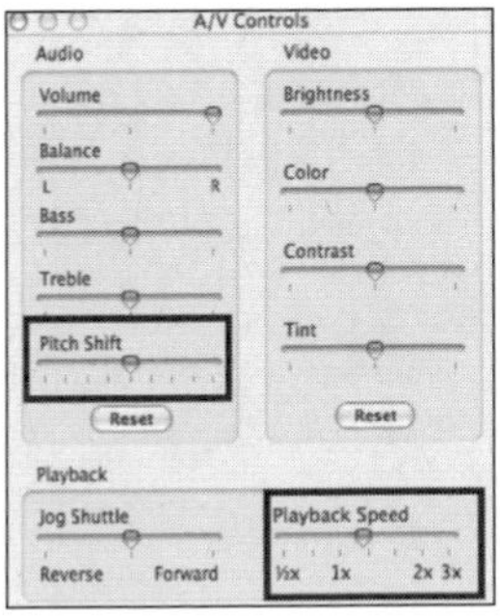

With QuickTime Pro, you can edit movies by cutting and pasting, and save movies in a host of formats. (See

Fig. 8.11
QuickTime's Pitch Shift and Playback Speed controls

chapter 10 for more information on editing movies in iMovie and Windows Movie Maker.) After a movie is loaded, choose File > Export. At the bottom of the Export window, click the Export tab, and you can then convert the movie to many different formats (see Fig. 8.12).

If you want the Swiss army knife of video editing tools, consider purchasing QuickTime Pro.

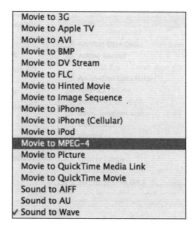

Summary

Fig. 8.12
QuickTime Pro Export File format options

There is widespread agreement that video sharing can be a positive influence on education. This chapter explores the various options available to you if YouTube is blocked by your school district or institution. The first place to start is to review your school district's Internet policy and then contact the school or district technology administrator and ask them if one or more of the following options are possible: allowing access to YouTube from your teacher computer for class demonstration; allowing specific YouTube videos to be accessed in the classroom; or allowing access to YouTube via proxy servers or anonymizers. If none of these options is permissible, you can explore education-friendly video-sharing websites such as TeacherTube.com, SchoolTube.com, and Archive.org. The second half of this chapter explains how to download videos to your computer in a variety of formats, how to play them back on your computer, and how to use QuickTime to change the speed and/or key of videos.

Equipment for Producing Quality Videos

Chapter Nine

This chapter will address the budget and equipment needed for producing videos on YouTube. It will cover the following topics:

- ▶ How YouTube formats videos
- ▶ Budget
- ▶ Video and audio file formats
- ▶ Resolution
- ▶ Using a webcam or built-in camera in your computer
- ▶ Choosing a video camera
- ▶ Video converters
- ▶ Video and audio accessories
- ▶ External microphones
- ▶ Microphone recording tips
- ▶ Computer video editing software

How YouTube Formats Videos

Before deciding what equipment you need to make quality videos, you should understand how YouTube handles videos. Most users shoot a video and then upload the file to YouTube (see chapter 10). YouTube then converts it to the

Flash (.flv) format (see chapter 8). Chapter 10 will cover considerations when shooting a video. You should record the highest-quality video possible and then let YouTube do the conversion. When selecting audio and video equipment, keep in mind the following recommendations from YouTube Help:

Recommended resolution: 1280 × 720 (16 × 9 HD) and 640 × 480 (4:3 SD)

Video file formats: H.264, MPEG-2, or MPEG-4 preferred

Audio file formats: MP3 or AAC preferred

This chapter will explain the technical terms above and provide you with a broad overview of the equipment you will need to create quality YouTube videos.

Budget

You can spend a little or a lot of money on video and audio equipment. For the purposes of this book, we will focus on semi-professional and consumer-level options. While you can spend many thousands of dollars on equipment, this chapter assumes a budget ranging from $300 to $3,000.

TIP   If your school has a video production department, check to see if it has some equipment you can borrow (cameras, microphones, etc.). Perhaps you can borrow gear until you purchase your own equipment for the music department.

Video File Formats

By now you should have a basic understanding of which audio and video file formats can be used to upload videos to YouTube. These file formats are often referred to as codecs. As mentioned in chapter 4, *codecs* (short for "compressor-decompressor") are used to reduce the size of large music and video files to make them a more manageable size.

You can upload YouTube videos in most of the file formats created by digital cameras, camcorders, and video-editing software. These include:

- .wmv (Windows Media Video)

- .avi (Audio Video Interleave) (Windows)

- .mov (QuickTime) (Mac and Windows)

- .mpg (Moving Picture Experts Group: MPEG-2, MPEG-4) (Mac and Windows)

The most common formats are QuickTime (.mov) and Windows Media Video (.avi). Your video camera and editing software should have one of these file formats as its default setting.

Resolution

Another key term used in video production is *resolution*. YouTube formats videos to fit its onscreen player, and when you upload your video, it is converted to Flash format. You can upload any resolution video and YouTube will convert it, but it is best to upload your video in a format that conforms to YouTube's specifications. Otherwise the video may not appear the way you intend it to look.

The physical size of a video is measured in *pixels*, which is short for "picture elements." The more pixels a picture has, the higher the quality. There are two types of resolution: standard definition, or SD, and high-definition, or HD. A standard-definition television has a resolution of 640 × 480 pixels. The newer high-definition TVs pack a lot more punch (pixels) than SD TVs. Several HD resolutions are used for HD TV. However, the HD resolution that YouTube recommends is 1280 × 720. It is always best to upload the highest-resolution video possible, and let YouTube do the conversion. The resolution is controlled by the video editing software discussed further in chapter 10.

If YouTube gives you an error message when uploading a video, first check to see if it is in one of the accepted formats. The YouTube Help area also provides excellent support.

Audio File Formats

Like video, raw audio creates very large files. Standard audio files are either .wav (WAV) or .aif (AIFF). The WAV format originated on Windows computers, but is compatible with Macs. The AIFF file format (or Audio Interchange File

Format) is primarily used with Macs. WAV and AIFF are uncompressed audio file formats.

Compression is used to make audio files a more manageable size. Since videos include sound as well as picture, you should be aware of audio formats. YouTube recommends using one of two common audio codecs: MP3 or AAC. MP3 (short for MPEG-1 Audio Layer 3) is a common format for consumer audio storage. The best choice is to use the newer ACC (Advanced Audio Coding) format. AAC compresses files much more efficiently than the older MP3 format, yet its quality rivals uncompressed AIFF or WAV files.

Recommended Formats for YouTube

Below are the recommended specifications for YouTube videos. Make sure your video-editing software conforms to these settings.

Video: .mpg, .mov, .avi, or wmv

Audio: MP3 or ACC format

Resolution: 640 × 480 (SD) or 1280 × 720 (HD).
Use the HD setting if possible

Length: Do not exceed 10:59

File size: Not more than 1 GB

As indicated above, be aware that YouTube restricts the length of videos. A video cannot exceed 10 minutes and 59 seconds. The file size also must not exceed 1 GB (gigabyte).

Selecting Equipment

This section will deal with the options for recording your videos. Although you can create videos with an investment of a few hundred dollars, to create quality music videos, you will need to invest between $1,000 and $2,000. The areas we will cover include:

1. The camera and necessary accessories

2. The external microphone and stand

3. Computer video editing software to create the final version of your videos

Using a Webcam or Your Computer's Built-in Camera

It is likely that the computer you are using has a built-in camera. Most Mac and Windows computers come with a camera. This onboard camera with built-in microphone is referred to as a *webcam*. Webcams can be built in to a computer or purchased as a separate unit. Most Macs come with the iSight webcam, and many PC brands such as Dell have a built-in webcam option.

The advantages of webcams is that they have both a camera and microphone built in, are easy to connect to a computer, and are quite inexpensive. If your computer does not have a webcam, then you can purchase one. External webcams are available from companies such as Logitech (www.logitech.com) (see Fig. 9.1) and Microsoft (www.microsoft.com). There are many different models to choose from. Generally, the higher the cost, the better the quality of the video and audio.

Fig. 9.1
Logitech Quickcam Vision Pro

Note that while a webcam is an inexpensive option, it will not produce high-quality audio or video. Webcams are best used for primarily speech-related videos, such as audio tutorials, and not for live recordings of music ensembles. If you want to record a tutorial (see chapter 10), then a webcam could be sufficient. However, if you want to create a video with the highest-quality audio and video, then a stand-alone video/audio recorder is recommended.

Choosing a Video Camera

A handheld video camera is called a *camcorder*, and many versions are available. Since you will be using this camera for video and you will most certainly be recording some music performances, below are some recommendations.

First, you should consider purchasing a digital camcorder. (The older tape-based camcorders are referred to as analog cameras.) A digital camcorder can be easily connected to a computer and the video files can be edited using video-editing software. The more expensive the camera, the more bells and whistles are included.

When selecting a camera, make sure it has an external input for a microphone. Later in this chapter we will discuss and recommend specific microphones—the single most important factor for quality music recordings. Also, since only the higher-grade cameras tend to have an external microphone input, you will be getting a camera that will also serve you well in the video domain.

The Panasonic VDR-D310 (see Fig. 9.2) costs around $500 and records to DVD-RW and DVD-R (8 cm) discs. An advantage is that the discs can be removed for storage. A disadvantage is that you are limited to 30 minutes of recording per disc. Since the maximum upload time for YouTube is 10:59, this should be sufficient. It has a built-in microphone, but also offers the flexibility of connecting an external microphone.

Fig. 9.2

Panasonic VDR-D310 camcorder with external microphone input

The JVC Everio GZMG555 is another camcorder in the $500 range that uses a built-in hard drive for storage. The unit also features a built-in microphone and an external microphone input. Very few consumer camcorders have an external microphone input. If you are shopping for a camcorder, be sure to check the specifications to see if there is an external microphone input.

If budget is a consideration, consider a Flip Video Camcorder (www.theflip.com). Although none of the models at this writing feature an external microphone jack, the built-in microphone is acceptable for dialog and some low-end music applications. For the best recording quality, you should purchase a camcorder with an external microphone input. Specific applications for external microphones will be discussed later in this chapter.

Prosumer and High-Definition Camcorders

If you want to get really serious, consider one of the prosumer video cameras. *Prosumer* (a combination of "professional" and "consumer") is a term used to describe camcorders that are above the consumer level but not quite at the professional or pro level. A disadvantage is that prosumer camcorders are quite large and require a shoulder rest. They are also expensive—expect to pay in the $1,000 to $3,000 range for cameras such as the Canon XL2. An advantage of prosumer camcorders is that most models allow you to use different lenses for specific applications. High-end prosumer cameras also can record true high-definition video. The Sony Handycam HDR-SR10 can record in HD and sells for under $1,000. While these models are beyond the budget of most music departments, if the funds are available, a prosumer camera should be a consideration.

Video Converters

If you have to work with an existing video camera or camcorder that is not digital (in other words, it records to tape rather than an internal drive or disc), you can transfer the data to your computer with a video converter. These devices typically work by connecting the output of the analog camcorder to the converter and then connecting the output of the converter to your computer. Most models require a FireWire connection to the computer. All current Macs come with a FireWire port. Some Windows computers have the port (also called IEEE 1394), but it may not be standard. The Canopus ADVC-110 (www.canopus.com) is an example of a video converter in the $200 range. Although you will be much better off with a digital camcorder, converting from analog will work until you have the money to purchase one.

Accessories

Video accessories are also important to consider. A must is a floor-standing tripod. It is much better to place your camera on a tripod than to attempt hand-held recording. While there may be some isolated times when you will want to use the hand-held approach, a tripod will be the method of choice for most videos that you shoot. Be sure to purchase a quality tripod. Expect to spend $50 to $100 for a quality tripod. The Sony VCT series (www.sonystyle.com) offers many different models to choose from.

Another cool option is the Gorillapod Focus by Joby (http://joby.com). Designed for consumer camcorders, the Gorillapod (see Fig. 9.3) can either stand on a desk or be wrapped around an object. The latter can be a handy

Fig. 9.3
The Gorillapod Focus

way to mount your digital camera. Be sure to purchase a model that can hold the weight of your camcorder.

Lighting is a main consideration for shooting quality videos (see chapter 10). When you purchase your camcorder, also purchase an add-on video light such as the Sony HVL-FDH4 Video Flash Light (see Fig. 9.4). Make sure the light is compatible with your camcorder. You can search the manufacturer's website for lights made specifically for your brand of camcorder. If your camcorder does not have a way to connect an external light, you can purchase a stand-alone light.

Fig. 9.4
Sony HVL-FDH4

External Microphones

Since you will be making many videos where sound is the main component, you will want to invest in an external microphone designed for recording music. As mentioned previously, in order to connect an external microphone, you must have a video recorder with an external microphone input. One reason for using an external microphone is to get the microphone as close as possible to the recording source. For example, you might want to use a clip-on, or lavalier, microphone for dialog, solo voice, or solo instruments. Getting the microphone close to the source can greatly enhance the output quality. Another reason for purchasing an external microphone is that the quality may be better than the camcorder's built-in microphone. However, today's camcorders have decent built-in microphones and can be sufficient for some applications.

Several types of microphones are used for sound recording. Here is a brief overview of the most common types.

A *dynamic* microphone is typically used for live performance. Dynamic microphones include the Shure models SM-57 and SM-58. These microphones have an XLR connector and are usually plugged into an audio mixer or interface. Dynamic microphones are not typically used to record video sound. Another type of microphone is a *condenser* microphone. Condensers are typically more sensitive than dynamic microphones and are recommended for the best-quality music recordings.

Microphones also have specific recording pickup patterns. The most commonly used pattern is *cardioid*, so named because the mic picks up sound in a heart-shaped pattern. Other microphone types include *bi-directional* and *omnidirectional*. Bi-directional mics record in opposite directions (in front of and behind the mic). These are typically used in interviews where there are two people speaking who are facing each other. An omni microphone picks up sound equally in all directions, so if you are in an auditorium it will pick up both the stage sounds and the audience sounds. Another type of microphone is a *lavalier*, or clip-on microphone.

You should also consider whether the microphone is stereo or mono. A stereo microphone is basically two microphones in one. It has a left and right recording capsule built into the microphone. Most microphones only have one recording capsule and hence are referred to as mono microphones. For music recording, stereo microphones usually sound best.

For recording videos, you should purchase a lavalier or clip-on microphone and a stereo condenser microphone. The former is best for individual recording and the latter for large groups and ensembles.

Lavalier (Clip-on) Microphones

A lavalier or clip-on microphone is an excellent choice for spoken dialog as well as solo instrument and solo voice recording. You will want to budget in the $100 to $200 range for a high-quality stereo lavalier mic. Also, make sure that the microphone's cable connection is the same as the input of the camcorder. You can also purchase adaptors for most common video and audio cables. The most common connector is a 1/8" (3.5mm) stereo mini plug (see Fig. 4.6 in chapter 4).

Fig. 9.5
SmartMusic clip-on microphone

One inexpensive lavalier option is the SmartMusic microphone. Many music departments are using SmartMusic software (www.smartmusic.com), and you can connect the same microphone that is used for the software to your camcorder's external microphone input. SmartMusic has a clip-on microphone (see Fig. 9.5) for instruments and a vocal microphone that is attached to a headset. The microphones cost $19.95 each and are a terrific value. Note that both of these microphones are mono, not stereo.

Some other clip-on microphone options include the Microphone Madness MCSM-4 Mini Cardioid Stereo Lavalier Microphone (http://microphonemadness.com), which has a left and right microphone for stereo recording. This will produce a better-quality recording than the SmartMusic microphones. Expect to pay $75 to $150 for higher-quality lavalier mics.

Stereo Condenser Microphones

High-quality camcorders, those featuring an external microphone input, typically have a decent-quality built-in microphone (see Fig. 9.2). However, to capture recordings of large ensembles such as bands, orchestras, and choirs, you should consider investing in a high-quality stereo condenser microphone. The Sony ECM-MS907 Stereo Condenser Microphone can be attached to a microphone stand and moved into the best position for recording a musical ensemble. This all-purpose microphone does a nice job, but in many cases it might not be that much better than the camera's built-in microphone. As with other components, the higher the price of the microphone, the better the quality.

Microphones have three common parts—a capsule containing the microphone element, internal wiring, and a housing or case. A recommended microphone for instrumental and choral recordings is the Audio-Technica AT8022 stereo condenser microphone (see Fig. 9.6). This is actually two mics in one. It has two capsules, one facing right and the other facing left, so you will get a stereo image when recording. The AT8022 requires a battery to work with a camcorder. The price is in the $400 range, but it is worth every penny. It can be connected to traditional sound gear via the typical XLR microphone connector, and it also gives you the option of connecting to your camcorder via a stereo mini cable.

Fig. 9.6
Audio-Technica AT8022

Microphone Stand

Another essential item to have when using external microphones is a good mic stand, such as the QuikLok A85 and similar models. Don't skimp on this item, as you want to protect the investment you have in the microphone and also be able to put it in the best position for recording. Expect to pay around $100 for a quality microphone stand.

Using an Audio Mixer

You can also connect an audio mixer to your camcorder. For example, if you already own an audio mixer, such as one of the popular Mackie models (www.mackie .com), you can connect the output of the mixer to the input of the camcorder. You will most likely need to get an audio adapter to convert the mixer output to a stereo mini plug. Another option is to route the headphone output of the mixer to the camera input. Be sure to monitor the audio input level to avoid distortion. Using a mixer will allow you to use your existing microphones and, if you wish, use several microphones to record an ensemble.

Microphone Recording Tips

Setting up microphones for optimal recording is a complicated topic beyond the scope of this book. Yet if you intend to record large ensembles using external microphones to get the best possible results, "MidWest Clinic Recording 101," by Dr. Ross Walter (www.midwestclinic.org/recording_101/), is an excellent article that highlights five ways to make the best recording:

1. Choose an appropriate space.

2. Use the proper equipment.

3. Position the microphones for the best blend. Set the microphones 12 to 15 feet in front of the ensemble, at a height of about 15 feet.

4. Set the recording levels carefully.

5. Don't adjust any levels during recording.

Another excellent resource for audio and microphone technique is a document from the Shure microphone company called "Audio Systems Guide for Music Educators." It can be downloaded free from the Shure website at www.shure

.com/stellent/groups/public/@gms_gmi_web_ug/documents/web_resource/us_
pro_audiomusiceducators_ea.pdf.

Page 6 of the Shure Audio Systems Guide describes the suggested microphone
placement for recording large ensembles: 2 to 3 feet in front of the ensemble and
2 to 3 feet above it. This requires external stands that can be adequately extended.
The best way to decide on microphone placement is by trial and error. You want
to be close to the ensemble to get good quality sound.

Video Editing Software Options

After making your video recording, you will want to trim the beginning and
ending sections and make other edits to get the best sound. Some video cameras,
such as the Flip series, can upload files directly to YouTube right from the camera.
However, you and your students will want to edit most of your videos to make
them look their best. You will also most likely need to cut down the length of the
videos, as YouTube has a 10-minute, 59-second limit.

TIP   Get your students involved in the technical side of your projects, especially
the editing. Many students have experience with video editing software,
and if not, they tend to be fast learners.

There are many video editing programs available, falling under three main
categories:

1. Free programs

2. Consumer editing programs

3. Professional editing programs

This is not an all-inclusive list of video editing software, but features some of the
more popular programs used in education.

Free Programs

Free video editing programs include iMovie (Mac) and Windows Movie Maker
(Windows). These programs are relatively simple but quite powerful, and provide

the basics for beginners to get started. Both of these programs are discussed in depth in chapter 10.

Consumer Editing Programs

Consumer-level editing programs are usually a good choice for students at the middle and high school levels. There may even be some courses at your school where students can use the software. If you find yourself looking for more video effects or editing options, consider purchasing one of the following programs that fits your needs. In the consumer area some popular titles include:

- ▸ Final Cut Express (Mac)
- ▸ Adobe Premiere Elements (Windows)
- ▸ Pinnacle Studio (Windows)

Final Cut Express (Mac). This is a "lite" version of the professional editing software Final Cut Pro, and a significant step up from the free Apple software iMovie. The cost is a very reasonable $199. The current version, Final Cut Express 4, allows you to import iMovie projects. It includes sophisticated plug-in effects and filters to add a cinematic look to your project, with an expansive library of high-quality transitions and filters including Soft Focus, Vignette, Light Rays, and Line Art. Final Cut Express will work with both standard and high-definition video. You can add multiple audio tracks to facilitate transitions. Final Cut Express also lets you edit in the timeline by simply dragging clips into place. The program automatically converts a variety of file formats.

Adobe Premiere Elements (Windows). This is a lite version of Adobe Premiere Pro, one of the most popular video editing programs in the industry. It has the same look and feel as the pro version but without the high cost. One of the advantages of Adobe Premiere Elements is that you can create multiple audio and video tracks to facilitate easy editing. It also lets you automatically upload files to YouTube.

Pinnacle Studio (Windows). This software family includes Pinnacle Studio, Pinnacle Studio Plus, and Pinnacle Studio Ultimate. Prices range from $49.99 to $129.99. One of the advantages of using a program such as Pinnacle is it offers a host of add-on packages. Pinnacle's effects raise it above the free option, Windows Media Player.

Professional Editing Programs

The programs in this category are designed for professional use. They might be found in some high school or higher-education video courses. Some of the more popular software options include:

1. Final Cut Pro (Mac)

2. Adobe Premiere Pro (Windows and Mac)

3. Avid Media Composer (Windows and Mac)

Final Cut Pro 7 (Mac). Apple boasts that this program is the first choice of professional editors worldwide. Final Cut Pro 7 delivers high-performance digital nonlinear editing and native support for virtually any video format. Finish your edit with professional color grading, add sophisticated 2D and 3D motion graphics, and mix surround sound or stereo soundtracks. Output to multiple delivery formats and create a professional DVD in SD or HD resolution. Integration with the full range of Apple professional products further extends the Final Cut Pro platform. At $999, it is not a cheap alternative but you get a lot of punch for the investment. Apple does offer generous discounts to educators and schools. Be sure to check the education discount options at www.apple.com/education/shop/.

Adobe Premiere Pro CS4 (Windows and Mac). This is the most popular professional editing program for Windows users, with a cost in the $800 range. The program works seamlessly with professional video equipment from Panasonic and Sony. It also works with both standard and high-definition video. It is part of the Adobe Creative Suite, a suite of graphic design, video editing, and Web development applications.

Avid Media Composer (Windows and Mac) is a professional software package offering a variety of creative tools, media management, and high-quality effects. You can mix and edit multiple formats in real time, and combine HD, SD, DV, and film formats. Avid offers Media Composer at an attractive educational discount price of $294.95 (the list price is $2,495), so be sure to purchase from an academic dealer.

Which Program Should I Choose?

There are so many options—which program is best for you? Check with the other teachers in your school to find out what they are using. What programs are taught in the high schools in your district or community? Also ask your students what video-editing programs they are using at home. Having a support group is helpful since video editing programs can take time to learn and master.

Also, in a school system, it is a good idea to use the same family of software. For example, an elementary school could use iMovie, a middle school Final Cut Express, and a high school or college Final Cut Pro. Other software companies such as Pinnacle and Adobe offer a range of programs to choose from. The advantage of using products from the same family of software is that you can transfer skills from one program to the other quite nicely.

Summary

It is important to understand how YouTube handles videos, and the best video and audio file formats and resolution to use for your videos. There are several options for recording video, including webcams and camcorders. When selecting a camcorder, choose a model with an external microphone input. In addition, consider purchasing accessories such as a tripod for the camcorder and an external light. For quality music recordings, an external microphone is recommended, such as a lavalier or stand-alone microphone. A stereo condenser microphone will give you the best audio recording quality. Proper microphone placement is important, and a microphone stand is recommended. The final piece in your studio is the video-editing software. Free, consumer-level, and professional programs are available. The recommended equipment and software will help ensure that your videos will be of the best quality and in the appropriate format for YouTube.

Creating Music Videos and Student Applications

Chapter Ten

In this chapter you will learn:

- ▶ How to produce your own videos in iMovie and Windows Movie Maker
- ▶ How to upload videos to YouTube
- ▶ How to connect with the YouTube Community
- ▶ How to integrate social networking sites
- ▶ How to solicit comments from outside reviewers
- ▶ How to promote your videos on YouTube
- ▶ Ideas for creating your own videos
- ▶ Ideas for lessons where your students record and upload videos

Producing Your Own Videos

Now that you have some background knowledge of the required equipment and software for capturing video (see chapter 9), the next step is to put that knowledge into action. Producing your own videos for use with your students and showing your students how to produce their own videos is a lot easier than it sounds. The most difficult part begins long before you start filming. The careful preparation needed before you begin shooting is similar to planning a lesson. The lessons that are well prepared usually go well, and those that are improvised are often less than stellar. The time you spend planning will always be time well spent.

The following is a step-by-step guide illustrating how to produce your own videos for use with your music students. These are the same basic steps your students will take to create their own YouTube videos if you allow them to do so. It is meant to serve as a generic model for all types of videos. At the conclusion of this guide are suggestions for what to include in specific videos.

Currently, YouTube has a maximum video time limit of 10:59. Keep this in mind as you plan your video. Shorter is always better in most cases. If you have a longer project in mind, then consider uploading it in several parts, such as part 1, part 2, and so forth.

Step One: Determine the Need

Before you get started shooting your video, ask yourself how your music program can be improved.

> ### YouTube Teaching Strategy 104
>
> Create teaching videos for your students and upload them to YouTube to supplement your music curriculum.

Do your students have access to quality instrumental music lessons? Do you have small group instruction for your performance ensembles? Do your students need a little extra help learning music theory skills? What National Standards are being addressed effectively by your curriculum? What standards are being neglected?

Once you answer some of these questions, you should be able to determine the needs of your program, which might tell you how producing videos for your students will enhance your program. For example, if your teaching schedule limits the amount of time you have for individual and/or small group instruction, producing instrumental lesson videos might help your students. If you have a large number of students auditioning for an honors ensemble that requires them to play a given excerpt, it might be quite a valuable teaching tool to post a video of yourself performing that excerpt for your students to listen to and learn from. If your students are preparing for the AP Music Theory exam, you can create your own study materials for them. As with all other teaching materials, once you have created them, they can be used again and again. The time needed upfront to create the videos may be extensive, but the long-term prospect for using the videos is well worth the expense. You not only can post teaching materials; you can also post musical performances and other videos for your curricular use. And you can share these same steps with your students for their video projects.

Step Two: Start Planning the Video

Once you have determined the need for a video, the next step is perhaps the most important. Effective planning combined with creativity will determine the success of the video. Things to consider during the initial planning stage include:

- ▶ Content outline
- ▶ Creating the storyboard
- ▶ Script writing/editing/revising
- ▶ Location of the shoot

While these may seem like obvious and possibly tedious steps, they should not be ignored. Going through this process will make the actual video shoot a much less painful process.

For the sake of example, let's focus on a specific content area for a video: a trombone lesson. The first step would be to create an outline for the lesson, focusing on the specific technique or musical excerpt being taught, for example the Trio section from John Philip Sousa's "The Stars and Stripes Forever." When creating the outline, ask yourself the following questions:

- ▶ What is the best way to present what I want the student to learn?
- ▶ How much talking should I do?
- ▶ How much playing should I do?
- ▶ Should I play a recording of the piece?
- ▶ How long is the video going to be?

Once you have answered these basic questions, you can create a simple outline for the content in your video. In this example, your outline might look like this:

1. Introduction

   a. Briefly talk about John Philip Sousa

   b. Briefly talk about "The Stars and Stripes Forever"

2. Discuss the focus of the lesson: The Trio section of "The Stars and Stripes Forever"

   a. Why is this section important?

      i. The trombone has melody

   b. Discuss the role of the Trio section in Sousa marches

3. Perform the Trio section without accompaniment

4. After the performance, discuss suggested techniques and dynamics

   a. Demonstrate each

5. Perform the Trio section with accompaniment

6. Ending

   a. Provide encouragement and context

TIP As you plan, keep in mind the 10:59 limit of YouTube videos. If your lesson is longer than that, you will have to break it into parts.

Once you have completed your content outline, you should create a storyboard for the actual video shoot. A *storyboard* provides you with a visual roadmap that you can use during the filming of your video. To create a storyboard, simply divide a sheet of paper into four equal squares and sketch or type a suggested video angle/location/background based on your outline. You can also plan on your storyboard what text (if any) will appear during your video. The video in this example would most likely only include a single camera angle of the teacher holding and playing the trombone, but it could also include both a close-up of the teacher describing the history of the piece and a wide-angle shot while they perform it—perhaps sitting down to demonstrate proper posture. The storyboard for this example might look like this:

1. Introduction	2. Focus of the Lesson: Trio Section
Close-up shot of teacher in the band room discussing the life of John Philip Sousa and the origins of "The Stars and Stripes Forever."	Shot of teacher sitting down with the music on a music stand. Holding trombone, but not in playing position. Discuss the Trio section.
3. Perform the Trio Section	4. Discuss Technique and Dynamics
Switch camera angle to wide angle — include full posture. Turn on metronome, and perform the entire Trio section twice.	Switch back to camera angle used in shot #2. Discuss the dynamic markings that Sousa included as well as technique suggestions.
5. Perform Trio Section w/Accompaniment	6. Ending
Switch back to the camera angle used in shot #3. Have someone press Play on CD accompaniment in stereo. Perform Trio again.	Use the camera angle used in shot #1. Discuss the role of the trombone in the Trio section and encourage students to practice.

Once you have completed the storyboard, the next step is to write the script. While some might skip this step and opt to speak extemporaneously, more often than not this will lead to multiple takes, and cause the video shoot to be much longer than if there is a script available. It is strongly recommended that you take the time to write the script and either print it out in a large font so that you can read it while filming, or memorize it in short sections and plan your shots accordingly.

The last step in the planning stage is to choose a location for your video shoot. Lighting is perhaps the most important factor (see chapter 9) in this choice, and the best way to find a good location for your video is to experiment with some test shots and see how they look. Off-the-shelf digital video cameras as well as built-in webcams are often far more forgiving than much more expensive ones. Your classroom or home studio is probably the most obvious place to shoot your videos, but remember that people look pretty pale under fluorescent lighting. If you don't like the way you look, try adding some halogen lightbulbs to the mix. For a more artistic feel, you might even add some lighting gels—ask your school A/V or TV studio person for some assistance. You can get really carried away with this step. Just remember, the video might be viewed by millions, so always try to look your best.

Last but certainly not least, think about the best time of day to shoot your video. If you are working at home, this might not be an issue at all, but if you are shooting your video in school, you need to consider the extraneous noise that occurs during the school day. Things like the school bell, announcements, and student interruptions can really cause havoc while shooting your video. You might be best off coming in before school or waiting until after school to have a quiet environment to shoot your video in.

Step Three: Get Your Gear Ready

Now that you have prepared your script and storyboard and planned your shoot, it is time to make sure that you have all of the necessary hardware and software ready (see chapter 9). The simplest approach is to use the built-in video camera on your computer, which normally includes some type of basic video-editing software. On a Mac, you most likely will have a built-in video camera (or webcam) and microphone as well as iMovie from the iLife Suite, which is included free on every Mac. On a PC, you may very well need to purchase a separate webcam (see chapter 9 for suggestions) as well as video-editing software, though Windows Movie Maker is a free option and a good place to start. For more advanced stand-alone video cameras and editing software and microphone recording techniques, refer to chapter 9.

The most important things to consider when preparing to shoot your video include:

- Hard drive space—most videos are quite large

  It is a good idea to purchase a stand-alone hard disk drive to both store and edit your videos. There are countless brands to choose from, and they are quite inexpensive. Saving videos to an external hard drive saves your computer's available hard disk space, thus improving system performance.

- Deciding whether you are going to capture your video on a camera or directly on your computer

  Capturing your video on a video camera provides you with far greater portability options than if you record it directly to your computer's hard drive using a built-in webcam. Capturing video on a camera also eliminates the need to use your computer's hard disk space to store the video

- Choosing your camera (see chapter 9)

- Deciding which software program(s) you will need to edit your video (see chapter 9)

- Determining the file format of your video (see chapter 9)

- Deciding if you need screen-capture software

If you plan on using some sort of computer screen capture during your video (especially helpful when creating software tutorials), you have a number of options. There are literally hundreds of screen-capture software titles available, many of which are shareware or freeware (search for "video screen capture" to find these). Recommended titles include:

- SnapZPro (Mac)
- iShowU (Mac)
- ScreenCast (Mac or PC)
- CamtasiaStudio (PC)
- Jing (Mac or PC)
- Snagit (Windows)

Each of these computer screen-capture titles allows you to save files in a variety of formats. Be sure to check the default settings before incorporating them into your video project.

Step Four: Shoot Your Video

Now that you have everything ready, you can begin filming your video. For the trombone lesson mentioned above, for example, you could shoot the video in both the band room and the teacher's office, using a stand-alone camcorder as well as a floor-standing tripod to hold the camera steady during filming.

Here is a list of tips for shooting video with a camcorder:

- **Avoid zooming in and out.** Position the camera at the desired distance from your subject. Using the zoom option does not take advantage of the full video quality of your camera. If you need to zoom in and out while filming, do so slowly.
- **Make sure the lighting is adequate.** If your subject is not backlit, they will appear to be very dark; if they are lit too brightly, they may appear very pale.
- **Don't pan the camera too much or too quickly.** Try to maintain a single shot when filming something like a person talking or performing. If filming a large group, be sure to pan (move the camera back and forth) slowly, rather than making quick pans.

▸ **Keep it steady.** If available, use a tripod. Holding a camera in your hands makes it difficult to take a steady shot of your subject.

▸ **Use an external microphone to record audio** (see chapter 9). Some video cameras have an audio input. Whenever feasible use an external microphone to capture the best possible audio recording. This is especially important when recording musical performances.

▸ **Always use the highest resolution possible.** Many video camera models allow users to choose the resolution. Always try to capture in the highest resolution possible. You can always compress the file later. Currently, YouTube recommends 1280 × 720 (16 × 9 HD) and 640 × 480 (4:3 SD). There is no required minimum resolution—in general, the higher resolution the better, and HD resolution is preferred. For older content, lower resolution is unavoidable. See YouTube Help for more info: www .google.com/support/youtube/bin/answer.py?hl=en&answer=132460.

▸ **Stick to the storyboard.** If you have taken the time to create a storyboard, use it to guide you through the filming process.

▸ **Set the white balance.** It is important to focus the video camera on something white before recording your video. This will avoid issues with color and brightness later.

Once you have addressed each of these tips, go ahead and shoot your video. You might find that it will take you a bit longer than you initially anticipated. Plan on shooting multiple takes of each scene from your storyboard so they can be edited together using the video-editing software. Reading from a prepared script during the video will help cut down on the number of necessary takes. If, however, you are speaking extemporaneously during the video, it may take you a number of takes to get it right.

When using a video camera, don't worry about recording, stopping, rewinding, and recording again to save space on your video camera. Just record each take at the end of the previous take, and decide which takes to use when you edit the video on the computer. You just might find that there are usable pieces in each take that you can splice together later. While it is always optimal to get one clean take, you might need to edit a few together.

Computer screen-capture software allows you to select an area on the computer screen to capture, including the entire screen. When launched, the software typically requires you (they all function in a similar manner) to select the video format and how much of the screen to record. Most software allows the user to record audio simultaneously. While recording, the software will capture everything that happens on your screen, including opening and closing applications, moving the mouse, as well as any sound or voiceover. Think of computer screen–capturing software as someone looking over your shoulder and recording your every move on the computer.

TIP   Make sure the video is less than 10 minutes, smaller than 1 GB in size, in an acceptable format, and you're ready to upload it. Consider breaking longer projects up into several projects 10 minutes or less, and call them part 1, part 2, and so forth.

Step Five: Edit Your Video

Chapter 9 lists many of the software titles available for video editing. Both Mac and Windows computers have free video editing software preloaded when they come out of the box. On the Mac side, there is iMovie (see Fig. 10.1), and any version of the iLife Suite can handle the basic editing functions necessary in this tutorial. At the time of this writing the most current version of iMovie is iMovie '09, which will be illustrated below. On the PC side, Windows Movie Maker (see Fig. 10.2) comes as part of the Windows operating system (Windows XP and Vista). Both of these titles provide users with powerful editing options. For additional editing software options, see chapter 9.

Fig. 10.1
Apple iMovie

Before we explore these two programs, it is important to review how to get video from your camera onto your computer's hard drive. All video cameras come with some type of proprietary cable that connects the camera to the computer through either a USB or a FireWire port. Both iMovie and Windows Movie Maker have functions that will import the video from the camcorder directly into the program. It is recommended that you connect your camera to your computer before launching the video editing software. This will ensure that the software recognizes your camera as a peripheral when it launches.

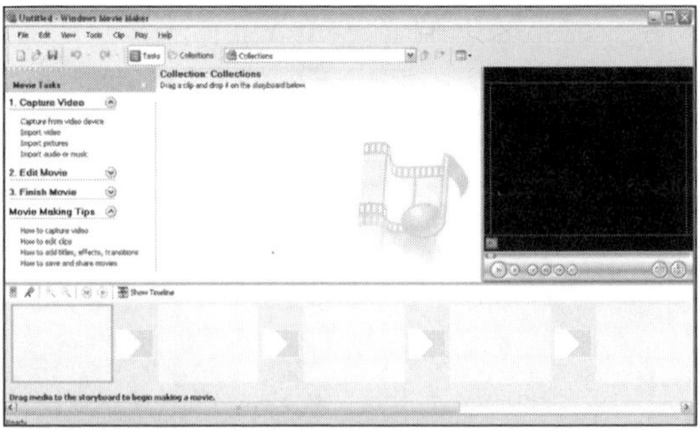

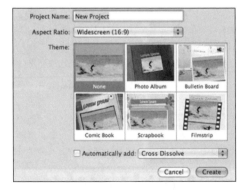

Fig. 10.2
Windows Movie Maker

Editing Video with iMovie

The first step in editing video with iMovie is to get the raw video footage transferred from your camera into the computer. Before launching iMovie, follow these steps:

1. Connect your video camera to the computer through the available connection (USB or FireWire).

2. Once connected, turn the camera on. Be sure that it is set to either VTR mode, Play mode, or VCR mode (whichever is available).

Once you have completed these steps, launch iMovie by double-clicking on the iMovie icon. Once the program opens, click on the File menu and select New Project. You will be greeted by the New Project menu (see Fig. 10.3). Here you can name your project, choose from a variety of project templates, and specify the aspect ratio of your film. For optimal results in YouTube, select the Standard 4:3 ratio rather than Widescreen. You can also select the default transition setting between video clips from this menu by selecting the Automatically Add check box and choosing from the many options in the drop-down menu. Once you have made your selections, click Create.

Once the project opens, you will see the iMovie project environment (see Fig. 10.1). If you would like to import the video you have taken

Fig. 10.3
iMovie New Project menu

from your camcorder, select File > Import from Camera (make sure your camera is connected to your computer before launching iMovie). If you do not have your video camera correctly connected to your computer, iMovie will automatically use the video picture from your built-in webcam, if one is installed. Assuming that your camera is properly

Fig. 10.4
iMovie Import From

connected, you will then see the Import From menu (see Fig. 10.4). Here you can select individual clips to import by clicking on Manual import (see Fig. 10.5) and selecting only the clips you'd like to import, or you can import all of the clips by selecting Import All. Once you click the Import button, you will see the Import All menu (see Fig. 10.6), which allows you to create a new event name, add clips to an existing event, and automatically analyze the video clips for stabilization (iMovie will actually eliminate most of the unsteady movements during the video). Once you have made your selections, click Import.

Fig. 10.5
iMovie Manual Import

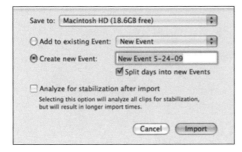

Fig. 10.6
iMovie Import All menu

If you have video clips already on your computer that you've made using computer screen-capture software or that you've downloaded from the Internet, you can add those clips to your iMovie project by choosing File > Import and selecting Movies if the movie is already on your hard drive, Camera Archive if you imported the film from your camera in the past, or iMovie HD Project if you'd like to incorporate an existing project.

Once you have all of your video source material selected, these clips will appear in the iMovie Event Library at the bottom of the screen (see Fig. 10.7). This library contains all of the video clips that you have imported into your computer. To begin creating your movie, start by highlighting the desired video clip (or section) and dragging it from the Event Library window to the Project window in the upper left corner of the screen (see Fig. 10.8). To add clips, repeat the process and add each clip to the end of the previous video clip. You may drag as many clips as you like into this Project window but keep in mind that YouTube has a 10-minute/1 GB time/size limit.

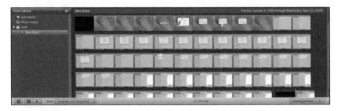

Fig. 10.7
iMovie Event Library window

Fig. 10.8
iMovie Project window

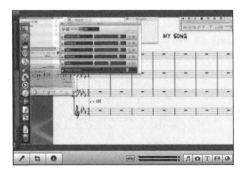

Fig. 10.9
iMovie Video Preview window

Fig. 10.10
iMovie Play controls

You can preview your video clips in the Video Preview window (see Fig. 10.9) at any time by pressing the Play button. To see the video clip in full-screen mode, select the Full Screen Mode button (see Fig. 10.10).

In addition to video clips, you may add audio, pictures, titles, credits, video transitions, maps and backgrounds, and video special effects to your project. To access these features, select the appropriate icon from the toolbar below the Video Preview window (see Fig. 10.9). To add audio to your video, click the musical note icon and select the desired audio file from your file browser. To add a picture to your video, click on the camera icon and select the desired picture file from your file browser. To add titles and text to your video, click on the "T" icon to access the Titles menu (see Fig. 10.11). To select a style of text animation, click on the desired selection and drag it to the Project window.

To add a transition from one clip to another in your video project, click on the transition icon to access the Transitions menu (see Fig. 10.12). To select a style of transition, click on the desired transition and drag it in between the video clips that you would like to transition. To add video special effects, click on the "i" icon to access the Inspector (see Fig. 10.13). Here you can click on the Video Effects menu (see Fig. 10.14) and select the desired effect for your video clip.

Fig. 10.11
iMovie Titles menu

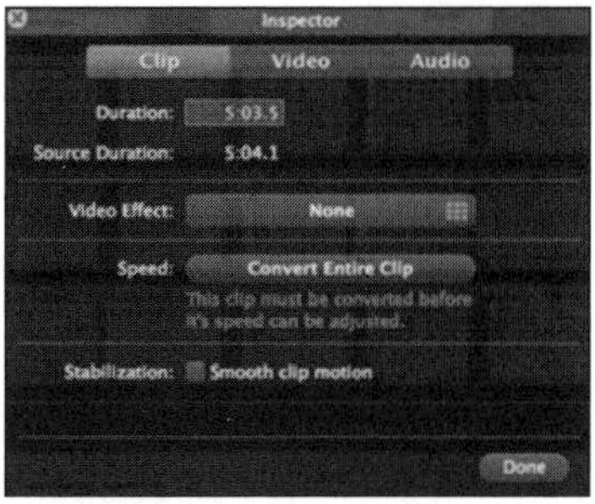

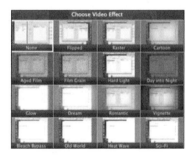

Fig. 10.13
iMovie Inspector

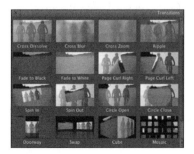

Fig. 10.14
iMovie Inspector

Fig. 10.12
iMovie Transitions menu

Once you have added all the text, audio, effects, and transitions that you'd like, preview your finished product by clicking on the Full Screen Play button. If you are satisfied with the results, save your movie. To do so, click on the Share menu and select the YouTube option. You will then see the Publish to YouTube menu (see Fig. 10.15). This menu provides a very convenient way to upload your movies directly to your YouTube account.

Fig. 10.15
iMovie Publish to YouTube menu

First, enter your YouTube account information by clicking the Add button and entering your YouTube account name. Next, type your password into the appropriate field. Then, select the Category that you would like your video to be displayed under. Next, type in a title, description, and relevant tags for your video. Finally, select the Medium setting under Size to ensure the best quality for your video. Once you have entered this information, click Next. You must then agree to the YouTube Terms of Service regarding copyright and click Publish. Your Internet browser will then open and take you to your YouTube account. If your account information is correct, the video will automatically begin uploading to your YouTube account. If you would prefer to save your video to your computer's hard drive before uploading it to YouTube, choose Share > Export Movie…, select the size (640 × 480 is the standard size for YouTube), and click Export.

For a video tutorial on creating videos with iMovie, visit: www.apple.com/support/ ilife/tutorials/imovie/.

Editing Video with Windows Movie Maker

As with iMovie, the first step is to transfer the raw video footage from your camcorder onto your computer hard drive by connecting the camera to the computer, turning the camera on, setting the camera to VTR Play, or VCR mode, and launching the software. To launch Windows Movie Maker, click on the Start menu, then choose All Programs > Windows Movie Maker (the program may be located in the Accessories menu). Next, choose File > New Project. To capture the video from your camera, choose Capture Video from the Movie Tasks section (see Fig. 10.16). Then select your video camera from the available devices window and click Next. You will then be asked to name your footage and select the folder where you wish to store it. If you have an external hard drive, select it here and click Next.

On the next screen you can select the video quality for your project. If you are storing your video on an external hard drive, select Best Quality for Playback on My Computer. This selection will actually save your video in the WMV (Windows Media Video) format. If you plan on creating a DVD for the video, select Digital Device Format. You can also select Other Settings to capture the video in other formats; you should select the first option for YouTube videos.

Fig. 10.16
Windows Movie Maker
Movie Tasks menu

Click Next to move on. On the next screen you will be asked to select your desired capture method. You can choose either "Capture the entire tape automatically" or "Capture parts of the tape manually." If you select the first option, the computer will upload everything from your video camera, which will take quite some time, depending on how much video you have recorded. If you select the manual option, you can choose the exact clips to upload. Select the first option if you want to be able to edit all of the footage that you shot. Click Next, and the video will begin transferring to your computer. If you know the exact clip(s) you want to upload, choose the manual option and click Next. You will then see a screen that provides a preview of the video as well as playback controls and a Start Capture and Stop Capture button. Once you have selected and named all of the clips you wish to upload, select Finish. If you plan on incorporating content from computer screen-capturing software, you should click Import Video from the Movie Tasks menu (see Fig. 10.16) and select the file(s) that you wish to import into the project.

Now that you have all of your video material on your computer, it's time to edit the footage into a finished, polished video. To begin, select Create New Project from the File menu (you can also click CTRL+N). Next, click on Collections at the top of the screen (see Fig. 10.17) and select the video clips that you would like to use in your project. If you have just imported video from your camcorder, you should see it in the window. Select the

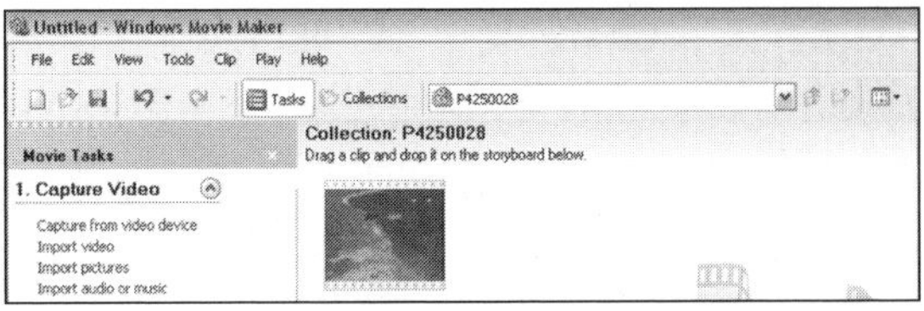

Fig. 10.17
Windows Movie Maker Collections area

desired video and click Play to preview. The video will play in the video playback window (see Fig 10.18).

Adding Video Clips

To add a video clip to your project, drag it from the Collections window into the Timeline at the bottom of the screen. Similar to the editing interface of iMovie, the Timeline provides a visual representation of the order in which the video clips will be played. To add additional clips, just repeat this process. Each clip you drag will be added to the

Fig. 10.18
Windows Movie Maker Video Playback window

end of the previous clip. You can add as many clips as you like in Windows Movie Maker, but keep in mind that YouTube has a 10-minute/1 GB time/size limit.

Once you have all of your clips in your timeline, you can then add things such as titles, credits, video transition effects, and special video effects. To access these editing functions, expand the Edit Movie section on the left side of the screen (see Fig. 10.19). Here you can select "View video effects" to preview all of the various special effects you can add to your video clips (see Fig. 10.20), "View video transitions" to preview the transition effects between video clips (see Fig. 10.21), or "Make titles or credits" to add titles and credits to your video project.

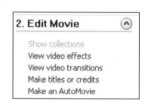

Fig. 10.19
Windows Movie Maker Edit Movie section

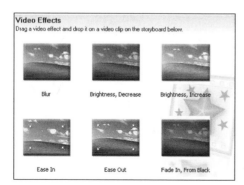

Fig. 10.20
Windows Movie Maker Video Effects

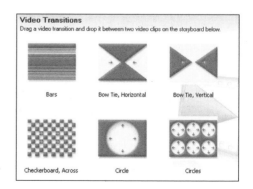

Fig. 10.21
Windows Movie Maker Video Transitions

Viewing Your Video

In order to see your video after adding titles, effects, and transitions, click on the Rewind Storyboard button (Ctrl+Q) and then click the Play button (Ctrl+W) (see Fig. 10.22). If you are satisfied with the final product, save your project. To Save, click on the Finish Movie section on the left side of the screen and select the "Save to my computer" option (see Fig. 10.23). While you can also save your movie to a CD, the Web, e-mail, or your camera, you should select the "Save to my computer" option when preparing videos to be uploaded to YouTube.

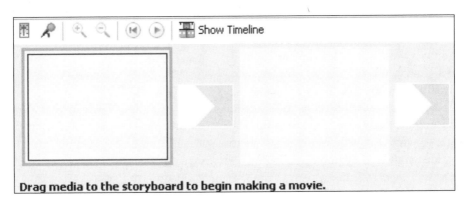

Fig. 10.22
Windows Movie Maker view video

Windows Movie Maker saves movies as .wmv files, which is one of the acceptable formats for uploading videos to YouTube. To ensure the best quality, however, follow these steps to save:

Fig. 10.23
Windows Movie Maker Finish Movie section

1. Choose "Save to my computer."

2. Enter a name for your movie, select the location to save your movie, and click Next.

3. On the Movie Settings page, click on "Show more choices" and then click "Other settings."

4. Select Video for broadband (512 Kbps) and click Next.

5. Click Finish.

Unlike iMovie, Windows Movie Maker does not have an option for uploading finished videos directly to YouTube. Therefore, it's time to look at the process for uploading videos to YouTube. For a YouTube video tutorial on how to create movies with Windows Movie Maker, go to www.youtube.com/watch?v=JZXK68NS7gU.

Step Six: Upload Your Video to YouTube

Whether you have used iMovie, Windows Movie Maker, or more advanced video-editing software to create your movie on a Mac or PC, the uploading process to YouTube is exactly the same (although you can upload your videos directly to YouTube from iMovie). In order to upload videos to YouTube, you must first have a YouTube account. Refer to chapter 3 for details on how to set up an account if you have not already done so. The following step-by-step instructions will help you to upload your videos to YouTube:

Fig. 10.24
YouTube Video File Upload window

1. Log in to your YouTube account.

2. Click on My Videos from the menu under your account name.

3. Click on New > Video Upload.

4. Click on Upload Video, and then select the movie that you would like to upload.

5. Enter the title for your video on the video upload screen (see Fig. 10.24). This is the title that will appear above your video on YouTube.

6. Enter a description for your video. This description will appear to the right of your video. Provide a concise description of what viewers will see during the video. You can also include a link to a website in this description if you want to.

7. Enter tags—these are words that will help locate your video when people search for videos on YouTube and Google. While this is not required, it helps others to find your work.

8. Choose a video category. There are quite a few categories to choose from, but you might consider selecting either Education or Music. You can only select one category for your video.

9. Decide whether you want your video to be Public or Private. If you select the "Share with the world" option, anyone will be able to view your video. If you select Private, you can invite up to 25 people to view your video, but it will not be available to anyone else.

10. Click Save Changes.

Once your video has been successfully uploaded, it will immediately appear live on YouTube. Try searching for the title of your video to check that it plays correctly. If for some reason it doesn't, you can always delete the video from the My Videos page in your account settings. You can also include annotations and captions in your videos by clicking the Annotations button on the My Videos page. Annotations and captions are the text bubbles and captions that appear layered on top of the video while it is playing. While there are some educational purposes for this feature, it is not necessary. You can also decide whether to allow comments on your video, comment ratings, video ratings, whether others can embed your video on their websites, and whether others can post video responses to your video. See chapter 3 for more information on these features.

For more information on all of the video uploading options available on YouTube, including the recently added HD video, visit the YouTube Video Uploading Help site at http://help.youtube.com/support/youtube/bin/topic .py?hl=en&topic=16560.

Step Seven: Publicize Your Video

Now that your video is on YouTube, you should let others know it is there. There are a few easy ways to accomplish this task:

▶ **Use the Share options that are located underneath your video once it is posted to YouTube** (see Fig. 10.25). If you have a MySpace account, you can post your video directly to your MySpace page by selecting the MySpace option. You can e-mail anyone a link to your video by selecting the Send Video option. By selecting the Facebook option, you can post your video directly to your Facebook account. You may also click "More share options" to upload your video to other social networking websites such as Twitter and Digg.

| ♡ Favorite | ⇥ Share | ✛ Playlists | ⚑ Flag | |
| MySpace | Send Video | Facebook | | (more share options) |

Fig. 10.25
YouTube Share options

▶ **You can embed your video on any website** by copying the code that appears in the Embed window to the right of your video on YouTube. Once you have copied the code, you can use the HTML editing function that comes with any website-editing software to paste this embed code into the source code of your website. You can customize the embedding function by clicking on the gear icon to the right of the Embed window (see Fig. 10.26).

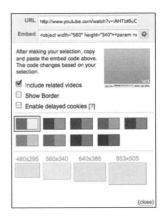

Fig. 10.26
YouTube embedding options

▶ **You can send a message to your YouTube Channel subscribers and Group members** to let them know you posted a new video. See chapter 3 for a detailed description of how to set up a group specifically for use with your students. Anyone who subscribes to your YouTube channel (such as your students) will receive an automatic notification that you have posted a new video. The Group menu allows you to easily send messages to all group members.

▶ **Promote your video.** This option requires you to pay YouTube to promote your video. This is most likely an unnecessary option for music educators who teach in a school environment, but if you plan on using YouTube to publicize your private teaching studio or business venture, it might be a worthwhile investment to investigate the video promotion options that YouTube provides. For more information on promoting your videos, click on the Promote Video button that appears under your video in the Video Upload section of your YouTube Account Settings.

▶ **Get users to comment on, rate, and share your video with others.** On YouTube, the more these three interactive features are used, the more attention your video will receive. If you are an active blogger, post a link to the video in your blog. If you are sharing the video with your students, require them to comment on the video and rate it. Popularity on the Internet is measured by how many people link to, talk about, and share your work.

Suggested Video Topics for Music Educators

The list below offers suggestions for some of the many topics a music educator might consider making a video on for use in their music programs.

YouTube Teaching Strategy 105

Instrumental/Vocal Music Lessons

- ► Basics: How to set up the instrument, how to produce a sound
- ► Practice tips: Overview of the best ways to practice a given instrument
- ► Warm-up exercises: How to properly warm up on a given instrument or voice type
- ► Technique: How to play high/low notes, breathing, scales, articulations
- ► Repertoire: Videos on specific pieces of music (All State selections)

YouTube Teaching Strategy 106

Instrument Care Lessons

- ► Basic instrument care
- ► How to perform simple repairs

YouTube Teaching Strategy 107

Music Theory Lessons

- ► Fundamentals of music, with screen shots of sheet music
- ► How to incorporate audio files into your soundtrack
- ► Scrolling scores

YouTube Teaching Strategy 108

Software Tutorials

- ► Basic functions of software used in class
- ► Specific tutorials on functions required for given projects

YouTube Teaching Strategy 109

Project Examples

If you require students to score films or do other types of multimedia projects, try creating a project yourself and posting it to provide students with an example.

YouTube Teaching Strategy 110

Program Information Videos

▸ Provide an overview of the requirements for participation in your music program

▸ Provide informational videos about music department events, including marching band shows, concerts, parades, trips, and other functions

▸ Create recruitment videos for students

▸ Create Back to School Night presentations

YouTube Teaching Strategy 111

Upload Student Ensemble Performances

▸ If performing copyright-protected works, first you must obtain any required permissions from the publisher(s) whose work appears in the video.

▸ Show performances of original student work

▸ Take videos of yourself conducting for critique and reflection

▸ Take videos of yourself teaching for critique and reflection

YouTube Lesson Plans

Graduate students in Dr. Frankel's Intermediate/Advanced Application of Music Technology course at Columbia University were asked to write a lesson plan based around using YouTube in the music classroom. While quite a few students submitted lesson plans, the following three exemplify the types of learning activities that can be facilitated by the website.

One Is the Loneliest Number:
Creating a One-Man Barbershop Quartet on YouTube

By Stephanie Gravelle

A cappella groups have swept the choral nation. Every major university boasts at least one such ensemble, with names like Fundamentally Sound, DisChord, and A Whole Step Up. They have become mini-Greek organizations complete with hazing rites, secret handshakes, and vocal traditions. At any high school choir camp, strains of "In the Still of the Night" and "Uptown Girl" can be heard long into the night, sung by a spontaneously arranged quartet composed of kids from different cities.

Because of today's technology, a would-be barber-shopper does not need to search for three other voices to fulfill a craving for some vocal harmonization. There are numerous examples of barbershop enthusiasts who create video montages containing multiple tracks with themselves singing each of the parts of the quartet. Some examples include:

- ▶ www.youtube.com/watch?v=8JWTD-Zcsrs
- ▶ www.youtube.com/watch?v=h_j9QbUXVIY
- ▶ www.youtube.com/watch?v=wC4eGVseOd4

Lesson Objective

Each student will create a four-part a cappella arrangement of a song, record each part, and post a mosaic video to YouTube.

MENC National Standards

1. Singing, alone and with others, a varied repertoire of music.

4. Composing and arranging music within specified guidelines.

5. Reading and notating music.

6. Listening to, analyzing, and describing music.

7. Evaluating music and music performances.

Purpose

This assignment gives the singers in an a cappella group a chance to construct an arrangement all their own and share it with a broad audience. Arrangers deal with an array of musical problems, such as harmony, texture, vocal range, and style. Students should be familiar with four-part harmony and the software needed to create their own video.

Materials Needed

- A favorite public-domain song

- A video camera

- Computer with the following software:

  Video: FinalCut Pro, Adobe Premiere, or Media Composer

  Audio: Any digital audio workstation (DAW) software, including GarageBand, Audacity, Pro Tools, Logic, or Sonar

Anticipatory Set

Watch a YouTube video of a multitrack tag or full song from the examples listed above.

Procedure

- Have students select a public domain song to create an a cappella arrangement of.

- Have students record a bass track for their arrangement into the available DAW software. Some may choose to start with the lowest part; others the melody.

- Export each individual part as a separate audio file.

- Have students record a video while singing each individual part in the arrangement. This can be done either while actually recording the part, or the students may choose to lip sync the part. It is much easier to videotape the actual performance than to try and line up the video with the audio later.

- ▸ Record each accompanying part using the original track as a guide for audio and visual cues.

- ▸ Import all of the separate audio and video tracks into the available video editing software.

- ▸ Create a mosaic/multitrack video.

- ▸ There are quite a few tutorials that can be found online on how to create a split screen such as those found in the suggested examples above. Each video software title also includes Help guides that explain how to create the split-screen effect.

- ▸ Post each completed project to YouTube.

- ▸ Require students to post comments about each performance.

Check for Student Understanding

Discuss with students why it is beneficial to post original music on a site like YouTube. What are the pros and cons of singing with only one vocalist?

Closure

Once all the assignments are posted on YouTube, the class will have a screening day. The other members of the class will critique each student's video, and perhaps one or two arrangements could be selected and performed by a large group at an upcoming concert. Another option is to screen the actual video during a concert. Students would introduce their pieces to the audience and, instead of sharing the stage with the rest of the ensemble, could have a moment in the spotlight as a group of one.

Extensions

- ▸ Have students in the instrumental music program record themselves performing duets, trios, or quartets, playing each individual part in the same manner.

- ▸ Have students record videos of other students in the class performing their arrangement.

Film Scoring Lesson Plan

By Pamela Golkin

Technology has become an integral part of our students' lives. To ignore this is to ignore the progress of the world and its capacity for creativity. This project is one that will easily span a full semester, with an emphasis on promoting creativity through the use of technology. The project is designed for high school students, primarily seniors. The objective is to score a film in a way that creates a visual understanding of an original music composition. The film will have to reflect the nature of the student's original music in some visual color, shape, or form. At the completion of the project, the videos will be uploaded onto a private YouTube Web page supervised by teachers, where the class can view other students' work and comment on those videos.

Lesson Objective

Students will compose a musical score to accompany a given film clip following specified guidelines.

MENC National Standards

4. Composing and arranging music within specified guidelines.

5. Reading and notating music.

6. Listening to, analyzing, and describing music.

7. Evaluating music and music performances.

8. Understanding relationships between music, the other arts, and disciplines outside the arts.

Purpose

To learn how to use GarageBand, Sibelius, iMovie, and iTunes (or suitable PC equivalents) as a guide to creating an original score that coincides with film. In addition, students will be encouraged to help each other to learn the technology. Students will be asked to give constructive criticism of their peers, as well as encourage them through the creative process.

Although this is not a project that is geared toward group participation, it can easily be converted to one, where the students, in small two- or three-person groups, would create this music video. Don't be surprised if students end up creating more than one film for this project.

Materials Needed

  - ▸ Mac computers with GarageBand, iMovie, iTunes, and Internet access.* If only PCs are available, software programs such as Mixcraft, Sonar, Pinnacle, and Windows Movie Maker can be used
  - ▸ Microphones and piano keyboards for the computers are optional
  - ▸ A computer projector, so the teacher can show students how each program is operated
  - ▸ Public-domain film clips

*If students have learned how to use the notation software Sibelius, they can create a film score for their video using this program. Although it will make composing the music a little more challenging, it would be a great way for the students to create music from scratch while learning about notation. It would be helpful for students to have a music theory background before using this program.

Anticipatory Set

In doing this project, it is important to talk about YouTube and find out what students think about this Internet application. Teachers can discuss access to music and film through the Internet and intellectual property rights.

In order to obtain film materials that are copyright and royalty free, teachers can go to www.archive.org. Because it is impossible to screen what students see on the Internet, teachers could download about five to ten videos off this website, which students could then manipulate to create an original film. This way students do not need to look on the Internet for videos. Students could be encouraged to use homemade videos in their films, provided the material is appropriate for a school environment.

Procedure

Note: This is a long-term project in which students will need a lot of time and access to computers.

  - ▸ In the first few classes, GarageBand or equivalent DAW software would be taught. Giving the students mini projects would be a good idea, so they can practice using the program. Creating tracks, loops, and being able to input audio will be the primary focus of students' initial learning of GarageBand or an equivalent DAW.

▸ Following this, students will learn how to use iMovie, or equivalent PC video editing software. iMovie will allow students to splice the film(s) that they are working with to make one cohesive video.

▸ Once the video is completed the students will import it into GarageBand or an equivalent DAW to create the score for their film.

▸ To upload the videos to YouTube, they will have to be exported from GarageBand into iTunes. iTunes then converts the video and music to a file that can then be uploaded onto YouTube.

Check for Student Understanding

For this project to be successful, teachers must make themselves accessible for students if they need help. There is a lot to learn in these programs. Many applications require reinforcement and a supervising teacher.

Closure

It is important for each student's video to be shown at the end of the project. When a student is able to see his/her work up on a big screen they get a true sense of pride and ownership. Students will be encouraged to comment on each other's videos through the YouTube website, as well as in class when the videos are shown.

Extensions

This is a project that could easily be extended to the rest of the school. The teacher could sponsor an original score and music video contest, or talent show. Using the same guidelines for the in-class project, this extension would allow the rest of the students in the school to participate in creating this project during their free time.

Using YouTube for Performance Critique

By Daniel Antonelli

Lesson Objective

Students will learn about the process of critique by viewing videos on YouTube and posting their critiques, as well as posting their own performances on the site for class critique.

MENC National Standards

1. Singing, alone and with others, a varied repertoire of music.

2. Performing on instruments, alone and with others, a varied repertoire of music.

6. Listening to, analyzing, and describing music.

7. Evaluating music and music performances.

Purpose

▶ Students will learn to improve their posture/technique using YouTube as a visual tool

▶ Implementing technology (YouTube) in the classroom

▶ Students will learn to analyze and give constructive criticism by examining videos from peers and professional musicians

▶ Furthering constructive criticism

▶ Helping students develop a critical eye through a visual aid (YouTube) in addition to written directions only

▶ Learning how to accept, give, and apply constructive criticism from peers

▶ Fostering social skills/working with peers

Materials needed

▶ Computer with Internet access

▶ Digital video camera

▶ Basic video-editing software

Procedure

Students will view videos assigned by the teacher of professional performances demonstrating proper technique to analyze, critique, and further discuss in a classroom setting. A few examples will be viewed and analyzed in class to provide students with more experience. The teacher will then assign appropriate YouTube videos for students to analyze as homework, and hand in a written analysis of the YouTube video.

Students will then record themselves practicing their instrument or voice, and post it on YouTube. The teacher will view the video and provide visual and aural feedback showing correction and instruction and post it on YouTube as a video response for the student to view.

Students will form small groups according to their instrument/voice and then view each other's practicing videos on YouTube for peer critique.

<u>Closure</u>

Students will post comments on each other's videos, focusing on constructive comments for performance improvement.

<u>Extensions</u>

Discuss how effective YouTube was as a learning tool, and if students were comfortable using it.

Summary

Producing, uploading, and promoting videos on YouTube is essentially free if you already own a computer with Internet access. This incredible tool allows music educators to connect with students in ways never before imaginable. The tutorials included in this chapter provide a basic introduction to video editing. For more opportunities for professional development, consider taking a multimedia course such as those offered by TI:ME, or a video-editing course. There are numerous online courses and graduate courses that focus on creating videos, as well as countless books. Remember that the hardest part of creating a video is developing the content. Everything else is relatively simple once you get the hang of it. Start by creating one video for your students per school year and see how it goes. You just might find that shooting, editing, uploading, and sharing videos will be a frequent event. Also, consider projects where students upload their own videos to YouTube. This can be a valuable learning tool for students in a variety of ways.

Notes

Chapter 1

[1] IMDb.com, "America's Funniest Home Videos," http://www.imdb.com/title/tt0098740/ (accessed March 16, 2009).

[2] Meghan Keane, "YouTube Goes Legit, Begins Streaming Approved CBS Content," Wired.com, October 10, 2008, http://blog.wired.com/business/2008/10/youtube-goes-le.html (accessed March 16, 2009).

[3] YouTube Symphony Orchestra FAQ, http://www.google.com/intl/en/landing/ytsymphony/faq.pdf (accessed June 16, 2009).

[4] Anne Midgette, "Live, From Carnegie Hall: It's the YouTube Symphony Orchestra," *Washington Post*, December 2, 2008, page C07.

[5] Ibid.

[6] Mike Harvey, "Britons Join YouTube Symphony Orchestra," Times Online, March 3, 2009, http://entertainment.timesonline.co.uk/tol/arts_and_entertainment/music/article5836109.ece (accessed March 13, 2009).

[7] Ibid.

[8] YouTube Symphony Orchestra, www.youtube.com/symphony/ (accessed March 13, 2009).

[9] Roi Carthy, "Kutiman Killed the Video Star," TechCrunch, March 11, 2009, http://www.techcrunch.com/2009/03/11/kutiman-killed-the-video-star/ (accessed June 16, 2009).

[10] Ibid.

[11] Ibid.

[12] Kutiman-Thru-you-01-Mother of All Funk Chords, http://www.youtube.com/watch?v=tprMEs-zfQA (accessed June 16, 2009).

[13] Kutiman-Thru-you-03-I'm New, http://www.youtube.com/watch?v=EsBfj6khrG4 (accessed June 16, 2009).

[14] Lawrence Lessig, *Remix: Making Art and Commerce Thrive in the Hybrid Economy* (New York: Penguin, 2008).

[15] Jessica E. Vascellaro and Ethan Smith, "YouTube, Universal Music Discuss Alliance," *The Wall Street Journal,* March 5, 2009, http://online.wsj.com/article/ SB123620507812933263.html?mod=todays_us_marketplace (accessed March 16, 2009).

[16] Ibid.

[17] Corey Vidal, MySpace Page, http://www.myspace.com/coreyvidal (accessed March 16, 2009).

[18] Meghan Keane, "YouTube Goes Legit, Begins Streaming Approved CBS Content," Wired.com, October 10, 2008, http://blog.wired.com/ business/2008/10/youtube-goes-le.html (accessed March 16, 2009).

[19] Ibid.

[20] Wikipedia, "YouTube," http://en.wikipedia.org/wiki/Youtube (accessed March 16, 2009).

[21] Ibid.

[22] Alexa, http://www.alexa.com/site/ds/top_sites?ts_mode=global&lang=none (accessed March 16, 2009).

[23] Wikipedia, "YouTube," http://en.wikipedia.org/wiki/Youtube (accessed March 16, 2009).

[24] Marc Prensky, *Don't Bother Me Mom—I'm Learning!* (St. Paul, MN: Paragon House Publishers, 2006).

[25] John Palfrey and Urs Gasser, *Born Digital: Understanding the First Generation of Digital Natives* (New York: Basic Books, 2008).

[26] Kevin Smith, *Tuba Lessons: Parts of a Tuba,* http://www.youtube.com/watch?v= aFhchjTiTT8&feature=related (accessed March 17, 2009).

[27] "Finale Notation Software Tutorial" search results, http://www.youtube.com/ results?search_type=&search_query=finale+notation+software+tutorial&aq=f (accessed June 16, 2009).

Chapter 2

[1] "Music education" search, www.youtube.com/results?search_type=&search_query=music+education&aq=f (performed June 1, 2009).

Chapter 3

[1] YouTube Help, "Channel Profile Definition," www.google.com/support/youtube/bin/answer.py?hl=en&answer=57960 (accessed March 24, 2009).

[2] YouTube Help, "YouTube Group Definition," www.google.com/support/youtube/bin/answer.py?hl=en&answer=67403 (accessed March 23, 2009).

Chapter 5

[1] James Frankel, *The Teacher's Guide to Music, Media, and Copyright Law* (New York: Hal Leonard, 2009), p. 1-2.

[2] Ibid.

[3] Title 17, United States Code, §107.

[4] 17 USC §107.

[5] 17 USC §107.

[6] Frankel, *Teacher's Guide to Music, Media, and Copyright Law,* p. 137.

[7] Chloe Albanesius, "EFF Gets Involved in Election Video Takedown Spat," *PC Magazine,* October 21, 2008, www.pcmag.com/article2/0,2817,2332981,00.asp (accessed March 26, 2009).

[8] Electronic Frontier Foundation, "Mom Sues Universal Music over DMCA Abuse," June 24, 2007, www.eff.org/deeplinks/2007/07/mom-sues-universal-music-dmca-abuse (accessed March 26, 2009).

[9] Tim Arrango, "Rights Clash on YouTube, and Videos Vanish," *The New York Times,* March 22, 2009, www.nytimes.com/2009/03/23/business/media/23warner.html (accessed March 26, 2009).

[10] YouTube.com, "YouTube Copyright Policy: Video Identification Tool," www.google.com/support/youtube/bin/answer.py?hl=en&answer=83766 (accessed March 27, 2009).

[11] YouTube.com, "Copyright Infringement Notification," www.youtube.com/t/dmca_policy (accessed March 28, 2009).

[12] YouTube.com, "General Copyright Inquiries: Guiding Principles," www.google.com/support/youtube/bin/answer.py?hl=en&answer=83749 (accessed March 28, 2009).

[13] YouTube.com, "How to Make Sure Your Video Does Not Infringe Someone Else's Copyrights," http://help.youtube.com/support/youtube/bin/answer.py?hl=en&answer=143460 (accessed June 22, 2009).

[14] YouTube.com "Copyright: Filing a Counter Notice," http://help.youtube.com/support/youtube/bin/answer.py?answer=59826&topic=10554#dmca (accessed March 28, 2009).

[15] Frankel, *Teacher's Guide to Music, Media, and Copyright Law,* p. 137.

[16] Ibid.

Chapter 6

[1] Search for "Bach, St. Matthew's Passion," http://www.youtube.com/results?search_type=&search_query=bach+st+matthew+passion&aq=0&oq=bach+st+ma (accessed April 4, 2009).

[2] Search for "classical music," http://www.youtube.com/results?search_type=&search_query=classical+music&aq=f (accessed April 5, 2009).

[3] Search for "folk music," http://www.youtube.com/results?search_type=&search_query=folk+music&aq=f (accessed April 10, 2009).

[4] Search for "Oh Susanna," http://www.youtube.com/results?search_type=&search_query=oh+susanna&aq=0&oq=oh+sus (accessed April 11, 2009).

[5] Search for "jazz," http://www.youtube.com/results?search_type=&search_query=jazz&aq=f (accessed April 11, 2009).

[6] Search for "bebop," http://www.youtube.com/results?search_type=&search_query=bebop&aq=f (accessed April 11, 2009).

[7] Search for "Miles Davis," http://www.youtube.com/results?search_type=&search_query=miles+davis&aq=f (accessed April 11, 2009).

[8] Search for "Charlie Parker," http://www.youtube.com/results?search_type=&search_query=charlie+parker&aq=f (accessed April 11, 2009).

Recommended Reading

Fahs, Chad. *How to Do Everything with YouTube*. New York: McGraw Hill Publishers, 2008.

Sahlin, D. and C. Botello. *YouTube for Dummies*. Hoboken, NJ: Wiley Publishing, 2007.

Miller, Michael. *YouTube for Business*. Indianapolis, IN: Que Publishing, 2009.

Index